Rethinking Theatrical Documents in Shakespeare's England

RELATED TITLES

The Arden Introduction to Reading Shakespeare
ISBN 9781472581020
Jeremy Lopez

Imagining Cleopatra: Performing Gender and Power in Early Modern England
ISBN 9781350058965
Yasmin Arshad

Playing Indoors: Staging Early Modern Drama in the Sam Wanamaker Playhouse
ISBN 9781350109506
Will Tosh

Shakespeare and the Gods
ISBN 9781474284271
Virginia Mason Vaughan

Shakespeare and the Politics of Nostalgia: Negotiating the Memory of Elizabeth I on the Jacobean Stage
ISBN 9781350067226
Yuichi Tsukada

Shakespeare on the Record: Researching an Early Modern Life
ISBN 9781350003514
edited by Hannah Leah Crummé

Shakespeare's Theatres and the Effects of Performance
ISBN 9781408146927
edited by Farah Karim-Cooper and Tiffany Stern

Rethinking Theatrical Documents in Shakespeare's England

Edited by Tiffany Stern

THE ARDEN SHAKESPEARE
LONDON • NEW YORK • OXFORD • NEW DELHI • SYDNEY

THE ARDEN SHAKESPEARE
Bloomsbury Publishing Plc
50 Bedford Square, London, WC1B 3DP, UK
1385 Broadway, New York, NY 10018, USA
29 Earlsfort Terrace, Dublin 2, Ireland

BLOOMSBURY, THE ARDEN SHAKESPEARE and the Arden Shakespeare logo are trademarks of Bloomsbury Publishing Plc

First published in Great Britain 2020
This paperback edition published 2021

Copyright © Tiffany Stern and contributors, 2020, 2021

Tiffany Stern and contributors have asserted their right under the Copyright, Designs and Patents Act, 1988, to be identified as the authors of this work.

For legal purposes the Acknowledgements on pp. xv–xvi constitute an extension of this copyright page.

Cover design: Charlotte Daniels
Cover image: *Marks of Genius* exhibition display (© Bodleian Library, University of Oxford)

This work is published open access subject to a Creative Commons Attribution-NonCommercial-NoDerivatives 3.0 licence (CC BY-NC-ND 3.0, https://creativecommons.org/licenses/by-nc-nd/3.0/). You may re-use, distribute, and reproduce this work in any medium for non-commercial purposes, provided you give attribution to the copyright holder and the publisher and provide a link to the Creative Commons licence.

Bloomsbury Publishing Plc does not have any control over, or responsibility for, any third-party websites referred to or in this book. All internet addresses given in this book were correct at the time of going to press. The author and publisher regret any inconvenience caused if addresses have changed or sites have ceased to exist, but can accept no responsibility for any such changes.

A catalogue record for this book is available from the British Library.

A catalog record for this book is available from the Library of Congress.

ISBN:	HB:	978-1-350-05134-8
	PB:	978-1-3502-4885-4
	ePDF:	978-1-350-05136-2
	eBook:	978-1-350-05135-5

Typeset by RefineCatch Limited, Bungay, Suffolk

To find out more about our authors and books visit www.bloomsbury.com and sign up for our newsletters.

CONTENTS

List of Illustrations viii
List of Contributors x
Acknowledgements xv

Introduction 1
Tiffany Stern

Part One Documents Before Performance

1 Writing a Play with Robert Daborne 17
Lucy Munro

2 A Sharers' Repertory 33
Holger Schott Syme

3 Parts and the Playscript: Seven Questions 52
James J. Marino

4 Undocumented: Improvisation, Rehearsal, and the Clown 68
Richard Preiss

Part Two Documents of Performance

5 Rethinking Prologues and Epilogues on Page and Stage   91
   Sonia Massai and Heidi Craig

6 Title- and Scene-Boards: The Largest, Shortest Documents   111
   Matthew Steggle

7 What Is a Staged Book? Books as 'Actors' in the Early Modern English Theatre   128
   Sarah Wall-Randell

Part Three Documents After Performance

8 'Flowers for English Speaking': Play Extracts and Conversation   155
   András Kiséry

9 Shakespearean Extracts, Manuscript Cataloguing, and the Misrepresentation of the Archive   175
   Laura Estill

10 Typography *After* Performance   193
    Claire M. L. Bourne

11 Shakespeare the Balladmonger?   216
    Tiffany Stern

Part Four Lost Documents

12 Lost Documents, Absent Documents, Forged Documents   241
Roslyn L. Knutson and David McInnis

Afterword: 'What's Past Is Prologue'   260
Peter Holland

Index   273

ILLUSTRATIONS

4.1 *The Book of Sir Thomas More*, B.L. MS Harleian 7368, fol. 7r. By permission of the British Library. 75
5.1 Rate of publication and rate of inclusion of Prologues and Epilogues in First Editions. 93
5.2 First Editions featuring Prologues and Epilogues, per Type of Play. 96
6.1 Signs imagined by William Percy, superimposed onto an image of the Blackfriars Playhouse, Staunton, Virginia. By permission of the American Shakespeare Center's Blackfriars Playhouse. 116
7.1 *The Geneva New Testament* (1557), B.L. C.17.a.15. By permission of the British Library. 141
9.1 'Songs from Otway's Plays' in Peter and Oliver Le Neve (1661–1729), and Thomas Martin (1697–1771), *Manuscript Collection* (*c.*mid seventeenth century), B.L. Add MS 27406, f. 114 v. © The British Library Board. 185
10.1 *A Pleasant Conceited Comedie Called, Loues labors lost* (London: Cuthbert Burby, 1598), A4v–B1r. By permission of the Folger Shakespeare Library. 200
10.2 *A Pleasant Conceited Comedie Called, Loues labors lost* (London: Cuthbert Burby, 1598), E1r. By permission of the Folger Shakespeare Library. 205
10.3 *A Pleasant Conceited Comedie Called, Loues labors lost* (London: Cuthbert Burby, 1598), E2v–E3r. By permission of the Folger Shakespeare Library. 206

10.4	*A Pleasant Conceited Comedie Called, Loues labors lost* (London: Cuthbert Burby, 1598), E3r. By permission of the Folger Shakespeare Library.	207
10.5	*A Pleasant Conceited Comedie Called, Loues labors lost* (London: Cuthbert Burby, 1598), G3v–G4rr. By permission of the Folger Shakespeare Library.	208
11.1	Anon, *No-body, and some-body* (1606), title page. By permission of the Folger Shakespeare Library.	225
11.2	Anon, *A Ballad of the Lamentable and Tragical History of Titus Andronicus* (*c*. 1660), Huth 50 (69). By permission of the British Library.	228

CONTRIBUTORS

Claire M. L. Bourne is Assistant Professor of English at Pennsylvania State University, where she teaches courses on Shakespeare, early modern drama, and book history. Her first book – *Typographies of Performance in Early Modern England* – is forthcoming from Oxford University Press. Her scholarship on early modern book design and use has been published in *English Literary Renaissance*, *The Papers of the Bibliographical Society of America*, *Shakespeare*, and several collections, including ones on Restoration Shakespeare, Christopher Marlowe, and early modern marginalia. She has received support for her research from the Folger Shakespeare Library, the Huntington Library, the Bibliographical Society of America, the Beinecke Library, the Harry Ransom Center, and Penn State's Center for Humanities and Information.

Heidi Craig is Assistant Professor of English at Texas A&M University. She edits the *World Shakespeare Bibliography,* and, with Sonia Massai and Thomas L. Berger, is the co-editor of a digital edition of dramatic paratexts printed to 1660. Her first book project, *A Play without a Stage: English Renaissance Drama, 1642–1660*, considers the production and reception of early modern drama during the theatrical prohibition; a second book project examines the role of rags and rag-pickers in early modern textual culture. Articles from these projects are published or forthcoming in *English Literary Renaissance, Huntington Library Quarterly* and *Literature Compass*. She is the grateful recipient of research support from the Huntington Library, Newberry Library, Folger Shakespeare Library, Marsh's Library and the Malone Society.

Laura Estill is a Canada Research Chair and Associate Professor of English at St. Francis Xavier University in Nova Scotia. She edits the *World Shakespeare Bibliography* and *DEx: A Database of Dramatic Extracts*. Her publications include *Dramatic Extracts in Seventeenth-Century English Manuscripts: Watching, Reading, Changing Plays* (2015) and, with Diane Jakacki and Michael Ullyot, *Early Modern Studies after the Digital Turn* (2016). Her work has appeared in *Shakespeare Quarterly, Papers of the Bibliographical Society of America, Digital Humanities Quarterly, Studies in English Literature*, and other journals. With Tamara Atkin, she is currently editing *Early British Drama in Manuscript* (forthcoming).

Peter Holland is McMeel Family Chair in Shakespeare Studies and Associate Dean for the Arts at Notre Dame. He was editor of *Shakespeare Survey*, co-General Editor, with Stanley Wells and Lena Orlin, of *Oxford Shakespeare Topics* and, with Adrian Poole, of the 18-volume series *Great Shakespeareans* (Bloomsbury Academic, 2009–13). Among his books are *English Shakespeares: Shakespeare on the English Stage in the 1990s* and a major study of Restoration drama, *The Ornament of Action*. He has also edited many Shakespeare plays. In 2007, he completed publication of a five-volume series of essays, *Rethinking British Theatre History*. In 2007–8, he served as President of the Shakespeare Association of America. He is the author of more than one hundred articles on a wide range of topics in Shakespeare studies.

András Kiséry is Associate Professor of English at The City College of New York (CUNY). He is author of *Hamlet's Moment: Drama and Political Knowledge in Early Modern England* (2016) and co-editor of *Formal Matters: Reading the Materials of English Renaissance Literature* (2013), and *Worlds of Hungarian Writing: National Literature as Intercultural Exchange* (2016). He is now working on two longer projects, about early modern English literature and the European book trade, and about the birth of media studies in Weimar-era European sociology, history, and philology.

Roslyn L. Knutson is Professor Emerita at the University of Arkansas at Little Rock. Her books include *The Repertory of Shakespeare's Company, 1594–1613* (1991), *Playing Companies and Commerce in Shakespeare's Time* (2001), and *Christopher Marlowe, Theatrical Commerce, and the Book Trade* (2018), co-edited with Kirk Melnikoff (University of North Carolina-Charlotte). A pioneer in the field of repertory studies, she has published essays on playhouse commerce in numerous journals, annuals, and collections. An on-going project is the wiki-style *Lost Plays Database*, which she founded with David McInnis (University of Melbourne) and co-edits with him and Matthew Steggle (University of Bristol).

James J. Marino is Associate Professor of English at Cleveland State University and author of *Owning William Shakespeare: The King's Men and Their Intellectual Property* (2011). His essays have appeared in *ELH, ELR, Shakespeare Quarterly*, and elsewhere.

Sonia Massai is Professor of Shakespeare Studies at King's College London. She has published widely on the history of the transmission of Shakespeare on the stage and on the page. Her publications include her books *Shakespeare's Accents: Voicing Identity in Performance* (forthcoming) and *Shakespeare and the Rise of the Editor* (2007), collections of essays on *Ivo van Hove: from Shakespeare to David Bowie* (2018), *Shakespeare and Textual Studies* (2015) and *World-Wide Shakespeares: Local Appropriations in Film and Performance* (2005), and critical editions of *The Paratexts in English Printed Drama to 1642* (2014) and John Ford's *Tis Pity She's a Whore* for Arden Early Modern Drama (2011).

David McInnis is the Gerry Higgins Senior Lecturer in Shakespeare Studies at the University of Melbourne. He is author of *Mind-Travelling and Voyage Drama in Early Modern England* (2013), co-editor (with Claire Jowitt) of *Travel and Drama in Early Modern England: The Journeying Play* (2018), and editor of Dekker's *Old Fortunatus* for the Revels Plays series (2019). With Matthew Steggle, he edited *Lost Plays in Shakespeare's England* (2014), and he is preparing a second co-edited collection and a monograph on lost plays. With Roslyn L. Knutson and Matthew Steggle, he is co-editor of the *Lost Plays Database*.

Lucy Munro is Professor of Shakespeare and Early Modern Literature at King's College London. She is the author of *Children of the Queen's Revels: A Jacobean Theatre Repertory* (2005) and *Archaic Style in English Literature, 1590–1674* (2013) and the editor of plays including Dekker, Ford and Rowley's *The Witch of Edmonton*, Fletcher's *The Tamer Tamed*, and Brome's *The Demoiselle* and *The Queen and Concubine*. She is currently completing a book entitled *Shakespeare in the Theatre: The King's Men* for Bloomsbury Arden Shakespeare and working on editions of Shirley's *The Gentleman of Venice* and Marston, Barksted and Machin's *The Insatiate Countess*.

Richard Preiss is the author of *Clowning and Authorship in Early Modern Theatre* (2014) and co-editor, with Deanne Williams, of *Childhood, Education, and the Stage in Early Modern England* (2017). He is currently editing Robert Armin's *The Two Maids of More-clacke* for *The Routledge Anthology of Early Modern Drama*, as well as completing a monograph on the ecology of early modern London playhouses.

Matthew Steggle is Professor of Early Modern English Literature at the University of Bristol. He has worked as contributing editor to the *Cambridge Works of Ben Jonson* (2012); and to the *Norton Shakespeare*, Third Edition (2015). His books include *Laughing and Weeping in Early Modern Theatres* (2007); and *Digital Humanities and the Lost Drama of Early Modern England: Ten Case Studies* (2015). He co-leads (with Roslyn L. Knutson and David McInnis) the Lost Plays Database, and (with Martin Butler) the AHRC-funded *Oxford Works of John Marston* project.

Tiffany Stern, FBA, is Professor of Shakespeare and Early Modern Drama at The Shakespeare Institute, University of

Birmingham. She specializes in sixteenth- to eighteenth-century drama, Shakespeare, theatre history, book history, and editing. Her books are *Rehearsal from Shakespeare to Sheridan* (2000), *Making Shakespeare* (2004), *Shakespeare in Parts* (with Simon Palfrey, 2007) and *Documents of Performance in Early Modern England* (2009). She has edited the anonymous *King Leir* (2001), Sheridan's *The Rivals* (2004), Farquhar's *Recruiting Officer* (2010), and Brome's *Jovial Crew* (2014), and co-edited, with Farah Karim-Cooper, *Shakespeare's Theatres and the Effects of Performance* (2013). She is author of over fifty chapters and articles on sixteenth- to eighteenth-century drama, and is general editor of New Mermaids and Arden Shakespeare 4.

Holger Schott Syme teaches theatre history and early modern drama at the University of Toronto. His publications include *Theatre and Testimony in Shakespeare's England: A Culture of Mediation* (2012), the co-edited *Locating the Queen's Men, 1583–1603* (2008), and essays in *Shakespeare Quarterly*, *Shakespeare Survey*, *Theatre Survey*, the *Review of English Studies*, and elsewhere. He is currently writing a book on Shakespeare in Berlin, 1918–2018, and regularly blogs about theatre of the past and present on dispositio.net.

Sarah Wall-Randell is Associate Professor of English at Wellesley College. She is author of *The Immaterial Book: Reading and Romance in Early Modern England* (2013), which examined scenes of reading in Spenser, Shakespeare, and Wroth. Her essays on early modern literature and the history of books have appeared in *Renaissance Quarterly*, *SEL*, *Marlowe Studies*, and in edited collections including *Christopher Marlowe, Theatrical Commerce, and the Book Trade* (2018) and *Gathering Force: Early Modern British Literature in Transition, 1557–1623* (2019).

ACKNOWLEDGEMENTS

The chapters presented in this book were tested, refined, and developed at a meeting at The Folger Shakespeare Library, Washington DC. I am so grateful to my fairy Folger godmother – and to Owen Williams, in particular – for inviting me to run a symposium on a subject about which I am passionately interested, Shakespeare's Theatrical Documents. And I am delighted that the contributors to that symposium, who gave such fantastic papers, were prepared to rework their papers as book chapters: their energy and excitement has made editing this book a delight.

I also owe a debt of gratitude to a number of other institutions. *Rethinking Theatrical Documents in Shakespeare's England* had its inception when I was at the University of Oxford; it was developed while I was at Royal Holloway, University of London; and it was completed in my new academic home, The Shakespeare Institute, University of Birmingham. Grateful thanks to friends and colleagues at all three places, in particular: at Oxford, Nicholas Halmi, Laurie Maguire, Simon Palfrey, Emma Smith, Bart Van Es, Laura Varnam; at Royal Holloway, Roy Booth, Harry Newman, Deana Rankin, Anne Varty; at the Institute, Michael Dobson, Ewan Fernie, John Jowett, Chris Laoutaris, Abigail Rokison-Woodall, Elizabeth Sandis, Simon Smith, Erin Sullivan and Martin Wiggins.

Working with Margaret Bartley at the Arden Shakespeare is always a delight. She, and Lara Bateman, guided me through the process of completing *Rethinking Theatrical Documents in Shakespeare's England* with patience and good humour. Thanks too, to the anonymous reader who gave such generous and supportive feedback on each chapter and who has made this a better book.

My hugest debt of gratitude is for my family, old and new, who have seen me through this and many other projects: Elisabeth Stern, Jonty Stern, Joy Moore, Alison Grimley and Allan Grimley. Daniel Grimley said 'yes' when I asked him to marry me. This book is dedicated to him.

Introduction

Tiffany Stern

Theatre and book history, which are rooted in the same set of facts, the same interests, and often the same material texts, have traditionally attracted scholars with different priorities and approaches. Each cognate field, theatre and book, has, as a result, developed its own ethos; the two are often treated as though they are separate, and sometimes as though they are in conflict. Even the attempt to join the two, the 'stage to page' or 'page to stage' discipline (the order of the words reveals the priorities of the user) joins its topics by desperate rhyme, as though fearing there is no more real connection between the two.

This edited collection finds ways in which the two fields can learn from and give to one another and, on occasion, solder their separations. It is the result of a Folger Shakespeare Library Symposium that brought theorists, book historians and theatre historians together in what turned out to be a feverish and passionate dialogue. Over a week of collaboration and sharing, 'documents' and their attendant 'playbooks' were found to be more entangled, and often in odder ways, than either theatre or book history separately had suggested.

The book thus relates to, but differs from, the field of 'performance studies'. That field places performance – now and historically – at the core of its discipline, importantly redressing a 'Shakespeare studies' long obsessed with text without considering the occasion for which it was written. The focus of 'performance studies' on 'performance' in its own right has made it receptive to new theoretical and intellectual frameworks: important recent performance studies work considers staging in the light of cognitive science, for instance. Yet in replacing a print-focus with a production-focus, 'performance studies' reverses rather than resolves a two-part hierarchy. This book, by contrast, aims to keep both early modern text and performance in view as it presents the rich complexities of their conjoined relationship. Its intention is to explore the way plays negotiate with both page and stage, providing information and approaches that relate to, arise from, complicate, and complement 'Shakespeare studies' and 'performance studies' too.

Rethinking Theatrical Documents expands the available documentary evidence (looking at 'different' documents on the stage/page divide like staged title-boards, staged books and 'play ballads'); considers the meaning of lost documents (including lists of plays with their performance dates, repertory accounts, and performance venues); explores never existing 'documents' (clowns' improvisations); and reconceives the way that we analyse the documents we have, such as the printed play, prologues and epilogues, actors' parts, and commonplaced play extracts. But its aim is to think anew about what even constitutes 'documents' in the first place, and, as a consequence, what constitutes 'plays', what constitutes 'playbooks', and what the nature is of the relationship between events seen and heard in performance and words read on the page.

The book confronts a fact that modern scholarship tends to avoid: that the stage/page tension it inherits is itself early modern in origin. For the very word 'playbook' combines 'play', which has its roots in the Middle Dutch 'pleyen', to dance or leap, with 'book', which has its roots in the Old Dutch 'buok', a written document; the 'playbook' was, in its very name, a paradox in which performance was confounded in text and text in performance. No surprise, then, that early modern playwrights did not have one fixed model for the way the playbook negotiated with production. So James Shirley can regret the way a printed play 'wanteth ... that Ornament, which the *Stage* and *Action* lent it';[1] Nicholas Downey can be comforted by the fact that S.H.'s play is printed 'Before some *Players* braine new drencht in sacke / Do's clap each terme new fancies on it's backe';[2] and Cleveland can be delighted because the 'majestick splendour' of Ben Jonson's printed works survives to triumph over 'a gawdy show / Of boords and canvass, wrought by Inigo' (Inigo Jones had designed the scenes and costumes for many of Jonson's masques).[3] As this shows, printed plays might 'mean' differently – in these instances, less than performance, free of performance, and better than performance respectively – according to author and/or text. Our modern assumption that printed playbooks represent one thing, often hides the difference not just between printed play and performance, but also between printed play and printed play.

The fact, moreover, that all plays, whether printed or not, intertwined performance with the text behind them – as manifested by early modern terminology – shows how complex the relationship between the two was from inception. Performance was often, in the period, described as a literalized book, for instance. The person in charge of overseeing a production, the 'prompter', was also called the 'book holder' (and, occasionally 'book keeper'), because he held the manuscript 'book' of the play in his hands throughout the production and guided and corrected actors against it. Indeed, so linked was prompting actors with the fact of the 'book' that the verb 'to hold the book' was an alternative for the verb 'to prompt': Will Summers in Nashe's *Summer's Last Will* [perf. Whitgift's household? 1592] asks the prompter to 'holde the booke well', in order that 'we be not *nonplus* [at a loss about what to say] in the latter end of the play'.[4] Thus behind all performances was a book that was both a physical presence and a notional ideal. Acting was judged by its ability to be faithful to that 'book'. Henry Wotton relates how some apprentices had, in 1613, 'secretly learnt a new Play without book, intituled, *The Hog hath lost his Pearl*'.[5] His vocabulary reveals that actors who had perfectly learned their lines – 'off-book' is our modern, still book-focused, term – were said to be 'without' the book, even though they will only have been given 'parts' (bits, rather than the whole of the book) to memorize. Collectively conveying to the audience the book from which their parts descended, however, was what actors' perfection was. Thus whenever books are staged, as Wall-Randell argues (Chapter 7), performance and text meld into one another in particularly complex ways.

Similarly, the vocabulary for reading printed books was often performative. When Middleton and Rowley published the masque *The World Tost at Tennis* (1620), their printer or publisher – or perhaps they themselves in the guise of the printer/publisher – gave it a dedication 'To the . . . well reading *Vnderstander, well-vnderstanding Reader*', jokily conflating the playgoer who stands under the stage with the playreader who understands fully the printed text. As masques were sometimes printed in advance of performance, and were often intended to be read during it, this text may even have been conceived as an aspect of performance.[6] Yet a similar point is made by the stationer who writes an epigraph to Beaumont and Fletcher's *King and No King*, a text only ever available to be read after performance. It has the lure, '*A Play and no Play, who this Booke shall read, / Will judge, and weepe, as if 'twere done indeed.*'[7] Here a pun on the title of the play is also a pun on the relationship between play and book – this book, it is claimed, has an urgency that will make its events seem so 'real' that 'weeping' and 'judging' – what a good performance provokes – will be the result. The suggestion is that reading *King and No King* will seem 'real' in that the reader will feel as though the play is really being staged. That may connect to the fact that publication itself was sometimes seen as an extension of performance (or performance a prediction of publication), so that Beaumont calls the printing of Fletcher's *Faithful Shepherdesse* 'This second publication'– the first 'publication' being the making-public of the text on stage.[8] So just as performance was instinct with text, so text was instinct with performance, the one always gesturing towards, because always somewhat being, the other.

That introduces an issue at the heart of this collection: that playbooks, in manuscript or print, tended to hover between text and performance, containing aspects of both. We know, for instance, that whatever the origin and meaning of published playbooks, they were sometimes later used as prompter's books – printed texts being easier to read than manuscript texts; hence printed plays that are marked up with manuscript production notes.[9] We know too that documents designed for staging sometimes made it into print – as when the 'scrolls' containing stage letters, songs, or prologues, often from different sources and dates from the dialogue, are printed in playbooks.[10] But plays, as this book shows, continued to resolve, during and after performance, into further documents, being taken away by audiences as snippets for commonplace books, or printed and then commonplaced (Kiséry, in Chapter 8, teases out why play snippets were thought useful for conversation), or rethought as ballads (Stern in Chapter 11 explores marketing plays as or in other texts).

Here it is important to realize, as Claire Bourne reminds us (Chapter 10), that even the term 'document' is loaded. It stood, in the early modern period, for 'teaching' or 'instruction' rather than, as now, for the inscribed paper that contains them. So 'he that goes to see a Play' was described as having 'a Morall presented to his eye, that should convey some profitable document to his heart', the document here being not a paper but a lesson.[11] That means that performance was itself a 'document', and that theatrical events, for which there may never have been paper witnesses (explored in Preiss's Chapter 4 on the lost essence of clowning, improvisation) are 'documents' too. This book, in considering what constitutes documents at their broadest, extends its understanding not only of how 'documents' relate to 'plays', but also of what 'documents' and 'plays' actually are.

It also seeks to expand the approach and methodologies we have for discussing such documents. Theatre and book historians have traditionally been averse to speculation and often list or catalogue the tremendous discoveries they have made, leaving other scholars to make the information work. Authors for *Rethinking Theatrical Documents* were encouraged to interpret, think imaginatively, even speculate. They opened up new areas and approaches for known documents including playbooks (Bourne, Chapter 10); Daborne's letters (Munro, Chapter 1); actors' parts (Marino, Chapter 3); prologues and epilogues (Massai and Craig, Chapter 5); and cataloguing (Estill, Chapter 9). Equally, the book allowed for fresh thought, speculation, and analysis of what might be learned from documents that, like Syme's performance lists (Chapter 2), Steggle's title- and scene-boards (Chapter 6), and most of the plays discussed by Knutson and McInnis (Chapter 12), no longer exist.

Rethinking Theatrical Documents consists of four sections: 'Documents Before Performance', 'Documents of Performance', 'Documents After Performance' and 'Lost Documents'. It starts with documents out of which a play was constructed and learned (including sources, plots, drafts, casting lists, repertory lists, actors' parts); moves on to documents from which a play was performed (including prologues and epilogues, staged title-boards and staged books); considers the documents into which a play resolved after performance (including passages in miscellanies and commonplace books, and ballads); and finally explores the documents that survive when a play itself does not. An Afterword points at the future for the critical field defined by the book. Made up, throughout, of 'provocations' in the form of mini-chapters, the book hopes to replicate the collaborative conversations out of which it was formed, and to harness their vigour and excitement.

The first section, 'Documents Before Performance', is on papers that shaped what performance was. It starts with Lucy Munro's 'Writing a Play with Robert Daborne', which revisits the letters of Robert Daborne to Philip Henslowe in 1613–14, a rich documentary resource that has been much underused, to describe the lived experience of playwriting: reading source materials, plotting, drafting, reading to the company and revising. Written during a period in which Daborne was scripting plays for the Lady Elizabeth's Men, the letters show how the messy circumstances of Daborne's own life impaired his ability to meet his commitments. Tracing working practices that were both idiosyncratic to Daborne and crucial to the collaborative structures of the early modern theatre industry, the chapter explores the relationships between playwrights, financiers and actors, the dynamics of authorial collaboration, and the financial processes and institutions with which aesthetic production was entwined.

Holger Syme's 'A Sharers' Repertory' considers a pre-play document that must have existed though no examples of it survive: the list of plays and performance dates that companies would have drawn up in order to help organize their daily offerings. It undertakes a fresh analysis of Henslowe's *Diary* in the light of surviving casting information from the 1620s and 1630s in order to explore which roles a 'lead' player was really expected to take on. Added to this information is what can be learned from a newly developed database that includes wordcounts for all roles in all early modern plays – it suggests that the assumption that lead roles were always played by the company's lead actor is anachronistic. Thus its 'lost' repertory document, considering how repertories will really have been assembled, and how companies will have spread their major roles among the sharers, becomes a new means of rethinking the early modern star system itself.

The third chapter, James J. Marino's 'Parts and the Playscript: Seven Questions', reconsiders actors' parts. It argues that many standard hypotheses implicitly depend on the notion that actors could make changes to their parts in the playhouse, without examining the possibility or feasibility of such changes. Its seven questions are about the way parts will have affected the early modern repertory. How, for instance, did actors relearn parts when they changed; what revisions were most difficult or most potentially disruptive of performance; and what limits does a part-based repertory set upon revision? By thinking through some of the greater questions to which parts give rise, it refocuses attention onto plays in pre-performance or pre-revised-performance as well as performance form.

Richard Preiss' 'Undocumented: Improvisation, Rehearsal, and the Clown' is on passages that were never inscribed. It compares what we know about the way companies distributed parts for study, rehearsal, revision, and line-learning with what we know about the clown, who forgot, altered, or added to parts programmatically. How do we reconcile a production system that prioritized efficiency with a clowning technique seemingly designed to provoke error and miscue? Identifying improvisation not as a contingency but as an expedient, the chapter uses extemporization to interrogate the distinctions we draw between the phases of a play's life, such as composition and performance, or rehearsal and premiere. Why, if improvisation was so routine, did playwrights insist so obsessively and paradoxically on staging its failure? When is a play a 'rehearsal' and when is it a 'performance'?

The second section, 'Documents of Performance' looks at documents that tread a careful line between performance and book. It starts with Sonia Massai and Heidi Craig's 'Rethinking Prologues and Epilogues on Page and Stage', which explores the oddity of prologues and epilogues: seemingly theatrical documents that found their way into printed playbooks. Providing the first systematic overview of the different role that prologues and epilogues played once rendered into reading texts, and considering their rate of inclusion in early modern printed playbooks, it asks whether some types of printed playbooks were more likely than others to include prologues and epilogues. Touching upon the way prologues and epilogues changed over time and the extent to which they may, and may not, relate to the prologues and epilogues that were spoken on stage, it reveals the fraught and ambiguous nature of this peculiar form of paratext.

A different kind of performative paratext, the 'Title- and scene-board', is the topic of the next chapter by Matthew Steggle. It investigates the early modern theatre's use of painted signs bearing, respectively, the title of the play being acted and the location of the action. Drawing on examples from the stage directions of the amateur dramatist William Percy, who seems to envisage a hierarchy of different information contained within written signs around the playing area, it shows how the information contained in signs affected the watching experience of early modern theatre. It places these little texts as new members of the family of 'documents of performance', arguing that title- and scene-boards set out an interpretive frame for the play's theatre audiences, and hence are part of the way we need to understand the performed play as textual object.

Sarah Wall-Randell's chapter asks 'What is a staged book?' It questions the ontological status of a book on stage asking whether books are merely physical objects like any other prop, or something more active or interactive. Exploring lines spoken by actors as though read from books, and asking which actual books were staged – can books 'play' themselves? – the chapter speculates about a 'company library' that was both a resource for playwrights and a supplier of stage props. If sources or references might also become props, then we must think in a new way about the interpenetration of play and the real in early modern theatrical mimesis.

The third section, on 'Documents After Performance' looks at the documents that a play is rendered into after performance has taken place. One obvious one is extracts in commonplace books: what András Kiséry calls 'Flowers for English Speaking'. His chapter is on the notes taken from plays which, in terms of scholarship hitherto, have generally been treated as 'literary' extracts. But, as the chapter explores, dramatic dialogue in the period was closely associated with spoken discourse, and among oral modes, with the conversational rather than with formal oratory. Arguing that most early seventeenth-century notes from plays – whether from printed playbooks or from the stage – are documents not of theatrical performance, or 'literature', but, of colloquialisms and colloquial style, it posits a culture of oral, conversational performance, complicating what plays were used for, and why.

Laura Estill's 'Shakespearean Extracts and the Misrepresentation of the Archive' is also on play extracts, and explores a different way in which they have been misunderstood. It considers how scholarship itself, privileging the Shakespearean over the non-Shakespearean, has misrepresented surviving documents. Dramatic extracts from Shakespeare seemingly outnumber those from other dramatists in pre-1600 manuscripts – but only because centuries of Shakespeare-centric cataloguing and scholarship have alerted scholars to 'Shakespearean extracts' more than to other extracts. Likewise dramatic extracts are more fully catalogued than the other materials found with them in commonplace books. Making a case for under-researched non-Shakespearean/dramatic commonplace examples, the chapter argues that we cannot properly comprehend early modern dramatic texts and their reception until we are more thoughtfully alert to their contexts.

Claire M. L. Bourne's 'Typography *After* Performance' analyses what type itself can reveal about staging. It starts from the fact that playbooks themselves are the major documents after performance. Many playbooks were also after performance in that they were designed to accord with (as in, to take after) the effects of performance. The chapter explores playbook typography and the arrangement and appearance of dramatic material on the page to show how readers were taught to encounter, navigate, and experience the print instantiations of this genre. Using Q1 *Love's Labour's Lost* (1598) as a case study, it explores a varied range of typographic strategies that help 'vitalize' for readers the play's non-verbal theatricality, especially in set-pieces that involve onstage reading and/or performance. Just as the play's plot turns on the (un)successful reading and performance of textual matter, so Q1 positions readers in the conceptual space between the idea of the play as a book and the idea of the play as a theatrical event, providing one of the best examples of an early modern playbook that functions as a 'theatrical document for readers'.

Another beyond play document was the ballad, which seems sometimes to have been written for, sometimes exploited by and sometimes sold at, the playhouse. In 'Shakespeare the Balladmonger?' Tiffany Stern looks at Shakespeare's use of ballads in his plays; and also his or his theatre's use of 'play ballads' – printed ballads that tell the entire narrative of his dramas. Asking whether Shakespeare promoted links between ballads and plays, or simply used them when they were there, the chapter raises questions about the form and nature of theatrical marketing around, before and after performance. Did ballads promote plays in performance or print – or did performance or print promote ballads? Were ballads specifically sold at playhouses, and if so, with the tacit acceptance, or at the insistence of the company? Complicating notions of the relationship between high and low literature, audience and actor, orality and text, performance and print, the chapter asks whether Shakespeare's company, and/or its playwrights, ever specifically marketed ballads to market plays, and whether a ballad should ever be considered part of a playtext.

The final section is on 'Lost Documents'. Knutson and McInnis consider 'Lost Documents, Absent Documents, Forged Documents', pointing out that countless documents from the early modern playhouse are no longer extant; routine events occurred in playhouses and among parties interested in theatrical business that did not provide a record at all; and forgers, motivated by professional self-importance and the allure of discovering evidence, filled gaps in received knowledge with documents of their own making. This chapter, on the continuum of lost-to-extant documents, moves beyond the paperwork generated by plays during the processes of composition and performance to consider evidence related to the culture of the early modern playhouse world in the categories of repertory, playwrights, provincial and court venues, and governmental action. Throughout, it considers the theoretical underpinnings of working with lost documents and the resources scholars have developed to raise the visibility of data from documents no longer extant. Although frustrated by incalculable losses from and about the early modern playhouse world, the chapter argues nonetheless that an awareness of what existed at one time is itself knowledge that keeps us both wary of assumptions and disciplined in the construction of narratives unsupported by the surviving documentary record.

An Afterword by Peter Holland adds to the rich range of what might constitute a 'document', and points the way for further productive investigation in the page/stage field.

Through these twelve brief chapters and Afterword, *Rethinking Theatrical Documents in Shakespeare's England* reflects upon and hopes to shift the way that page and stage, stage and page are addressed and separated. Documents should not, it suggests, be analysed and put in their place as ephemeral papers that give way to a play: rather, the playhouse should be understood to be frantically generating paratexts before, during and after performance, and redistributing them in wider society in ways that question what was text and what performance. This collection, which brings together, explores, analyses and theorizes a rich variety of entangled documents, some known and some relatively unknown, intends to shake up the critical, editorial, historical and material fields that depend upon 'page and stage' (or 'stage and page'). By using collective intervention to rethink both theatre history and book history, it provides new ways of understanding plays critically, interpretatively, editorially, practically and textually.

Notes

1 James Shirley, *The bird in a cage* (1633), A2r.

2 S. H., *Sicily and Naples, or, The fatall union A tragedy* (1640), A1r.

3 John Cleveland, *J. Cleaveland revived poems, orations, epistles* (1659), 43.

4 Thomas Nashe, *A pleasant comedie, called Summers last will and testament* (1600), H4v.

5 Henry Wotton, *Letters of Sir Henry Wotton to Sir Edmund Bacon* (1661), 155.
6 Thomas Middleton and William Rowley, *A courtly masque: the deuice called, the vvorld tost at tennis* (1620), A3r.
7 Francis Beaumont and John Fletcher, *A King and No King* (1639), titlepage.
8 John Fletcher, *The faithfull shepheardesse* (1610?), π3v.
9 Leslie Thomson, 'A Quarto "Marked for performance": Evidence of What?', *Medieval and Renaissance Drama in England*, 8 (1996), 176–210.
10 The subject of Tiffany Stern's *Documents of Performance in Early Modern England* (Cambridge: Cambridge University Press, 2009).
11 John Spencer, *Kaina kai palaia Things new and old, or, A store-house of similies, sentences, allegories, apophthegms, adagies, apologues, divine, morall, politicall, &c.* (1658), 274.

PART ONE

Documents Before Performance

1

Writing a Play with Robert Daborne

*Lucy Munro**

This chapter looks at a form of document about the theatre that is often overlooked because few examples survive: the letter. Specifically, it explores a set of letters written by the playwright Robert Daborne to the theatrical financier Philip Henslowe in 1613–14, letters that trace the often messy and protracted processes through which Daborne's plays reached the stage. They concern plays written for Lady Elizabeth's Men, a company payrolled by Henslowe, who also acted as their business representative in contexts such as the commissioning of plays.[1] Daborne worked on six plays between April 1613 and March 1614, the period around which most of the letters cluster: the tragedy *Machiavel and the Devil* (April–late June 1613); *The Arraignment of London*, written with Cyril Tourneur (*c*. June 1613); a collaboration with Field, John Fletcher and Philip Massinger, which may have been *The Honest Man's Fortune* (*c*. July–August 1613); *The Bellman of London* (August 1613–*c*. January 1614); *The Owl* (November 1613–March 1614); and *The She Saint*, which he started writing in March 1614.[2] All of these plays except *The Honest Man's Fortune* are now lost.

The letters often refer to other pre-performance documents, now lost: source materials; plots; contracts; sheets of plays in draft, 'fayr written' and revised versions; parts and playbills.[3] As scholars such as W. W. Greg, G. E. Bentley, Grace Ioppolo, Tiffany Stern and Bart Van Es have explored, they provide important insights into both the idiosyncrasies of Daborne's experience of playwrighting and the dynamics that informed industry-wide processes through which plays were commissioned and written.[4] At the same time, they evoke vividly the lived experience of writing plays for someone like Daborne, beset by financial pressures, ill health and a host of familial and legal engagements. Bringing the letters into dialogue with some hitherto overlooked documents that shed light on the origins of Daborne's writing career and his legal problems in 1613–14, this chapter will also explore a key question asked by this volume: what was text and what performance? As documents that emerged from a complex set of professional, emotional and bodily experiences, Daborne's letters deal with performance in two ways: they are directed towards the ultimate performance of the plays they help to propel into existence, and the financial and aesthetic rewards that performance will bring; and they are performances in themselves, aiming to produce short-term financial gain in the shape of advances or loans.

In order to trace these interactions, this chapter imagines Daborne as the author of a self-help manual for the aspiring Jacobean playwright, dealing with the complete process from the acquisition of sources through financial negotiations and drafting to the submission of the final manuscript of the play. We might imagine his manual beginning thus:

WRITING A PLAY
Pithy Counsel for all Seekers After Wit and Profit
By *Robert Daborne*, gent.

The first step: Seek out a book to assist thy labours

Daborne asks Henslowe on more than one occasion to provide him with books that are apparently to be used as source material for plays: 'if you will let me have pervsall of any other book of yours I will after ffryday intend it speedyly & doubt not to giv you full content' (Article 73; Greg, 69); 'send me the Book you promysed' (Article 87; Greg, 77). The relationships between these 'books' and Daborne's plays have not been precisely delineated: the title of *The Bellman of London* suggests that his source was Thomas Dekker's pamphlet, but *The Owl*, to which Daborne may refer when he mentions 'my other [play] out of your book' (Article 91; Greg, 79), probably did not draw heavily on Drayton's satire of that title, which is 'as rich in obscure satirical allegory as it is poor in narrative interest'.[5] There was clearly, however, a close relationship between Daborne's reading and writing, and the letters also suggest that company managers or financiers may routinely have lent books or other source materials, such as older playbooks, to playwrights. Sarah Wall-Randall discusses in her chapter in this volume the possibility that there were 'company libraries', and further evidence of such collections of books may survive in a previously unknown inventory of the household goods of Elizabeth Condell, apparently drawn up after her death in 1635, which includes 'one booke called the ffayry Queene [. . .] one booke called the Turkish history one booke called Jeffery Chaucers works one booke called Decameron'.[6] Elizabeth was the widow of a longstanding member of the King's Men, Henry Condell, and it is possible that these books – which served as sources for a number of early modern plays – were among the resources available to playwrights working for the King's Men.

The second step: Enter into conference about thy plot

Plays emerged not only from reading but also from conversations between writers. 'Mr. Dawborne and I', Nathan Field wrote to Henslowe around June 1613, 'haue spent a great deale of time in conference about this plott, which will make as beneficiall a play as has come these seuen yeares' (Article 100; Greg, 84). As noted above, it is not unlikely that the play that Daborne and Field were plotting together was *The Honest Man's Fortune*, written in 1613, in which only the hands of Field, Fletcher and Massinger have so far been traced. This may mean that Daborne's contribution to the play was limited to what Stern calls the 'Plot-scenario', especially given that he also worked on three other plays, *Machiavel and the Devil*, *The Arraignment of London* and *The Bellman of London*, in summer 1613.[7] If so, conversation or 'conference' was potentially as valuable to dramatists as writing itself and, something that Daborne perhaps had in mind when he wrote to Henslowe around August 1613 asking for an additional 10s. because 'I did think I deservd as much mony as mr messenger' (Article 76; Greg, 70–71).

The third step: Set a price for thy labour

Whether or not Daborne was granted his extra 10s., by the early 1610s £20 seems to have become the standard total price of a new play. Daborne agreed this amount for *Machiavel and the Devil* in April 1613, and he probably expected to get the same for *The Arraignment of London*, as he tells Henslowe that he could 'have 25[l] for it as some of the company know' (Article 81; Greg, 73–74). Later in the year, however, Daborne agreed to take 'but twelv pownds and the overplus of the second day' (that is, a share in the profit from the second performance) for *The Bellman of London* (Article 84; Greg, 75). Greg notes that this is 'low for a new play' and asks '[w]as it a re-writing of an old piece?' (75), but Daborne's comments suggest that he cut his price and deferred some of his earnings in order to secure money to deal with an immediate emergency. '[G]ood sir', he tells Henslowe explicitly, 'consider how for your sake I hav put my self out of the assured way to get mony and from twenty pownd a play am come to twelv', pleading with the other man 'in my extremyty forsake me not' (Article 84; Greg, 75). In December he offered *The Owl* for 'but ten pounds & I will vndertake vpon the reading it your company shall giv you 20ˡ rather then part with it' (Article 91; Greg, 79). Here there is no mention of the 'overplus', perhaps because Daborne's financial need was pressing him even further; in an undated letter belonging to the same period he tells Henslowe emphatically 'if you doe not help me to tenn shillings by this bearer by the living god I am vtterly disgract' (Article 95; Greg, 81).

The fourth step: Enter into bonds for the true fulfilment of thy promise

On 17 April 1613, Daborne drafted and signed a memorandum stating that 'before *the* end of this Easter Term' (i.e. 31 May) he would 'deliver in his Trageody cald matchavill & *the* divill into *the* hands of *the* said phillip' for £20 in instalments (Article 70; Greg, 67). On the same day Daborne and Henslowe signed a Latin bond in which Daborne agreed to pay Henslowe the sum of £20; a note in English on the back of the bond states:

> The Condici*on* of this obligac*ion* ys suche That if the w*i*thin ^ʳbounde˥ Robert daborne his executors or assignes doe deliuer vnto the w*i*thin named Phillipe henslow his executors or assignes one playe called Machivell and the divell vppon or before the last daie of Easter terme now next ensuinge the daie of the date of theise pr*ese*ntes w*i*thin written, accordinge to a memoraindu*m* or note made vnder the hande of the saide Robert daborne of the daie of the date of theise pr*ese*ntes w*i*thin written, without fraude or Coven,

That then this present obligacion to be voyde and of none effect, Or els to stande and be in full force and vertue.

(Article 71; Greg, 68)

The English text is not a translation of the Latin text, as some have assumed; instead, it supplies the crucial terms under which Daborne would be released from his bond. If he delivers *Machiavel and the Devil* to Henslowe by the end of Easter Term he will receive a total of £20 in instalments; if he does not deliver the play in a timely fashion, he will owe Henslowe £20. Henslowe later adopted a similar approach for *The Owl*, but he increased the stakes; on 10 December 1613, Daborne bound himself in the sum of £40 for the delivery of 'one plaie fullie perfected and ended Called by the name of the Oule [...] att, or vppon the tenth daye of ffebruarie next ensuinge' (Article 92; Greg, 80).

These bonds were apparently part of a broader practice. New evidence allows us to trace Daborne's association with the theatre industry back to 27 September 1606, when he bound himself in the sum of £50 to Robert Keysar, then the manager of the Children of the Queen's Revels at the Blackfriars playhouse.[8] The idea that this bond secured the composition of a play or plays gains strength if we look at Keysar's other financial engagements around this time. On 6 May 1606, Thomas Middleton bound himself to Keysar in the sum of £16 for the payment of £8 10*s*. by 15 June, a sum that Keysar said had not been paid when he sued Middleton at King's Bench in Trinity Term 1609. Middleton claimed, however, that he had fulfilled his obligation by delivering to Keysar on 7 May a tragedy called *The Viper and her Brood*.[9] Similarly, Thomas Dekker became bound to Keysar in the sums of £10 and £14 on 4 June 1606; these bonds, like Daborne's, are likely to have been for the provision of plays.[10]

The fifth step: Make bold for an advance

The memorandum that Daborne drew up for *Machiavel and the Devil* on 17 April 1613 specified that he would receive a total sum of £20, 'six pounds whearof the said Robert acknowledgeth to hav receaved in earnest of the sayd play [...] & must hav other four pound vpon delivery in of 3 acts, & other ten pound vpon delivery in of the last scean perfited' (Article 70; Greg, 67). In practice, the process through which he accumulated his payment was more *ad hoc*. By 25 April Daborne was writing to Henslowe asking him for 20s. to pay for his servant to be bailed from Newgate Prison 'vpon taking a possession for me' (Article 72; Greg, 68). On 3 May he wrote again asking 'for one 20s. more' of the £20, promising to deliver the three acts 'fayr written' on 'ffryday night', but on 8 May, having failed to deliver on his promise, he wrote to ask for another 20s. (Articles 73 and 74; Greg, 69). By this point, Daborne had received half of the total that he was due for the play. On 16 May he asked for a further 20s., and on 19 May he wrote out an acquittance to Henslowe acknowledging that he had received £16 in total, having apparently received another £5 (Articles 75 and 77; Greg, 70–71). Although Daborne wrote at the bottom of the acquittance '[t]his play to be delivered in to mr hinchlaw with all speed' (Article 77; Greg, 71), he was still working on *Machiavel and the Devil* when he made further requests for money in the following weeks: on 5 June he asked for 40s., of which he received 20s.; on 10 June he asked for and received 20s.; on 18 June he asked for 40s., which does not seem to have been provided; and on 25 June he again asked for 40s., of which he received 20s (Articles 78–81; Greg, 71–74). By 25 June he had therefore received a total of £19, leaving only 20s. to be disbursed on the submission of 'ye last scean perfited'. It is easy to see both why Henslowe would want to bind a playwright in a sum that would be forfeited if the play was not delivered, and why he was willing to keep giving advances: he always retained the threat of a lawsuit to recover the sums stated in the bond.

The sixth step: Balance thine obligations

Daborne's activities as a playwright took place against a backdrop of legal and familial turmoil that intensified after his father's death in August 1612. On 26 November 1612, Daborne's mother, Susanna, and a group of his father's creditors entered a bill against him at Chancery, alleging that he was blocking the sale of his father's Blackfriars properties.[11] The situation became even more fraught in the following years when Daborne sued his uncles, James and Edmond Travis, another kinsman, William Taylor, and John Sherrington.[12]

The law consumed much of Daborne's time and money. On 5 June 1613 he asked Henslowe, 'I beseech you as heatherto so you would now spare me 40^s which stands me vpon to send over to my counsell in a matter concerns my whole estate', and over the next few months his letters regularly refer to the problems of his 'term busines' (Articles 78–79; Greg, 72). In a letter of 18 June, he refers specifically to the Court of Common Pleas, and he does so in the context of the pressure that his legal obligations put on his ability to write: 'had not necessity inforct me to the common place bar this morning to acknowledg a ffynall recovery I would this day hav delivered in all' (Article 80; Greg, 73). His business in the Common Pleas may have been extensive: in the same term he was also sued by John Harris, who claimed that 'Robertum Daborne de London generosum' owed him the sum of £6.[13] On 30 July 1613, Daborne wrote to Henslowe describing the desperate state of 'my occations vntill I have made sale of that estate I have' (Article 83; Greg, 75), and he remained in a state of acute poverty over the following year, leading to further liquidation of his personal property and estate. On 12 December 1614 he sold property in Aldenham, Hertfordshire, which had apparently belonged to his father, to Henslowe for £50; this transaction may be the subject of an undated letter in which he writes 'I hav bin befor the doctor & aknowledged the deed with the chardg of 13^s I pray sir send me the 20^s you promysed'.[14] Around 31 July Daborne had written asking for 10s. in order to attend 'my lord willoughby [. . .] I know not how proffitable it may be to me & without your kindnes hearin I cannot goe' (Article 98; Greg, 83); the sale of his property to

Henslowe a few months later may indicate that this attempt to secure aristocratic patronage was unsuccessful.

The seventh step: Write thy play

Daborne has been described as suffering from writer's block, but he may simply have lacked the time to write. He certainly made unfulfilled promises: 'I will now after munday intend your busines carefully'; 'I can this week deliver in *th*e last word'; 'neather will I fayle to bring in the whole play next week' (Articles 75, 79, 85; Greg, 70, 72, 76). However, his letters also picture him writing before witnesses – 'yo*u*r man was w*i*th me whoe found me wrighting the last scean' (Article 88; Greg, 78) – and he consistently sends with them draft material in varying degrees of completion in order to secure advances or demonstrate his good faith: 'some papers I have sent you though not so fayr written all as I could wish'; 'I send you the foule sheet and *th*e fayr I was wrighting as yo*u*r man can testify'; and (in a very rushed hand) 'take these papers which wants but one short scean of the whole play' (Articles 74, 89, 96; Greg, 69, 78, 82). He is harassed and over-committed, frequently working on more than one play, starting another as soon as he finally finishes one, and trying out various forms of collaboration, from 'plotting' to doling out an act of *The Arraignment of London* to Cyril Tourneur.

The eighth step: Listen to thy body

In addition to providing an insight into the financial and emotional pressure to which Daborne was subjected, his letters also suggest the physical strain that dividing his time between the playhouse and the lawcourts was putting on their author. He appears often to have written at night, telling Henslowe on 18 June 1613, when he was in the throes of the final stages of *Machiavel and the Devil*, 'I sat up last night till past 12 to write out this sheet' (Article 80; Greg, 73), and promising to send in his manuscripts 'one [i.e. 'on'] ffryday night' (Article 73; Greg, 69), 'one Tuesday night' (Article 75; Greg, 70) or 'one Munday night' (Article 80; Greg, 73). He complains occasionally of ill health that compromises his ability to make personal contact with Henslowe and plead his case more effectively. A letter of 23 August 1613 opens 'I hav ever sinc I saw you kept my bed being so lame that I cannot stand' (Article 84; Greg, 75), his ailment leading him to negotiate his price for *The Bellman of London* by letter rather than in person. Similarly, a letter of 31 December reads 'I hav bin very ill this week of an extream cold ells I had come this night vnto you' (Article 94; Greg, 81).

The ninth step: Employ thy studies in rhetoric

Rhetoric was, of course, a central component in the construction of early modern plays, a fact that Daborne acknowledges in the preface 'To the Knowing Reader' in the 1612 edition of his play *A Christian Turned Turk* when he refers to oratory as '*an vnseparable branch of Poesy*'.[15] But the role of rhetoric was not limited to its part in composition of Daborne's plays – his letters to Henslowe being studded with purposeful and heightened language. He makes liberal use of professions of loyalty and friendship, such as his declaration 'wher I deale otherways then to your content may I & myne want ffryndship in distress' (Article 78; Greg, 72), and he also uses the language of financial indebtedness to underscore these claims: 'you shall find me thankfull & performing more then ever I promisd or am tyed to' (Article 72; Greg, 68). Exaggeration and hyperbole feature regularly, as in the statement 'rather then I would be vnthankfull to you I would famish' (Article 89; Greg, 78), and Daborne frequently resorts to the transgressive register of the religious oath, giving his writing the tang of spoken dialogue: 'before god . . .' (Articles 79, 81, 96, 97; Greg, 72–73, 82); 'by god' (Article 98; Greg, 83); 'by the living god . . .' (Article 95; Greg, 81); 'god is my judg' (Articles 79, 91; Greg, 72, 80). To label these techniques rhetorical does not, of course, mean that Daborne was not feeling frustration, anger or desperation as he wrote, or that he did not suffer from intense poverty; rather, his letters suggest that their author was using every resource available to him.

The tenth step: Offer pithy and profitable advice

Daborne's letters to Henslowe also offer insights into his role within the networks surrounding Henslowe and Lady Elizabeth's Men, and they display his intimacy with the affairs of both. 'I pray sir', he writes around August 1613, 'let the boy giv order this night to the stage keeper to set vp bills against munday for Eastward hoe & one wendsday the New play' (Article 76; Greg, 71), showing not only his knowledge of the company's repertory but also a desire to order their affairs that may have its roots in his own former position as a patentee for the Children of the Queen's Revels. On 28 March 1614 he similarly deploys his knowledge of Henslowe's theatrical dealings, confiding that 'mr Pallat is much discontented with your neglect of him I would I knew your mynd to giv him answer' (Article 97; Greg. 82); he refers here to the actor Robert Pallant, a member of Lady Elizabeth's Men who appears to have been brought into the company by Henslowe in June 1614 (see Article 106; Greg, 86).

The eleventh step: Deal with other companies

Daborne's knowledge of the theatre industry and the various strains to which he was subjected inform the threats that he repeatedly made in autumn 1613 to take one of his plays to a rival company, King's Men. Such an action put his relationship with Lady Elizabeth's Men at risk; yet more surprisingly, perhaps, he was prepared to involve Henslowe as an intermediary in this process. On 29 October, for example, he writes to Henslowe

> to know your determination for the company wheather you purpose they shall have the play or noe, they rale vpon me I hear bycause the kingsmen hav given out they shall hav it [...] I hav sent you 2 sheets more so that you hav x sheets & I desyre you to send me 30ˢ more which is iust eight pound besyds my rent which I will fully satisfy you eather by them or the kings men as you please.
>
> (Article 86; Greg, 76–77)

Henslowe has already paid out a significant sum in advance for the play, money that Daborne cannot repay, so he instead offers that the King's Men will pay Henslowe for it. '[T]he kings men', he writes again on 13 November, 'hav bin very earnest with me to pay you in your mony' (Article 88; Greg, 78). The correspondence thus suggests that companies might be vulnerable to losing out on a play not just at the commissioning stage – as Field feared in June 1613 that 'Mr. Dauborne may haue his request of another Companie' for the plot that they had been discussing (Article 100; Greg, 84) – but at a point at which scenes had been drafted and the true value of the work might become apparent.

The twelfth step: Read thy play

Daborne's letters reveal another aspect of the composition process that is often invisible in other sources: the reading of a complete or almost complete play by the dramatist to either the playing company or someone with a responsibility for commissioning plays.[16] In May–June Daborne repeatedly offers to read *Machiavel and the Devil* to Henslowe or Edward Alleyn: 'if you please to appoynt any hower to read to mr Allin I will not fayle'; 'one Tuesday night if you will appoynt I will meet you & mr Allin & read some for I am vnwilling to read to *the* generall company till all be finisht'; 'I can this week deliver in *the* last word & will *that* night they play thear new play read this' (Articles 74–5, 79; Greg, 69–70, 72). It is not always clear whose opinion counts for most when the play is read. 'I will vndertake vpon the reading it [*The Owl*] your company shall giv you 20ˡ rather then part with it' (Article 91; Greg, 79), Daborne writes on 9 December 1613, suggesting that the company's decision is all-important; this impression is reinforced by his reluctance to read *Machiavel and the Devil* to the company until it is more complete. In a later letter, however, Henslowe's own judgement is prioritized: 'if you doe not like this play [*The Owl*] when it is read you shall hav the other [*The She Saint*] which shall be finished with all expedition' (Article 96; Greg, 82).

The thirteenth and last step: Take pains to alter thy play

When Daborne refers to Henslowe's judgement, he suggests that taste and aesthetic evaluation played a role in the commissioning of plays, and similar ideas inform his references to the final step in his composition process: revision. In a letter of 25 June 1613, Daborne offers as a mark of the worth of *Machiavel and the Devil* the work that he has put not just into the original composition but into the honing of the text: 'for thear [i.e. the company's] good & myn own I have took extraordynary payns with the end & altered one other scean in the third act which they have now in parts' (Article 81; Greg, 73). This is a remarkable reference to the impact that a playwright's revision of the text might have on the actors who have to work with that text. As James J. Marino notes in his essay in this volume, '[c]hanging a script that actors had already learned imposed specific practical necessities'; here, Daborne's stated desire to improve *Machiavel and the Devil* complicates the process through which the actors were learning their lines and preparing the play for performance. Yet what also is striking in Daborne's comment is the way in which he aligns his own interest in the polish and aesthetic worth of the play with that of the company. Their interests are not always identical – as Daborne's willingness to consider taking his plays away to the King's Men suggest – but both have an investment in the worth of their output. Moreover, Daborne obviously thinks that Henslowe will agree with him that this process of revision will add value to the finished play.

If this chapter has fantasized about casting Robert Daborne in the role of professional guru, offering his hard-won experience to the aspiring Jacobean playwright, it has also suggested the extent to which that very experience might have undermined his ability to offer uplifting maxims. Daborne's letters offer a window onto the complex, embodied process of playwrighting in the early seventeenth century, one that is shaped not only by the conscious choices of the writer but also by the messy circumstances of his life and his commitments beyond the stage. We do not, of course, know how typical Daborne's experience was: while many playwrights suffered from poverty, and many became entangled with the law, few seem to have met with the perfect storm of familial and legal turmoil that Daborne faced in 1613–14. Nonetheless, his letters allow us to sketch out a network of textual and physical interactions between individuals and institutions that blur the boundaries between text and performance, work and life. They remind us that textual transactions are informed by personal, emotional and bodily experience, and that the pre-performance life of a play might be nearly as eventful as its eventual performance on stage.

Notes

* I would like to thank the members of the Folger symposium on Theatrical Documents and, especially, Tiffany Stern for their help with this essay.

1 See Dulwich College Muniment 52, consulted as a digital photograph in the 'Henslowe-Alleyn Digitisation Project', gen.

ed. Grace Ioppolo, http://www.henslowe-alleyn.org.uk (accessed 1 July 2018), and in W. W. Greg's transcriptions in *Henslowe Papers: Being Documents Supplementary to Henslowe's Diary* (London: A. H. Bullen, 1907), 23–24. Subsequent parenthetical references for Daborne's letters, which are to be found in Muniments Series 1 and MSS 1, are to these sources.

2 I agree with Martin Wiggins that *The Arraignment of London* and *The Bellman of London* are likely to have been separate plays, rather than the same play, as Greg assumed. See Wiggins, *British Drama, 1533–1642: A Catalogue: Volume VI: 1609–1616* (Oxford: Oxford University Press, 2015), #1740 (389) and #1717 (332); Greg, 75.

3 A broader consideration of these 'absent documents' appears in Roslyn L. Knutson and David McInnis's essay in this volume.

4 Greg, *Henslowe Papers*, esp. 65–85; Bentley, *The Profession of Dramatist in Shakespeare's Time* (Princeton: Princeton University Press, 1971), esp. 69–79, 105–106, 211–213; Ioppolo, *Dramatists and Their Manuscripts in the Age of Shakespeare, Jonson, Middleton and Heywood: Authorship, Authority and the Playhouse* (London: Routledge, 2005), esp. 11–44; Stern, *Documents of Performance in Early Modern England* (Cambridge: Cambridge University Press, 2009), esp. 23, 25, 47, 93; Van Es, *Shakespeare in Company* (Oxford: Oxford University Press, 2013), esp. 44–50.

5 Wiggins, #1747 (398–399).

6 John and Isabel Deodati v. Thomas Seaman and John Hatt, Chancery, 1638, The National Archives (TNA), C 3/400/76. Elizabeth Condell also owned copies of Lancelot Andrews's sermons and the works of Du Bartas.

7 See Stern, *Documents*, 8–35; on Daborne and *The Honest Man's Fortune* see Wiggins #1719 (333–337).

8 Keysar v. Daborne, King's Bench, TNA, KB 27/1404 (Trinity 1607), rot. 904d. Daborne's involvement with the theatre has usually been dated to 1608, Mark Eccles having located a later entry in the same suit in KB 27/1411, rot. 398 ('Brief Lives: Tudor and Stuart Authors', *Studies in Philology* 79 [1982], 1–135 [29]). He appears, however, to have been unaware of the earlier entry, which I owe to the unpublished notes of

C. W. Wallace and Hulda Berggren Wallace in the Huntington Library, San Marino. I am very grateful to Jonathan Mackman for providing me with translations of these Latin documents.

9 Keysar v. Middleton, King's Bench, Trinity 7 Jas I (1609), TNA, KB 27/1416, rot. 1056d; H.N. Hillebrand, 'Thomas Middleton's *The Viper's Brood*', *Modern Language Notes* 42 (1927), 35–38.

10 Keysar v. Dekker, King's Bench, Hilary 10 Jas I (1613), TNA, KB 27/1437, rot. 997r–v; David Mateer and Alan H. Nelson, '"When sorrows come": John Webster v. Thomas Dekker in the Court of King's Bench', *Shakespeare Quarterly* 65 (2014), 199–208.

11 Daborne et al. v. Daborne, Chancery, 1612, TNA, C 2/JasI/D2/3, C 24/408. See Wayne H. Phelps, 'The Early Life of Robert Daborne', *Philological Quarterly* 59 (1980), 1–10; Eccles, 31–32; S. P. Cerasano, 'Competition for the King's Men?: Alleyn's Blackfriars Venture', *Medieval and Renaissance Drama in England* 4 (1989), 173–186 (176–177).

12 These appear to be treated as one suit in witness depositions of December 1614 (TNA, C 24/409) and an order of June 1616 (TNA, C 33/140, f. 1015r–v). See also Cerasano, 177–178.

13 Harris v. Daborne, Common Pleas, TNA, CP 40/1914 (Trinity 1613), rot. 2189d.

14 TNA, Close Rolls, 12 Jas I, pt 31, C 54/2229, m. 40; British Library, MS Egerton 2623, fol. 24; Greg, Appendix 1, Article 3 (p. 126).

15 Robert Daborne, *A Christian Turn'd Turk* (London, 1612), A3v.

16 See Bentley, 76–79; Stern, *Rehearsal from Shakespeare to Sheridan* (Oxford: Oxford University Press, 2000), 59–61.

2

A Sharers' Repertory

Holger Schott Syme

Without Philip Henslowe, we would know next to nothing about the kinds of repertories early modern London's resident theatre companies offered to their audiences. As things stand, thanks to the existence of the manuscript commonly known as Henslowe's *Diary*, scholars have been able to contemplate the long lists of receipts and expenses that record the titles of well over 200 plays, most of them now lost. The *Diary* gives us some sense of the richness and diversity of this repertory, of the rapid turnover of plays, and of the kinds of investments theatre companies made to mount new shows. It also names a plethora of actors and other professionals associated with the troupes at the Rose. But, because the records are a financier's and theatre owner's, not those of a sharer in an acting company, they do not document how a group of actors decided which plays to stage, how they chose to alternate successful shows, or what they, as actors, were looking for in new commissions. The *Diary* gives us the outcome of a planning process, but it does not reveal much about that process itself – and in particular, it says almost nothing about the considerations a company of actors might have brought to the challenge of constructing a viable repertory. In this chapter, I will offer new readings of a number of extant performance-related documents in order to hypothesize about what we might know if the *Diary* of an actor-sharer such as John Heminges or Thomas Downton had survived.

That early modern theatre companies assembled their repertories with a great deal of forethought has been persuasively argued by Roslyn Knutson, whose foundational work established parameters for analysis both broad (that companies pursued fairly evident 'commercial tactics' in assembling a repertoire) and specific (what the schedule of performances was; how often new plays were introduced; the place of revivals; the mixing of plays from different genres; a taste for multiple plays on the same subject matter; the importance of serial or multi-part plays; and so on).[1] She traces in Henslowe's records strategies for the introduction of new plays (and the materials and costumes they required), the internal coordination of multi-part plays, and the external coordination of plays responding to titles in other companies' repertories – all of which would have required advance planning. Marketing, too, seems to have relied on at least a weekly planning cycle. Tiffany Stern has drawn our attention to accounts of playbills advertising upcoming shows with up to a week's notice, though, as she also notes, a strong demand for different plays could occasionally lead to overnight changes in programming, and the same presumably was the case if a new play proved surprisingly unpopular.[2]

In their attempts to reconstruct how repertories were built and performed, scholars have primarily focused on economics and markets on the one hand, and on dramatic content on the other: plays were scheduled because of their presumed popularity, and one of the primary grounds for popular appeal was what the plays were about. Actors appear in these analyses under two rubrics: the star and the cast. Stars are discussed as individuals (almost always Edward Alleyn or Richard Burbage) and considered a major reason playgoers came to the theatre. Casts are used analytically to establish the makeup of companies: 'the size and constitution' of the Queen's Men, for instance, can be deduced from a reading of their repertory that reveals the 'sameness rather than variety' of its casting demands.[3] But casts also consisted of specific actors – and even a repertory that regularly required a dozen adult players would not regularly have placed identical demands on each of those players.[4]

To understand more fully how early modern performance schedules took shape and to develop a more comprehensive view of the relationship between repertory and casting, we need to reconsider the importance of 'variety.' As I will argue in detail later, no sharer in a theatre troupe consistently took the largest role in all shows: staging plays was a company effort, and different kinds of plays were associated with different distributions of role sizes and modes of actorly exertion. Generic diversity thus must be analysed not just from the perspectives of marketing and economics, but also as an aspect of company management. In other words, repertories were not just designed to maximize revenues, but also to make the most of a troupe's talents while avoiding mentally and physically exhausting its sharers. We therefore need to reconstruct the programming and casting strategies early modern players adopted to achieve those goals.

Current accounts of early modern acting emphasize the importance of the companies' most famous actors, with Alleyn and Burbage as the paradigmatic embodiments of the type. As a result, in hypothesizing about casting choices, these players are often treated as the obvious choice for lead roles as a matter of course. John Astington makes this assumption explicit: 'given [Burbage's] position as leading actor we can reasonably infer he took the major roles in plays with a dominant central character: Henry V, Macbeth, Coriolanus, Antony, and so on.'[5] The same triple assumption is also applied to Alleyn: that there was such a thing as *the* leading actor; that Alleyn or Burbage was it; and that the 'leading actor' would as a matter of course play 'the lead' – here understood as the role with the largest share of the text. Andrew Gurr, considering a week of Admiral's Men's performances in August 1594, gives all title roles to Alleyn:

'Monday the 17th' he appeared 'as Marlowe's Lord High Admiral of France, on Tuesday as Tasso, on Wednesday as King Henry I confronting the clown Belin Dun, on Thursday he was the hero of *The Ranger's Comedy*, on Friday Galiaso and on Saturday he stalked as the heroic Cutlack.'[6] Astington, contemplating Alleyn's return to the company when it moved to the Fortune in 1600, gives him a similarly comprehensive list of roles, made up of revivals ('the multiple disguised roles in *The Blind Beggar of Alexandria*, Hercules ..., Hieronimo in *The Spanish Tragedy*, and Barabas in *The Jew of Malta*') as well as new parts: 'new additions to the repertory ... suggest that Alleyn also took the title roles in biblical plays of *Samson*, *Jephthah*, *Joshua*, and *Pontius Pilate*, as well as the great cardinal in two plays on the rise and fall of Wolsey.'[7] And S. P. Cerasano names a slew of other lost plays that may have featured the 'large roles' she believes were a popular feature of the Admiral's Men's repertory, since they provided 'natural roles for Alleyn': 'Mahomet', 'Godfrey of Boulogne', 'Antony and Vallia', 'Constantine', 'Harry of Cornwall', 'Zenobia'.[8] Of all these roles, Cutlack and Barabas are the only ones with a verifiable connection to Alleyn.

Much of the actual contemporary evidence for the parts Alleyn and Burbage played derives from anecdotal allusions and commemorative poems – sources likely to note their most memorable performances. If it were not for a surviving backstage 'plot', for example, we would certainly never have guessed that Burbage took the role of a mere messenger in the lost 'The Dead Man's Fortune'.[9] But even so, the very brief lists of roles Burbage and Alleyn verifiably played do not support the idea that they habitually took the lead. Consider what we actually know of Burbage. He was Gorboduc and Tereus in 'The Second Part of the Seven Deadly Sins', Hieronimo (presumably in Kyd's *Spanish Tragedy*), Hamlet, Lear, Othello, Malevole in the King's Men's remount of Marston's *Malcontent*, Volpone, Subtle in Jonson's *Alchemist*, Ferdinand in Webster's *Duchess of Malfi*, probably Richard III – and a messenger in 'Dead Man's Fortune.'[10] We thus know of eleven plays in which he acted; he took the lead role in six of them. What of the other five? Othello, the second lead in the eponymous play, is over 2,000 words shorter than Iago; Volpone is slightly shorter than Mosca; Subtle is substantially shorter than Face (by about 500 words); Ferdinand is the third-longest role in *Duchess*, after Bosola (well over 2,000 words longer) and the eponymous heroine, and barely longer than the next most substantial role, Antonio. Some of Burbage's leads were exceptionally large, especially Richard III (*c.* 8,800 words, over 31 per cent of the text) and Hamlet (over 11,500 words; 39 per cent). But others were not: Hieronimo, with *c.* 5,400 words, has 27 per cent of the text; Lear, just over 22 per cent (*c.* 5,600 words). Others still were dominant without being especially long: Malevole speaks *c.* 32 per cent of *The Malcontent*, but only has about 4,500 words.[11]

The evidence leads to two conclusions. First, that Burbage frequently acted major parts, taking outsized leads with disproportionate frequency. In the entire corpus of printed professional drama, only 8 per cent of all leads (33 out of 415) have more than 30 per cent of their play's text, yet a full third of Burbage's recorded roles fit that profile. But a second conclusion must be that other members of the Chamberlain's/King's Men were similarly capable of large roles. The same evidence that gives us Burbage's parts, after all, informs us that Henry Condell played Mosca, the lead in *Volpone* (*c.* 6,500 words; over 25 per cent); Nathan Field was Face, the lead in *The Alchemist* (*c.* 4,300 words; over 30 per cent); John Lowin played Bosola in *The Duchess of Malfi* (*c.* 5,800 words; over 25 per cent); and *someone* else played Iago (*c.* 8,400 words; over 32 per cent).[12] What is more, while anecdotes do often mention Burbage, other company sharers were also household names: the foolish playgoer in Webster's induction to *The Malcontent*, for instance, asks for 'Harry Condell, Dick Burbage, and Will Sly' – and instead of Sly, John Lowin then comes on.[13] Similarly, although Burbage is identified as the 'best actor' in Jonson's *Bartholomew Fair*, we ought to remember the full context for that identification:

COKES
...Which is your Burbage now?
LANTERN
What mean you by that, sir?
COKES
Your best actor: your Field?[14]

If Burbage was a synonym for 'best actor', so was 'Nathan Field'. Three years earlier, William Ostler, another prominent-but-now-forgotten sharer in the King's Men, and Antonio in *The Duchess of Malfi*, was apostrophized as 'the Roscius of these times' in John Davies's *The Scourge of Folly*.[15]

For Alleyn, although we have even less documentary evidence about his parts, a similar case can be made. He played most of Marlowe's outsized leads (Tamburlaine, Barabas, and Doctor Faustus) as well as Orlando in Greene's *Orlando Furioso*; Muly Mahamet in Peele's *Battle of Alcazar*; the title roles in the lost plays 'Cutlack' and 'The First Part of Tamar Cham'; and the secondary role of Sebastian in 'Frederick and Basilea'.[16] At first glance, this short list may seem to support Cerasano's assertion that the Admiral's Men's repertory 'require[d] a single, imposing actor who was capable of carrying many roles that placed him continually ... in the spotlight.'[17] But closer scrutiny of the evidence does not bear out this impression of relentless singularity. Take Everard Guilpin's well-known reference to Alleyn's 'Cutlack gait' in the 1598 epigram 'On Clodius'. The poem satirizes a 'Bragart' trying to learn to 'play the man' by copying actors. Cerasano uses the allusion to argue that Alleyn's 'unique swagger and overwhelming voice imprinted the part in the audience's memory' (50). But Guilpin's line undercuts such claims, since Clodius's 'passing big' persona is a hybrid of *two* theatrical antecedents:

Clodius, me thinkes, lookes passing big of late,
With Dunstan's brow and Alleyn's Cutlack's gate ...[18]

'Dunstan' may be the bishop in *A Knack to Know a Knave* – if so, and if Clodius's new persona is an assemblage of Alleyn roles, Guilpin is telling us that Alleyn played the fourth-largest role in *Knack*. Alternatively, 'Dunstan' was played by another actor, but impressed Clodius so much that he modelled his facial expression on that performance, while adopting Alleyn's posture. Or perhaps 'Dunstan' is an actor – either James Tunstall, a leading Admiral's Man until at least the summer of 1597, whose name is regularly rendered 'Donstone' by Henslowe; or Thomas Downton, one of the company leaders from October 1597 on, whose name also appears in many variations in the *Diary* and elsewhere.[19] Whoever is being alluded to, Guilpin's epigram does not support the notion that leads were Alleyn's exclusive domain.

Not that Alleyn's roles lacked impact: all three of his Marlovian characters are textually dominant. Doctor Faustus has a larger share of his play than any other early modern role (over 45 per cent; *c.* 5,000 words), and Barabas is close behind (*c.* 42 per cent; *c.* 7,500 words), as is the Tamburlaine of *Part 2* (*c.* 38 per cent; *c.* 6,600 words).[20] Both Tamburlaine in *Part 1* and Orlando in *Orlando Furioso* (in the printed text) also have an outsized textual presence, with *c.* 34 per cent each. Hence, five of Alleyn's six roles in extant plays come from that small group of parts with a share of 30 per cent or more of the text – compared to the third of Burbage's known roles that meet that standard. But the remaining three roles for which we have some information are of a different kind.

Muly Mahamet, although the longest part in Peele's *Battle of Alcazar*, only speaks around 17 per cent of the text (by word count, the shortest tragic lead in the entire corpus). Other major characters' word counts are quite evenly distributed, with Sebastian, Stukely, Abdelmelec, and the Presenter each taking 10–15 per cent of the script. Alleyn does not tower over this cast as in his Marlowe roles. Of the two backstage plots for lost plays, '1 Tamar Cham' gives Alleyn the title role, but he is always accompanied by Humphrey Jeffes's Otanes – and Otanes has several scenes alone on stage, which seem to represent soliloquies.[21] William Bird's Colmogra is present in almost as many scenes as Alleyn and unlike him has at least two opportunities for soliloquies. Finally, and most tellingly, in the backstage 'plot' for 'Frederick and Basilea,' it is Richard Alleyn (no relation) who plays Frederick; he appears in three scenes more than Edward Alleyn's Sebastian and speaks both the Prologue and the Epilogue. Basilea, played by a boy named Dick, has more scenes than anyone else (eleven).[22] Edward Juby's King, Martin Slater's Theodore, Thomas Towne's Myron-hamec, and Sam Rowley's Heraclius feature in seven scenes, as many as Sebastian. The narrative is impossible to reconstruct from the plot, but the document does not suggest that Edward Alleyn's part was especially prominent: he is never alone, and while he may be an important supporting character, the plot clearly focuses on the title figures.[23]

Alleyn's sample of roles is not quite as varied as Burbage's, but it supports the same conclusions: he sometimes played very large roles, sometimes regular-sized leads, and sometimes stepped back into the supporting cast. We do not know how many of the 190 or more lost Admiral's Men's plays had dominant leads, nor do we know which of them were designated Alleyn's. But he certainly did not play the leading role in 'Frederick and Basilea' – and he may well also have taken a supporting part in 'Tasso's Melancholy', 'Bellendon', 'Constantine', Rowley and Juby's 'Samson', Rowley's 'Joshua' – or Chapman's *The Blind Beggar of Alexandria*.

Despite their fame, Alleyn and Burbage did not define their companies, nor were they irreplaceable. We do know, after all, that neither the Admiral's nor the King's Men collapsed when they suddenly had to cope without them. But did company repertories change when their supposed stars died or retired? Scott McMillin has argued as much for the years of Alleyn's temporary withdrawal from playing (1597–1600), when 'the new plays written for the Admiral's men had no role as large as 600 lines; the company's dramaturgy can be charted according to the presence or absence of Alleyn'.[24] But what was that dramaturgy? We cannot say for the years before or during Alleyn's absence, since too many plays of the period are lost (as

Knutson and McInnis discuss in their chapter here). Nor can we track whether Alleyn's established roles disappeared from the repertory, since Henslowe stopped recording daily receipts in late 1597. The company picked up 93 plays in those three years, however, and even if McMillin were right about the extant nine texts, we cannot know how many of the 84 lost plays had large leads. But it is not in fact the case that those nine plays are notably deficient in long roles. Pisaro in Haughton's 1598 *Englishmen for my Money*, at over 6,200 words (nearly 29 per cent), is longer than one of the parts McMillin identifies as exceptionally large, Tourneur's *Atheist's Tragedy*'s D'Amville. Moreover, if we follow Martin Wiggins and others in accepting that the play published as *Lust's Dominion* is Dekker, Haughton, and Day's 'The Spanish Moor's Tragedy', recorded in Henslowe's *Diary* in February 1600,[25] it would seem that the Admiral's Men quickly found a suitable replacement for Alleyn: the part of Eleazer is longer than any associated with him (over 7,600 words, *c.* 40 per cent of the total text). In sum, the available evidence suggests that Alleyn's 'retirement' had no discernible effect on how the Admiral's Men went about their business.

Letting go of the notion that London's adult theatre companies had singularly dominant 'leading actors' necessarily affects our understanding of repertory planning. Take the first performance of 'Frederick and Basilea', recorded in Henslowe's *Diary* in the summer of 1597. It follows hard on the introduction of another new play, 'The Life and Death of Henry I' eight days earlier, which in turn comes fifteen days after the premiere of 'The Comedy of Humours' (usually identified as Chapman's *A Humorous Day's Mirth*). Conventionally, we might think Alleyn played the lead in 'Henry I' and in Chapman's play; we *know* he played a supporting role in 'Frederick and Basilea.' Perhaps convention has it right. If so, that supporting role might have been precisely what Alleyn needed after picking up two leads in quick succession: opening as Frederick a week after he had premiered his Henry may have been too tall an order. Equally plausibly, Alleyn's Henry I could have been paired with a secondary lead, or an even smaller part, in *Mirth* and the supporting role in 'Frederick and Basilea'. As the schedule developed over the coming weeks, Chapman's comedy and the new history play were often performed in close succession; taking the lead in both may have been a lot to ask of Alleyn, since unlike most comedies, Chapman's has a hefty lead in Lemot (*c.* 4,700 words; over 29 per cent). What if the three plays had three different actors in their longest roles? In that case, offering the three new shows one after the other from 7–9 June might have meant showcasing three different configurations of the company: one led perhaps by John Singer, their greatest comic actor; one with Edward Alleyn at its head; and one centred on Richard Alleyn.[26] Alternating plays with different actors in the leads would not only have allowed for a more diverse display of skills, it would also, crucially, have made for a more equitable distribution of labour among players who were, after all, formally equal sharers in the company. If so, the company in planning its schedule must have paid as much attention to who was playing how many large roles in any given week as to the other questions we usually consider central to repertory construction.

Two further data points support the notion that spreading the workload was a factor in managing the repertory. For one, plays with the kinds of outsized roles we might associate with a star system – the Barabases and Hamlets – are exceedingly rare, as we have already seen. Only 8 per cent of all extant plays, 33 in total, had leads with more than 30 per cent of the text, and they were not prevalent in any company's repertory (the fourteen such plays the King's Men owned were distributed over at least 40 years, from *Richard III* to Massinger's *The City Madam*). For another, two-thirds of those 33 plays are tragedies or histories; only nine are comedies. Tragedies, however, do not dominate the corpus as a whole: they only make up a third of all extant plays, a mix, as Knutson has shown, that was reflected in the repertory at the Rose.[27]

Generic diversity did not just enhance audience appeal, it also directly affected the division of actorly labour. Different types of plays, the data shows, favour a different distribution of roles.[28] Tragic leads are, on average, much larger than leads in other plays; speak almost 4,300 words, over 650 more than comic or tragicomic leads; and are responsible for almost a quarter of the entire text (over 23 per cent, compared to c. 19 per cent for other genres). Playing the lead in a tragedy was simply more work, on the level of the text alone, than playing the lead in another kind of play – and given the likelihood that these performances involved fights, they were probably more physically exhausting as well.[29] More comedies meant fewer overly-demanding lead roles.[30]

Second, the distribution of roles in comedies follows a different logic than in tragedies. While secondary leads, like the leads themselves, are shorter in comedies (by a far smaller margin of about 170 words), all other roles are more substantial. The fourth, fifth, and sixth longest part are all over 200 words longer than the equivalent roles in tragedies; their share of the text is correspondingly larger. The third longest role has an almost identical share of the text across all genres, but from the fourth on down, comedic roles are between 15 per cent and 30 per cent more textually present than tragic ones. Comedies thus tend to engage the entire ensemble: they may still have identifiable leads, but those leads are not usually textually dominant; the texts of comedies (and hence stage time and presence) are typically divided quite equitably among at least ten players. Tragedies put a much heavier emphasis on the two leading roles, who on average speak almost 40 per cent of the text and whose relative size compared to all other parts is also much greater than in comic plays.[31]

The benefits of a generically diverse repertory can be observed in casting records for the Caroline King's Men. The eight surviving cast lists, all but one from 1629–31, show patterns similar to those I have traced for Burbage and Alleyn; they also do not support narratives centred on a singularly prominent player.[32] By the 1620s, the company had at least two actors a conventional account might recognize as 'stars' (Joseph Taylor and John Lowin). Both frequently play the largest roles, but not exclusively. Taylor has the longest part in four of the eight performances, the second-longest in two others, the third-largest in a seventh play – and is not listed for the eighth. Lowin takes the lead in three shows and the second largest role in two more, but is also cast in a third, a fourth, and even a sixth-longest role in the other three plays.[33] One play, Carlell's *Deserving Favourite*, has a third actor, Richard Sharpe, as the lead (Lysander); he also takes the second-longest role in Wilson's *Swisser*. Only half of the lead roles are of noteworthy length: in a mix favouring comedy over tragedy 5:3, this is what we should expect. Lowin's Bosola in *Duchess of Malfi* and his Caesar in *The Roman Actor* have over 25 per cent of the text; Taylor's Antiochus in Massinger's *Believe as You List* does too, as does his Mirabell in Fletcher's *Wild Goose Chase* – the longest role in the sample, and an outlier for a comedic lead. The leads that follow generic norms, though, reveal the advantage of a diversified repertory for the workload of their actors. For instance, as Mathias in Massinger's *Picture*, Taylor played the lead; but with fewer than 4,000 words (around 19 per cent of the text), this would surely have been a less demanding task than roles such as Antiochus or Mirabell, though it was probably comparable to the even shorter Arioldus in *The Swisser* (his other comedic lead).

The small Caroline sample is not representative of the range of plays the company had in its repertory at that point, but even so, it affirms an ensemble-based approach to distributing workload and shows how a cannily constructed repertory supported that effort. Leading actors could take middle-of-the-pack roles (as Lowin does on two occasions); they could sit out some shows altogether (as Taylor does once); and even in a company that had two particularly prominent players, other actors could still play lead roles (as Sharpe did). Finally, *some* sharers seem to have specialized in supporting roles; for an actor such as Robert Benfield, the role of Antonio in *Duchess of Malfi* might have been an unusually demanding part (with *c.* 3,100 words), but he appears in the middle ranks in all eight cast lists. Sometimes, that position meant a role such as

Antonio; sometimes, a role of a mere 500 words or so (such as Rusticus in Massinger's *Roman Actor*).

Our limited knowledge of the King's Men's repertory in Burbage's prime leaves little scope for informed speculation, but one example, the second Henriad, allows us to trace a similar approach to casting in Shakespeare's work. Assuming the three Henry plays were staged in sequence or close proximity to one another, the trilogy seems tailormade for an equitable distribution of labour (even if each of the plays also could be, and surely was, performed individually). *1 Henry IV* has exceptionally balanced co-leads: Falstaff's part (*c.* 5,500 words, 23 per cent) is somewhat longer than the others, but Hal and Hotspur have to fight more than him; their parts are of almost identical length (*c.* 4,300 each, *c.* 18 per cent). And Henry IV is an unusually substantial fourth part, at almost 2,600 words (*c.* 10.5 per cent) – before the 1610s, only Puntarvolo in Jonson's *Every Man Out* is longer. When we turn to the trilogy's second part, though, things change radically: where *1 Henry IV* distributes its roles much like a comedy, *2 Henry IV* looks more like a tragedy. The part of Falstaff remains at almost the same length as in part one, but most others shrink dramatically; the lead is twice as large as the next part. That role, Hal (2,400 words, less than 10 per cent), is shorter than his father's in *1 Henry IV*; and only one other part, Henry IV, has more than 1,500 words. That makes good sense, too, from the perspective of distributed labour: Henry dies, after all, so whoever played him probably could take a break in *Henry V*. The Hal actor, on the other hand, was in for a serious workout, in one of Shakespeare's most demanding roles. But the trilogy carefully set him up for that challenge, with the relative breather in *2 Henry IV*.

The second Henriad, then, is constructed as we might expect from a playwright familiar with the interrelation of casting and repertory. The trilogy, like the repertory as whole, strikes a balance between the company's various, potentially competing interests: an equitable distribution of labour; making the most of everyone's talents and public appeal; and catering to the ambition, described by Tiffany Stern and Simon Palfrey, 'to "Act Great Parts"' – an ambition not limited to the 'master or chief players' in any company of actors.³⁴ Maintaining this delicate balance would have required a thorough knowledge of the relative lengths of the parts in the repertory and of the various sharers' needs, desires, and challenges. This would have had an effect on the acquisition of new plays, too, since additions to the repertory needed to respond to the same network of considerations as the scheduling of established parts of the repertory. It seems unlikely that such a complex task was handled entirely collectively; instead, it might have fallen to experienced sharers with quasi-managerial responsibilities (and possibly reduced stage time) – figures such as John Heminges in his last two decades with the King's Men.

Let me end by considering the question of repertory from the perspective of London's theatre industry four generations or so later. David Garrick's star status can hardly be questioned; from our modern understanding of the concept, we might expect him to have performed every night, as often as possible in roles for which he was famous. But that is not what the eighteenth-century theatrical records show. With the exception of his entirely atypical debut season, Garrick never appeared in more than 61 per cent of his company's performances. In his busiest season at Drury Lane, 1757–58, he performed 111 times.³⁵ He rarely acted his most famous roles more than a handful of times a year. After 1743–44, London audiences never had more than four chances a season to see his Hamlet. And Garrick frequently took on minor characters: Drugger in *The Alchemist*; Chamont in Otway's *The Orphan*; Lusignan in Aaron Hill's *Zara* (the latter no longer than 136 lines).³⁶

He explained to Francis Hayman in October 1745, 'I am not able to act two nights successively two principal carracters. I endeavour'd at it last season (contrary to my agreement) in King John, Tancred, &c & the whole town knows the consequence'³⁷ (he suffered a physical breakdown and did not return for months). An analysis of a typical season, 1753–54, confirms that he carefully managed his appearances. Only in new plays did Garrick act leads on more than two successive nights, appearing in the same role on up to six consecutive occasions. What caused strain was not repeating a role night after night (the norm for modern Anglophone actors) but playing different major roles in quick succession. The only time this happened on three consecutive nights that season it was followed by a four-day break. As a consequence, his famous roles were regularly played by other actors: Henry Mossop was Richard III twice as often as Garrick that season (four to two), Macbeth three times as often (three to one).[38]

Garrick's practice probably differed somewhat from early modern professional habits; the companies he worked in were larger, with more settled repertories. But we should take seriously his sense of the mental and physical limits to what an actor can do in any given week. Until he reduced his appearances in 1763, Garrick averaged about 92 performances a year; the most roles he ever played in one season was 29 (his average was 21). He acted many of those parts for 20 years or more, and not all of them were leads. Contrast that with what we conventionally assume Alleyn managed in the Admiral's Men's seemingly paradigmatic run from June 1594 to June 1595: 270 performances, playing 36 *leads*, while learning 20 of them from scratch.[39] How plausible is it that the limit of what was sustainable for an acting company had shrunk this drastically within four or five generations? Is it not more likely that the realities of the 1590s bore a closer resemblance to the 1750s than we have traditionally believed?

The reading of the Admiral's and King's Men's casting practices I have offered here encourages a rethinking of how a company of equal sharers would have approached the division of actorly labour. The most significant member of the company, from this perspective, would not be the one we have anachronistically identified as its 'star' but the one organizing a set of individuals into a collective. A Shakespearean character may serve as our patron as we begin to attend to these organizational endeavours. Appropriately, it is a worker. Not Nick Bottom, the hogger of leads in *Midsummer Nights*

Dream, but Peter Quince, a sharer in every sense: a manager of equals, a distributor of parts, and a man with a list.

Notes

1 Roslyn Lander Knutson, *The Repertory of Shakespeare's Company, 1594–1613* (Fayetteville: University of Arkansas Press, 1991); see esp. 20–55 for a detailed account of these parameters. For an overview of subsequent developments in repertory study, see Tom Rutter, 'Repertory Studies: A Survey,' *Shakespeare* 4 (2008), 336–350, and Rutter, 'Introduction: The Repertory-Based Approach,' *Early Theatre*, 13 (2010), 121–132.

2 See Tiffany Stern, *Documents of Performance in Early Modern England* (Cambridge: Cambridge University Press, 2009), 36–62, 264–265.

3 Scott McMillin and Sally-Beth MacLean, *The Queen's Men and Their Plays* (Cambridge: Cambridge University Press, 1998), 97–98.

4 In insisting on the construction of plays as systems of parts, James Marino's chapter in this volume pursues an argument related to mine: the ways in which changes to one part affected other actors' parts needed to be carefully managed. As I suggest here, the distribution of those parts across a repertory had casting implications that always affected the entire company, and required equally thoughtful management.

5 John Astington, *Actors and Acting in Shakespeare's Time: The Art of Stage Playing* (Cambridge: Cambridge University Press, 2010), 128. Cf. Bart van Es's assertion that the King's Men had *a* 'leading man', and that of the eleven 'dominant roles' Shakespeare wrote from 1599–1608, nine were written 'for' Burbage; see *Shakespeare in Company* (Oxford: Oxford University Press, 2013), 237–238.

6 Andrew Gurr, *Shakespeare's Opposites: The Admiral's Company, 1594–1625* (Cambridge: Cambridge University Press, 2009), 50.

7 Astington, 112.

8 S. P. Cerasano, 'Edward Alleyn, the New Model Actor, and the Rise of the Celebrity in the 1590s', *Medieval & Renaissance Drama in England*, 18 (2005), 50.

9 'Plots' were large single-page documents that listed entrances and sometimes the appearance of major props; in the handful of surviving examples, many of the actors playing the listed characters are named. 'The Dead Man's Fortune' cannot be reliably dated (or even assigned definitely to a particular acting company).

10 See Edwin Nungezer, *A Dictionary of Actors and of Other Persons Associated with the Public Representation of Plays in England before 1642* (New Haven: Yale University Press, 1929), 68–70. He also took unknown roles in Jonson's *Every Man in* and *Every Man out of his Humour*, *Sejanus*, and *Catiline*, and further plays by Beaumont and Fletcher.

11 Data about the length of roles is drawn from a database built using Martin Mueller's 'Shakespeare His Contemporaries' corpus and the Folger Shakespeare Digital Texts. It was assembled from the XML-tagged playtexts with code developed by my research assistant Lawrence Evalyn. Imperfections in the tagging mean it is prudent to use rounded rather than exact figures for word counts; the broader conclusions about company repertories and generic trends discussed later in this essay are sustainable despite this lack of precision.

12 See Gerald Eades Bentley, *The Profession of Player in Shakespeare's Time* (Princeton, NJ: Princeton University Press, 1984), 248–294.

13 *The Malcontent*, ed. W. David Kay, New Mermaids (London: A & C Black, 1998), Induction 11–12, 26SD.

14 *The Cambridge Edition of the Works of Ben Jonson*, ed. David Bevington, Martin Butler, and Ian Donaldson (Cambridge: Cambridge University Press, 2012), v. 4, 397, 5.3.64–67.

15 Nungezer, 262.

16 See Nungezer, 8.

17 Cerasano, 50.

18 *Skialetheia. Or, A Shadowe of Truth, Epigrams and Satyres*, ed. Alexander B. Grosart (Manchester: Charles Simms, 1878), 18.

19 See Nungezer, 117–119, 381.

20 Mueller's corpus includes only the 1604 A-Text, but this is likely closer to the version Alleyn would have performed than the B-Text published in 1616.

21 Reprinted in W. W. Greg, ed., *Henslowe Papers, Being Documents Supplementary to Henslowe's Diary* (London: A. H. Bullen, 1907), 144–148.

22 Reproduced and transcribed in W. W. Greg, *Dramatic Documents from the Elizabethan Playhouses* (Oxford: Clarendon Press, 1969), n.p.

23 Nonetheless, T. J. King insists that Edward Alleyn, as 'the leading actor of the company . . . plays Sebastian, the leading role' – a misrepresentation of what the plot indicates; *Casting Shakespeare's Plays: London Actors and Their Roles, 1590–1642* (Cambridge: Cambridge University Press, 1992), 30.

24 Scott McMillin, *The Elizabethan Theatre and The Book of Sir Thomas More* (Ithaca: Cornell University Press, 1987), 63.

25 Martin Wiggins and Catherine Richardson, *British Drama 1533–1642: A Catalogue*, vol. 4 (Oxford: Oxford University Press, 2014), 206–210 (#1235).

26 See *Henslowe's Diary*, ed. R. A. Foakes (Cambridge: Cambridge University Press, 2002), 58–59.

27 See Knutson, 40–41, 44.

28 To avoid the difficulty of fine distinctions between genres, which are not crucial to my argument, I am counting all history plays as tragedies (which reduces the average size of leads, since most chronicle plays are more evenly distributed than tragedies) and all romances and tragicomedies as comedies (which makes virtually no statistical difference, as these genres have nearly identical distribution patterns).

29 I am grateful to Ben Naylor for a spirited exchange on this question.

30 The one role that, as Richard Preiss demonstrates in his chapter here, eludes this text-based analysis is also the one that may have defied such generic distinctions: the clown. His part probably varied in length show-by-show, depending on the performer's

whim and the performance's needs, and those factors probably mattered far more than what kind of play the clown appeared in or what the playwright had set down for him.

31 This analysis ignores doubling, but distribution patterns suggest that actors beyond the third largest part would have had to double more in tragedies than in comedies. However, my reading of T. J. King's tabulations of casting records suggests a limited use of the practice across genres for the 8–12 'principal parts'. Even in the heavily doubled *Duchess of Malfi*, only two of the nine largest roles have a minor second part. See King, 96–143.

32 This information, gleaned from manuscript sources and a number of plays printed mostly in the 1630s, is summarized in King, 115–126.

33 Additional sources give Lowin the fourth-largest role in *Volpone* (Sir Politic), the third-longest in *The Alchemist* (Mammon), and perhaps the second-longest role in *Philaster*, Leon/Dion (Taylor being notably absent, Philaster is played by Hugh Clarke).

34 Tiffany Stern, *Shakespeare in Parts* (Oxford: Oxford University Press, 2007), 46. For the phrase, see King, 17.

35 Data collected from John Genest, *Some Account of the English Stage, from the Restoration in 1600 to 1830*, vol. 4 (Bath: H. E. Carrington, 1832); Arthur H. Scouten, ed., *The London Stage, 1660–1800. Part 3, 1729–1747* (Carbondale: Southern Illinois University Press, 1961); and George Winchester Stone, ed., *The London Stage, 1660–1800. Part 4, 1747–1776* (Carbondale: Southern Illinois University Press, 1962).

36 See George Winchester Stone and George Morrow Kahrl, *David Garrick, a Critical Biography* (Carbondale: Southern Illinois University Press, 1979), 481, 524–528, 564–568 and Appendices B and C.

37 Quoted in Kalman A. Burnim, 'The Significance of Garrick's Letters to Hayman', *Shakespeare Quarterly,* 9 (1958), 150.

38 See Stone, 377–433. I am indebted to Terry Robinson and David Taylor for conversations on this subject.

39 See *Henslowe's Diary*, 22–30.

3

Parts and the Playscript

Seven Questions

James J. Marino[*]

The scholars who pioneered modern dramatic bibliography knew very well that early modern plays were divided into acting parts or cue-scripts, but their theories focused on complete texts, the whole rather than the parts.[1] Even now, when Tiffany Stern and Simon Palfrey have returned actors' parts to critical attention, those parts have not been integrated into our standard textual models.[2] Although individual scholars have made individual efforts to ask how parts and cues illuminate specific textual problems, the default assumption remains that plays were changed wholesale, from top to bottom, and thinking about the parts remains optional rather than obligatory.[3] A hypothesis about the three *Hamlet*s or two *King Lear*s need not consider the cue-structure at all. This is both a mistake in itself and a cause of other mistakes.

It is a mistake in itself because once a script entered the players' repertory, further changes could only be executed through the medium of actors' parts. Players needed both to learn new cues and to remember not to give or to answer old ones. And they had to master the changed cue-structure well enough not to disrupt live performance. Giving the wrong cue, or failing to answer the right one, could stop a play. Changing a script that actors had already learned imposed specific practical necessities that any revision or adaptation needed to take into account.

One can only safely ignore these pragmatic realities by positing that all rewriting happened before the play entered repertory or else after its theatrical life. If one theorizes that a particular quarto was an unperformed draft, or that the 1623 Shakespeare Folio represents a post-theatrical literary redaction, theatrical parts become moot. Tiffany Stern's argument that the First Quarto of *Hamlet* derives from shorthand does not need to reckon with theatrical parts.[4] Likewise, Lukas Erne's argument that the so-called bad quartos are theatrical abridgements of longer literary texts can still be advanced if abridgement came before the division into parts.[5] But relatively few textual theories limit themselves to pre- or post-theatrical revision, especially since so many scholarly editions, including Erne's own edition, now resort to combined hypotheses.[6] Since the traditional hypotheses of touring adaptation, theatrical revision, and memorial reconstruction no longer seem sufficiently explanatory, editors propose that plays underwent more than one of these transformations.[7]

How players carried out the hypothesized adaptations or revisions, or whether they could carry them out, is routinely ignored. A textual theory that failed to consider the practices of early modern printers or scribes would be rightly dismissed. Theories that ignore the players' working practices are likewise unsound. Hypotheses that do not consider theatrical parts are in fact unacknowledged hypotheses about those parts. They inevitably imply subsidiary claims about the actors' scrolls. Failing to acknowledge those claims shields them from examination, even by the hypothesizer. And scholarly consensus about the provenances of particular dramatic texts should be taken with caution when such consensus ignores the evidence of parts and cues.

Failure to consider cue-structure also leads to particular errors, undermining many of our standard textual models. Arguments for playhouse revision must surely think about parts and cues. Theatrical revision was not infinitely flexible, because an early modern acting script was not equally mutable at every point. Its structure of interlocking, semi-independent scrolls eased certain changes and presented obstacles to others. No change was entirely impossible, if the players were sufficiently determined, but some would be extremely arduous or inconvenient. One cannot intuitively grasp the ease or difficulty of any change if one imagines the play only as a unified text. Those who revised early modern plays clearly understood the practical difficulties of enacting those revisions; scholars need to understand them, too.

And yet arguments about theatrical revision seldom distinguish between changes in the middle of speeches, which an actor might make on his own, and changes to cues, which needed coordination. The old hypothesis that the Folio text of *Hamlet* includes Richard Burbage's actor's gag is two hypotheses. Burbage could add 'O vengeance!' to a soliloquy unilaterally; adding 'O, o, o, o' to his last speech needs Horatio's cooperation. Scholars arguing that shorter quarto texts result from actors eliminating lines in performance must ask whether the dropped lines included cues and explain how the actors who did not get the cues that they expected were to respond. At the furthest extreme, plays performed by actors who worked in teams coordinated by scripted cues are discussed in terms designed for oral literature transmitted by individual story-tellers.[8]

Arguments that a play has been adapted for touring must also consider how the cast could learn a changed set of cues. The crudest versions of the touring-adaptation argument take the relative shortness of the text as *prima facie* evidence of a reduced cast. But, as Scott McMillin's work has shown, abbreviated plays made doubling harder.[9] And relearning a changed set of cues could make touring harder too, for no clear purpose. Proper attention to cue-structure can strengthen hypotheses about reduced casts, particularly when the evidence suggests that, for instance, a three-speaker-dialogue has been redistributed between two characters.[10] But other changes to cues would make a part harder to relearn, and thus riskier to perform, without any reduction in cast size or any benefit in performance. Why should Mistress Page and Mistress Ford's parts change so thoroughly in *Merry Wives*, when the changes do not eliminate either Mistress Page or Mistress Ford? Why is Page's part so different? Why would actors going out on tour do this to themselves?

Perhaps mostly damningly, claims of memorial reconstruction often identify particular actors as reporters without asking how well those alleged reporters recall their cue-lines. Such hypotheses usually measure the overall consistency of the actor's lines, but not the actor's cues.[11] But early modern players had strong incentives to remember cues and should not be assumed to have remembered the rest of their lines equally well. A player who remembers the bulk of his lines but not his cues is the opposite of what we should expect.

Some actors traditionally named as memorial reporters even seem to make the error that an early modern repertory player was least likely to make, giving one of his own cues to someone else. Scholars have long argued that *The First Part of the Contention between ... York and Lancaster* is a memorial reconstruction, based on a garbled speech by York in 2.2, and have labelled the actor playing Warwick the reporter.[12] For this to be true, Warwick must give away one of his own cues by mistake in the very speech that is held up as chief evidence of memorial report. York's botched account of his genealogy in the Quarto text ends with the word 'crown,' cueing Warwick. The more coherent Folio speech ends with 'traitorously,' cueing Salisbury instead (TLN 986). Here is the Folio version:

Yorke. ...
Till *Henry Bullingbrooke*, Duke of Lancaster,
The eldest Sonne and Heire of *Iohn* of Gaunt,
Crown'd by the Name of *Henry* the fourth,

Seiz'd on the Realme, depos'd the rightfull King,
Sent his poore Queene to France, from whence she came,
And him to Pumfret; where, as all you know,
Harmlesse *Richard* was murthered traiterously.
  Warw. Father, the Duke hath told the truth;
Thus got the House of *Lancaster* the Crowne.
  Yorke. Which now they hold by force, and not by
  right . . . .

(F, TLN 980–989)

And here is the parallel passage from the Quarto:

  Yorke. . . . Now sir. In the time of Richards raigne, Henry of Bullingbrooke, sonne and heire to Iohn of Gaunt, the Duke of Lancaster fourth sonne to Edward the third, he claimde the Crowne, deposde the Merthfull King, and as both you know, in Pomphret Castle harmlesse Richard was shamefully murthered, and so by Richards death came the house of Lancaster vnto the Crowne.
  Sals. Sauing your tale my Lord, as I haue heard, in the raigne of Bullenbrooke, the Duke of Yorke did claime the Crowne, and but for Owin Glendor, had bene King.
  Yorke. True. . . .

(Q1, C4v)

If the Quarto text represented the Warwick actor's memory of the Folio script, that actor would have to forget whether or not it was his turn to speak. Worse yet, Warwick's next speech in the Folio ends with the cue-word 'crown,' which means a memorial-reporter Warwick would be waiting for York to speak the cue that Warwick himself was meant to say. Two different actors responding to the same cue-word with two different speeches would obviously disrupt performance. But for an actor to wait for someone else to speak the cue he was meant to give would be more disruptive still. Nor would prompting resolve the trouble when the actor thought someone else was being prompted. If the actor playing

Warwick were to make this error on stage, no one would speak at all.

The problem here is not individual scholars' individual errors. These mistakes are pervasive. They are systematic and paradigmatic. We all make them, just as I myself have made them, because of our training. Our only saving grace is that no one catches us, because no one else checks the cue-structure either. That is both a professional mercy and an intellectual problem.

What would a theoretical model of early modern playtexts fully integrating parts and cues be like? I cannot pretend to have developed such a model, which will inevitably be the work of many hands. For now I would like to offer seven initial questions that might shape that model as it develops.

1. *Why do some characters change more than others?* W. W. Greg built his memorial-reconstruction hypothesis on a genuine insight: some characters' roles in early modern plays do change more than others.[13] Edgar and Goneril in *King Lear* change more than Edmund and Regan. Paris in *Romeo and Juliet* changes modestly but Capulet enormously. Greg's explanation does not bear up under scrutiny, but the phenomenon he saw still requires explanation.[14] The simplest hypothesis is that revisions have centred on some characters more than others. We know that such targeted revisions sometimes occurred. The additions to Kyd's *Spanish Tragedy*, for example, focus heavily on the part of Hieronimo, with some changes to the part of the boy playing Isabella.[15] This phenomenon is not an anomaly of failed reproduction, but a basic feature of early dramatic texts. Some roles change more than others because some rolls change more than others.

2. *Whose parts change most?* Greg's theory sought to identify the 'piratical' reporter by focusing on characters whose parts changed least, using *Merry Wives of Windsor*'s Host as the original example.[16] The best question about *The Merry Wives of Windsor* may not be why Mine Host's part changes so little from Quarto to Folio, but why Master Page's part changes so much. Not only do Page's lines and cues change, but also his entrances and exits, including his first entrance.

And when he is on stage other characters' roles must also change, because those characters inevitably exchange cues with him. Page is near the heart of a significant structural intervention in the script. Rather than imagining a failed attempt to transmit *The Merry Wives* entire and unchanged, we might more plausibly hypothesize an intervention or series of interventions centred on specific roles.

3. *How difficult would any change be to make?* Textual theories have often focused on why changes were made, demanding an explanation of the playwright or players' motives. The better question is not why, but how. Questions of motivation are necessarily speculative. Questions of opportunity are subject to demonstration. The question of why something was done to a play cannot logically precede the question of what was done to it. Asking what the players could do with their texts, arranged as those texts were into parts, allows us to measure the relative difficulty or ease of any particular changes. Scripts' division into parts made some changes surprisingly easy, some unexpectedly difficult, and others nearly impractical.

The difficulty of relearning dialogue depends on a number of factors, including the number and frequency of each player's cues. A stichomythia was harder to revise than a monologue. But the most important measure of difficulty is the number of players involved. The more actors who needed to relearn cues, the greater the difficulty of revision and the danger of accidental reversions during performance. Viewed from this perspective, the changes to Hamlet's soliloquies in the First Quarto, over which textual critics have long obsessed, are absolutely elementary. They involve only one actor and no changed cues. Monologues are, as Richard Preiss points out elsewhere in this volume, the easiest places for clowns to improvise, and equally amenable to scripted revision.[17] Hamlet in soliloquy can always speak more than is set down for him, or less than is set down for him, or something rather different than is set down for him, as long as he delivers the last word set down for him. From a practical standpoint the most important line in the 'To be or not to be' soliloquy is 'Nymph, in thy orisons be all my sins remembered,' which the First Quarto carefully retains. No matter how much Hamlet's First-Quarto soliloquies vary from the Folio or Second Quarto versions, they invariably preserve the cue.[18] *Hamlet*'s First Quarto, like all 'bad' dramatic texts, would profit from careful re-examination of the cue evidence.

4. *Which changes needed to be made simultaneously?* The number of actors involved in a particular change also reveals what I would call minimal revision events, interventions to the text that could only be made at once. The changes in Hamlet's soliloquies are one such minimal event: they could have been made entirely independent of any other changes. But other, seemingly less important, changes require more actors. Horatio and the Queen's conversation about Ophelia in the Folio and Second-Quarto *Hamlet* (4.5.1–20) adds or subtracts the additional part of a 'Gentleman' and switches a speech between Horatio and the Queen, requiring two or three actors' involvement (4.5.14–16). The First Quarto offers a completely different dialogue between Horatio and the Queen (scene 14); Horatio's part and the Queen's were demonstrably changed together, perhaps more than once. Similarly, the changes to 2.2 of *2 Henry VI* would require all three actors, York, Warwick, and Salisbury, to learn new cues. The changes to Page's role in *Merry Wives* necessarily involve a large number of other players, most prominently the actors playing Shallow, Slender, Evans, and Ford, and would indicate a major effort.

Such changes may or may not have been independent of other changes in the same play. Twentieth-century bibliography sought the tell-tale variant, the local detail revealing a global change in the script. One slip of the pen revealed the playwright's working draft; one garbled speech meant the whole play had been memorized. The traditional model presumes that changes were made simultaneously until proven otherwise; a part-based model might reverse that presumption. But a script divided into parts is uniquely amenable to mid-sized revisions. And a repertory company focused on managing and balancing its members' workloads, as Holger Syme has shown in the last chapter, might well count the labour of relearning parts in that workload, so that not all players would be considered equally available to master new cues at any given moment.[19] The best way to avoid unsupported presumptions is to think rigorously about which changes had to be made simultaneously, and to build any global theories upon those provable local examples.

While scholars have generally been reluctant to view the 1602 Quarto of *Merry Wives* as authorial or Shakespearean, the standard array of explanations – memorial reconstruction, theatrical adaptation, revision for performance at Court – all need to involve agents who thought in terms of parts.[20] Whether *Merry Wives* was revised by Shakespeare or adapted by other parties, the changes to Page's role very clearly needed to involve a number of other actors, but not the one playing Falstaff. Falstaff's part also changes significantly, but since he seldom interacts with Page that role was not necessarily revised at the same time. One can neither assume that Page and Falstaff were revised separately nor that they were revised together. The current textual model strongly favours the presumption of simultaneous change, positing the fewest possible interventions over a play's lifetime. This is so, oddly, even in cases such as that of *Merry Wives*, which critics have frequently imagined undergoing both revision and reconstruction, or both adaptation and memorial report. It is considered simpler to hypothesize that a play was revised once than that it was revised twice, but this introduces an unnecessary and unsupported hypothesis. Setting an unknown number to the lowest value possible is as arbitrary as setting it to the highest. If a bicycle's brakes, tyres, and handlebars have been replaced, it may be that some of those components were replaced simultaneously, but it would be illogical to presume so. Early modern plays were likewise divided into semi-independent components amenable to independent revision or replacement. But because the parts were only semi-independent, some changes to multiple parts were demonstrably made at the same time; textual theories must privilege those demonstrable facts.

5. *What changes were most potentially disruptive in performance?* Textual scholars have long assumed that cutting a play is easier than expanding it. Similarly, but not quite consistently, they have focused on the problem of 'drying' in performance, of momentarily forgetting one's lines and, in the terminology of the time, 'being out' (meaning, of course, 'out' of the part). But when acting a play whose cues have been memorized, revised, and re-memorized, 'drying' may be less dangerous than blurting. A player forgetting a line could be prompted by the prompter. A player speaking a speech that was no longer in the script could seriously derail a scene. The returned speech might cue the wrong player to speak next, or cue an earlier version of the scene which the other actors may or may not have learned. And no prompter in the world can unspeak a speech once the audience has heard it. Alternatively, the play might grind to a halt. The only thing worse than not giving the cue is giving a cue no one else on stage can answer.

Cutting a play had practical dangers, because a cut speech's ghost might return and go unanswered. Adding speeches risked the actor requiring the prompter; cutting speeches risked more substantial confusion, with no safety net. Certainly, early modern playing companies took these risks. But they did not ignore them.

Changing York's speech in *2 Henry VI* to end with 'traitorously' rather than 'crown' may use the cue change to manage performance risk. If one approaches the Folio text as a revision, rather than taking the Quarto as an erroneous copy, the cue change facilitates the change in who is cued.[21] 'Crown' cues Salisbury, 'traitorously' Warwick. The danger that Salisbury will speak the next speech from the Quarto script, which is meant to come later in the Folio, is forestalled because Salisbury does not hear the cue. Here it seems that the possibility of an actor answering a cue with an out-dated speech was foreclosed by changing the cue itself.

6. *What were the practical limits on playhouse revision?* This question moves from the demonstrable to the hypothetical, and where one sets the hypothesized limits will materially

change one's answers. How many actors' parts needed to change before those changes seemed impractical in the playhouse? At what point should one presume a literary revision, before or after a play's repertory lifetime, rather than a series of changes made within the repertory system? Changes affecting more than three players' roles at one time are fairly rare, but larger changes do exist. The changes surrounding Page in *Merry Wives* involve at least five actors, among the largest such changes in the surviving Shakespeare corpus. Perhaps this indicates something close to the maximum number of actors who could be asked to re-learn cues; perhaps it exceeds that maximum and indicates changes outside the playhouse, whether literary revision or some garbled form of post-performance transmission.

Neither is it clear how many changes to an individual actor's cues were tolerable or at what point the sheer number of changes suggests an actor has been replaced by a new actor memorizing the part afresh. The most obvious candidates for replacement are boy actors, who would eventually age out of women's parts as their voices changed. The transition to a new boy player presented an opportunity to revise both the boy's role and that of an adult scene partner. The example of Hieronimo and Isabella in the additions to *The Spanish Tragedy* is illustrative: rewriting the boy's role makes it easier to rewrite his senior partner's, since the new boy had to learn all his cues from scratch anyway.

The major differences between the Quarto and Folio versions of Mistress Page and Mistress Ford in *Merry Wives* can thus be easily explained by the inevitable casting of new boys, who could learn revised parts, in those roles. But it is not only women's roles that sometimes see major changes to the cue-structure. Page's radically altered role might indicate a part thoroughly rewritten for an experienced actor who could master numerous cue changes. Or it may indicate that the actor playing Page had been recast.

7. *Why does a new character's entrance sometimes shift a scene from textual variance to textual conformity?* Greg

noticed that when his proposed reporter, Mine Host, entered, the Folio and Quarto texts of *Merry Wives* often moved into close agreement. This happens less consistently than Greg first argued, and other character entrances in other plays have the same effect.[22] The Nurse, who is surely not a memorial reporter, creates the Mine Host effect once, but only once, in *Romeo and Juliet*, in 2.4.[23] And in 4.2 of *King Lear*, the entrance of a 'messenger' or a 'second gentleman' bringing news of Cornwall's death brings the divergent Quarto and Folio texts back to close conformity.[24] Even if memorial reconstruction is not happening here, something is.

There are at least two possibilities. The Mine Host effect could derive from separate revisions to relatively small groups of actors' parts. Romeo, Mercutio, and Benvolio's parts could only be revised together, but the Nurse's part did not need to be revised with them. Thus Romeo, Mercutio, and Benvolio can exchange revised cues freely, but need to give the Nurse the old ones. The entrance of a character who was not part of the targeted revision forces a return to the older version of the script. Alternately, players might have been divided into small working groups to study and master script changes together. In this scenario, Romeo, Mercutio, and Benvolio would have memorized their new cues together while the Nurse relearned his with other actors. The Nurse's entrance would thus still demand a return to unrevised and previously rehearsed cues.

Similarly, *King Lear*'s Messenger or Second Gentlemen enters a scene whose textual changes are isolated to Goneril and Albany's lines. The Quarto and Folio texts diverge when Albany enters, and converge again when Albany and Goneril begin exchanging cues with the messenger. The revisions have been kept limited and simple, learned by one man and one boy, and when those two actors are joined by a third they immediately revert to the earlier script. Why the messenger's entrance returns the Folio and Quarto to agreement may be less important than why Albany's entrance throws them out of agreement.

This explanation for the 'Mine Host' effect extends to Mine Host himself. Paul Werstine points to the way the Quarto and Folio texts of *Merry Wives* 'fly apart' after Mine Host's exit in II.i as one of Greg's strongest pieces of evidence.[25] But as in the *Lear* example, the alleged reporter's entrance interrupts a two-character scene. The Host's entrance prompts everyone on stage to closer textual fidelity, but 'everyone on stage' is Page and Ford. Those two characters have been playing a thoroughly rewritten version of the scene.[26] Every cue that Ford and Page give each other in 2.1 changes between the Quarto and the Folio. Even when their speeches to each other preserve the same general sense or elements of the same language, the cue words change without fail. That pattern requires those two parts to have been revised in tandem.

Whenever Ford and Page interact directly in this scene, the texts disagree. When they trade cues with other actors the textual agreement increases. Both characters speak cues found in both versions of the text, but not to each other. The textual agreement increases when Shallow and the Host arrive because Page and Ford stop cueing each other while Shallow and the Host are on stage. Page and Ford's parts have been rewritten and relearned together, but that rewriting must work around the other characters who come and go during the scene. As soon as the Host and Shallow depart, Page and Ford's parts immediately diverge again; Page exits in the Folio, but not the Quarto. But this change involves the same two actors whose earlier dialogue has altered. The Mine Host effect is not a sign of a global change to the play but merely a local inconvenience to be worked around as quickly as possible. The script reverts to unrevised text because the Host was not revised when Ford and Page were.

These seven questions do not yield answers about early modern playtexts. In many cases, they lead only to new questions. Early modern plays are far too messy and complicated for any easy solutions. But new questions, and new tools of analysis, may be what the study of early modern dramatic texts most needs. The good news, so late in our discipline's day, is how much work there is left to do.

Notes

* I would like to thank Richard M. Preiss, Brooke A. Conti, Tiffany Stern, and the members of the Folger Symposium on Theatrical Documents for their assistance with this chapter.

1 For a concise and sympathetic history of the New Bibliography, see Gabriel Egan, *The Struggle for Shakespeare's Text: Twentieth-Century Editorial Theory and Practice* (Cambridge: Cambridge University Press, 2010). For other perspectives, see Leah S. Marcus, *Unediting the Renaissance: Shakespeare, Marlowe, Milton* (London and New York: Routledge, 1996) and Paul Werstine's seminal essays 'McKerrow's "Suggestion" and Twentieth-Century Shakespeare Textual Criticism', *Renaissance Drama*, 19 (1988), 149–173; 'Narratives About Printed Shakespeare Texts: "Foul Papers" and "Bad" Quartos', *Shakespeare Quarterly*, 41 (1990), 65–86; and 'A Century of "Bad" Shakespeare Quartos', *Shakespeare Quarterly*, 50 (1999), 310–333.

2 See Simon Palfrey and Tiffany Stern, *Shakespeare in Parts* (Oxford: Oxford University Press, 2007) and Tiffany Stern, *Documents of Performance in Early Modern England* (Cambridge: Cambridge University Press, 2009).

3 For example, Paul Menzer, *The Hamlets: Cues, Qs, and Remembered Texts* (Newark: University of Delaware Press, 2008); James J. Marino, *Owning William Shakespeare: The King's Men and Their Intellectual Property* (Philadelphia: University of Pennsylvania Press, 2011), 75–106; Matthew Vadnais, '"Speake(ing) the Speech(es)": Reassessing the Playability of the Earliest Printings of *Hamlet*', in *Shakespeare Expressed: Page, Stage, and Classroom in Shakespeare and His Contemporaries*, ed. Kathryn R. McPherson and Sarah Enloe (Madison: Fairleigh Dickinson University Press, 2013), 81–92.

4 Tiffany Stern, 'Sermons, Plays, and Note-Takers: *Hamlet* Q1 as a "Noted" Text,' *Shakespeare Survey*, 66 (2013), 1–23.

5 Lukas Erne, *Shakespeare as Literary Dramatist* (Cambridge: Cambridge University Press, 2003, rev. 2013).

6 Lukas Erne, ed., *The First Quarto of Romeo and Juliet* (Cambridge: Cambridge University Press, 1997), 24–25.

7   See for example René Weis, ed., *Romeo and Juliet*, The Arden Shakespeare Third Series (London: Bloomsbury, 2012), 105–106, which simultaneously advances touring adaptation, rewriting by a playwright, theatrical abridgement, and memorial reconstruction.

8   Lene B. Petersen, *Shakespeare's Errant Texts: Textual Form and Linguistic Style in Shakespearean 'Bad' Quartos and Co-Authored Plays* (Cambridge: Cambridge University Press, 2010).

9   Scott McMillin, 'Casting the Hamlet Quartos: The Limit of Eleven', in Thomas Clayton, ed., *The Hamlet First Published (Q1, 1603): Origins, Form, Intertextualities* (Newark: University of Delaware Press, 1992), 179–194.

10 The theatrical manuscript of Fletcher and Massinger's *Sir John Olden Barnavelt* shows redistributions of this kind. See Paul Werstine, *Early Modern Playhouse Manuscripts and the Editing of Shakespeare* (Cambridge: Cambridge University Press, 2012), 168–172.

11 See Kathleen O. Irace, *Reforming the 'Bad' Quartos: Performance and Provenance of Six Shakespearean First Editions* (Newark: University of Delaware Press, 1994).

12 The Quarto speech is on C4r–C4v, reproduced in *King Henry VI, Part 2*, ed. Ronald Knowles, The Arden Shakespeare Third Series (London: Thomson Learning, 1999), 387–388. Compare *The Norton Facsimile: The First Folio of Shakespeare*, 2nd edn, ed. Charlton Hinman (New York and London: Norton, 1996), TLN 968–986 (all Folio quotations in this chapter are from this facsimile, using the through-line-numbers (TLN) of that edition. For the history of arguments about this speech see Knowles, 122–131, and Stanley Wells and Gary Taylor with John Jowett and William Montgomery, *William Shakespeare: A Textual Companion* (New York and London: Norton, 1987), 175.

13 See, 'Memorial Reconstruction' in *Walter Wilson Greg: A Collection of His Writings*, ed. Joseph Rosenblum (Lanham, MD: Scarecrow Press, 1998), 69–84.

14 For a seminal critique of the memorial-reconstruction hypothesis, see Laurie E. Maguire, *Shakespearean Suspect Texts: The 'Bad' Quartos and Their Contexts* (Cambridge: Cambridge University Press, 1996).

15 Marino, *Owning*, 90–94.

16 Greg, 79–82.

17 Richard Preiss, 'Undocumented: Improvisation, Rehearsal, and the Clown', in this volume.

18 See *The Three-Text Hamlet: Parallel Texts of the First and Second Editions and First Folio*, ed. Bernice W. Kliman and Paul Bertram (New York: AMS Press, rev. edn, 2003) and *The First Quarto of Hamlet*, ed. Kathleen O. Irace (Cambridge: Cambridge University Press, 1998).

19 Holger Syme, 'A Sharers' Repertory', in this volume.

20 For example, Giorgio Melchiori concludes that 'the Quarto is a reported text, a memorial reconstruction of an authorial acting version': *The Merry Wives of Windsor*, ed. Giorgio Melchiori, Arden Shakespeare Third Series (London: Thomson Learning, 2000), 42; John Jowett and the *Oxford Shakespeare* editors argue conversely that the play was memorially reconstructed and then 'subjected to theatrical adaptation and abridgement': Stanley Wells and Gary Taylor with John Jowett and William Montgomery, *William Shakespeare: A Textual Companion* (New York and London: Norton, 1997), 340; Richard Dutton's *Shakespeare, Court Dramatist* (Oxford: Oxford University Press, 2016) instead argues for the Folio text of *Merry Wives* as an authorial revision for court performance (245–258), which would of course require actors to remaster parts they had previously learned.

21 Steven Urkowitz argues for the *Henry VI* plays as theatrical revisions in '"If I Mistake those Foundations Which I Build Upon": Peter Alexander's Textual Analysis of *Henry VI Parts 2 and 3*', *English Literary Renaissance*, 18 (1988), 230–256 and 'Texts with Two Faces: Noticing Theatrical Revision in *Henry VI, Parts 2 and 3*,' in Thomas A. Pendleton, ed., *Henry VI: New Critical Essays* (New York: Routledge, 2001).

22 Werstine, 'Century', 313–315.

23 *An Excellent Tragedy of Romeo and Juliet* (1597), E2r; *The Most Excellent and Lamentable Tragedy of Romeo and Juliet* (1599), E3r.

24 *Mr. William Shak-speare His True Chronicle History of the Life and Death of King Lear* (1608), H4r; TLN 2311.

25 Werstine, 'Century', 313.

26 *Sir John Falstaff and the Merrie Wives of Windsor* (1602), C1r–C2v; TLN 551–769.

4

Undocumented Improvisation, Rehearsal, and the Clown

*Richard Preiss**

When a clown enters, we immediately recognize that he does not belong. The meter shifts to prose; his name is English, regardless of setting; he is not a lover, merchant, or king, but a servant, tradesman, or bumpkin; he is ignorant of the plot into which he has wandered, and unsure of what to do in it; his scenes go nowhere, degenerating into pratfall, patter, or miscarriage; he fails, at some level, to grasp the rules of being in a play – and he recognizes us, the audience, in turn. This chapter too does not belong; stage clowns have no place in a volume about documents. Clowning resists documentation: more than any other performer, clowns improvised, rendering the full scope of their contribution to early modern playing either invisible or lost. Lack of evidence, and the prejudice that clowns do not merit serious attention, has long been a methodological barrier to their study. This has given rise to certain distortions in theatre history.

Printed playbooks conceal as well as reveal. They appear to us organic, unified texts, composed at a single moment by a single, governing hand. That appearance has shaped our theories of how companies managed their repertories, assigned roles, distributed parts for study, rehearsed, revised, and overcame the cognitive challenge of remembering their lines.[1] Such theories posit a top-down model, in which the script, even understood as a composite of actors' scrolls, exerts total control over the play, and in which performance is a site merely of textual reproduction. The advantages of part-based composition, rehearsal, and revision are calibrated to that model. Distributing plays into parts maximized efficiency, encoding information into the text that allowed the disparate elements of performance to cohere at just the right moment.[2] As James J. Marino showed in the previous chapter, the coordinated cue-structure of those parts also had to be scrupulously maintained to minimize the greatest risk to performance: the disruption of actors' crossing their cues, or forgetting them, or forgetting to give them, thereby grinding the play to a halt.[3] Yet the frequency of complaints about the clown's infidelity to the script underscores the problem improvisation poses to this acting system – and at the same time suggests it may have been equally systemic, tolerated, and even encouraged. How did theatre compartmentalize these two seemingly incompatible modes of activity? How can we locate improvisation in printed playbooks, when they make no effort to distinguish it? How do we reconcile a system that prioritized economy with a technique seemingly destined to provoke error, confusion, and miscue?

If improvisation is the dark matter of early modern theatre, hidden below the surface of our texts, it may also be what held their performances together. Rather than stress the conflict between clowning and theatrical economy – and thus perpetuate the dichotomy of clown vs. author, performance vs. text – this chapter tries to integrate them, by analysing extemporality not as a glitch but as a feature, a generative principle of dramatic organization. As we will see, improvisation only pushes the distributive, decentralized logic of part-based acting further, interrogating fundamental categories in our histories of early modern theatre. What was a play? How did it get made, and when was it done? What was a playing company, and how did it function? If in our search for the undocumentable, finally, we find it everywhere traced, reflected, restaged – in a word, documented – what then is a 'document'?

The term 'clown' refers both to a stock character type – rustic, naïve, obtuse, lazy, clumsy, prosaic, appetitive, impertinent – and to the actor assigned those parts, a specialized member of company personnel. Despite their marginality, clown parts are a staple of early modern plays, irrespective of genre. Speech prefixes and stage directions will indicate simply 'clown' or 'the clown' as often as give their characters proper names, or will slip indiscriminately between these appellations; where playbooks survive with casting prescriptions, clown parts are always for one actor, never doubled. And despite the typical brevity of those parts, clown actors were the celebrities of early modern theatre, their names – Richard Tarlton, Will Kemp, John Singer, Robert Armin, John Shank, Thomas Greene, Tim Read, Andrew Cane – appearing in popular literature more often than those of dramatic leads like Alleyn and Burbage. The Queen Anne's Men's *Greenes Tu Quoque* (1614) by Cooke, indeed, took its very title from the name of their clown, a feat no other actor in the period could boast. Their personal styles (even their body types) defined the fare of their respective playhouses, and organized the commodity landscape of theatrical London: 'that's the fat foole of the Curtin', observes one balladeer, 'and the lean foole of the Bull'.[4]

The reason for this salience was simple: clowns were not confined to the play, and neither was theatre. Playbooks let us imagine that plays were the entirety of theatrical events, but what audiences saw was closer to a variety show, a medley of entertainments over which the clown presided as emcee.[5] There might be a pre-show pantomime, wherein he 'peeped' his nose from behind the arras, let the crowd tease him out, and pulled grotesque faces on demand; Tarlton was beloved for his bulbous, homely features, and two generations later Read kept a similar routine. There might be mid-play 'merriments', a broad class of interlude ranging from slapstick to lampoon. After the play there were jigs, farce afterpieces of song, dance, and sexual innuendo. These remained in high demand throughout the period, and occasioned such disorder in the audience that in 1612 they were briefly outlawed. Or there might be a concluding game of 'themes', in which the clown spontaneously versified on prompts yelled out by individual playgoers. Tarlton again pioneered this pastime, his zingers preserved in volumes like *Tarltons Jests*; Armin thoroughly specialized in it. Though clowns must have had reliable bits to which they repaired, most of this crowd-work had to be unscripted, which explains why performances ran four to five hours, far beyond the length of most plays.[6] Early modern theatre was heterogeneous, an amalgam of two antithetical modes of performance: the textual and the extemporal, the mimetic and the non-mimetic, 'play' and game. The clown belonged to the latter paradigm – the periphery our playbooks crop – and his dramatic roles were barely disguised extensions of his extradramatic persona. Generic vessels, they let him play himself.

To companies hastily mounting plays before impatient audiences, the clown was a safeguard against catastrophe: he could fill dead air. A 1633 jestbook relates how 'hee that presented the Clown' was 'called to enter (for the Stage was emptie)'; no lines are provided, and the player must create *ex nihilo*.[7] Edmund Gayton similarly recalls Prince Charles' Men sending out Cane, their 'most mimicall man', to 'pacify' a restless crowd.[8] In Goffe's *Careless Shepherdess* (1629), two fictional playgoers praise Read, whose diversions were largely gestural:

LANDLORD
   . . . I'ave laughed
Until I cry'd again, to see what Faces

> The Rogue would make ...
> To see him hold out's Chin, hang down his hands,
> And twirle his Bawble ...
>
> THRIFT   And so would I, his part has all the wit,
> For none speaks Carps and Quibbles besides him:
> I'd rather see him leap, or laughe, or cry,
> Then hear the gravest Speech in all the *Play*.
>
> (B2v–B3r)

Parodying this formula, the Cambridge satire *Pilgrimage to Parnassus* (*c.* 1598) hauls its clown out by a rope, ignorant even that he is a clown. 'What the devil should I doe here?' he asks. 'Dost thou not knowe a play cannot be without a clowne?' he is told. 'If thou canst but draw thy mouth awrye, laye thy legge ouer thy staffe, sawe a peece of cheese with thy dagger, lape vp drinke on the earth ... theile laugh mightily'.[9] His professional counterpart is the clown whose 'cinkapace of jests' Hamlet scorns in Q1 (1603), featuring catchphrases like 'Cannot you stay until I eat my porridge?' 'You owe me a quarters wages', 'My coat wants a cullison', 'Your beer is sour', and 'blabbering with his lips'.[10]

The antics Hamlet derides – 'speak[ing] more then is set down' – fall not outside the play, but in it.[11] Here too clowns were afforded extraordinary latitude, not only permitted but expected to embellish their parts. The safest vehicles were their monologues, typically found at the top or end of a scene, where the cleared stage reverted to a non-mimetic space. Here the clown could comment on the action, develop his character, or simply make sport, with minimal impact on cue-structure. These rants might be semi-scripted, or not; suggestions, or invitations; explored one way today, and differently the next. Thus Launce in *Two Gentlemen of Verona* can fight with his dog as long as he likes; the imprisoned Jeffrey in Marston's *Antonio's Revenge* (1600) can bewail his misery ('O hunger, how thou dominer'st in my guts! O, for a fat leg of ewe mutton in stewde broth ... I could belch rarely, for I am all winde. O colde, colde, colde, colde, colde ...'); *Lear*'s Fool can add to his prophecy, or subtract.[12] Usually, he adds: these scene-edges are a play's expansion joints, where comic material accretes. In 1606, *Mucedorus* begins with two lovers in the forest pursued by a bear; by 1610, it begins with Mouse – in the same forest, for no reason – tripping over that bear. Clowns get a disproportionate share of open-ended stage directions in early printed playbooks – '*speak anything, and exit*'; '*he playes or sings any odde toy*'; '*Jockie is led to whipping ouer the stage, speaking some words, but of no importance*' – as well as enigmatic dashes ('I shall, I shall–') and *et cetera*s ('Whoop, whow, &c.').[13] These are cues for limited improvisation, but how they affected others' cues is less certain. How long does an '*&c*' last? When Tarlton's Derrick in *The Famous Victories* enters chasing his runaway horse, calling out 'whoa there, whoa there, whoa there', the cue he gives is 'whoa there'.[14] Yet how many times does he give it? Three? More? Will his opposites come in early? Does he make a joke of pre-empting them? How much time was this meant to fill? Was the entire manic entrance unplanned to begin with, since the text has him re-enter one line later?

Recovering improvisation is tricky: beyond the few clear-cut examples, we run into nebulous questions of copy. If a text derives from performance, we cannot tell scripted from *ad lib*; if it doesn't, we cannot know if or where liberty was taken – and neither textual state is ever determinable or absolute. Scholars have tried to decode the signals playwrights used to license and restrain their clowns – assuming it was imperative to do both at once. A repeated cue, for example, might trigger misinterpretation: when the lovesick Valentine in *Two Gentlemen* sighs 'Silvia, Silvia', Speed calls out 'Madam Silvia! Madam Silvia!', and begins looking for her. Thus, it has been suggested, Shakespeare 'lengthened the leash' of his clowns, creating opportunities for self-contained stage business.[15] This is an optimistically short leash, however, presupposing the subservience of actor to dramatist. Improvisation did not always ask permission, as the clown from *The Tryall of Chevalrie* (1605) conveniently implies:

BOW
So, what's your name?
CLOW
My name, sir, is Bow wow.

(E1v)

'What's your name?' is the antithesis of a generous cue: his character's name is the one thing an actor does not get to invent.[16] A one-off joke, never revisited, it may have sprung from the clown's cue itself, the shorthand for his interlocutor as written on his part-scroll – Dick Bowyer, or '*Bow*'.

Whatever its origin, someone thought this amusing enough to write down; of all the replies he may have tried out, perhaps this got the best response. But such transcription was idiosyncratic. At one point in Wilson's *Three Ladies of London* (*c.* 1587), Tarlton breaks character to jibe at an enrapt spectator, whose mouth 'gapes to bite me'; later, he returns to the target, asking 'now sirra hast eaten vp my song? Ye shall eat no more today, / For euerybody may see your belly is grown bigger with eating vp our play'.[17] Despite clearly originating onstage, specific to a single performance, these lines end up in the book. The opposite is true of an incident in *The Famous Victories*, in which Tarlton once played the Chief Justice 'besides his owne part of the Clowne'. Having, as Justice, taken a punch from the Prince, Tarlton next appears 'in his Clownes cloathes', and 'askes the Actors what newes'; told of the assault, he admits 'the report so terrifies me, that me thinkes the blow remaines still on my cheeke'.[18] Specific to a single performance, this does *not* end up in the book; it survives only as anecdote. And there are ambiguous cases, which both include and omit. The title page of *A Knack to Know a Knave* (1594) advertises 'Kemps applauded merriments, of the men of Gotham'. Yet whatever transpired onstage does not persist on the page, amounting to twenty-eight lines in which some artisans dispute who should read their petition to the King, and never appear again.[19] Perhaps similar title page terminology – 'humours', 'veins', 'conceits' – denoted performed material only loosely

IMPROVISATION, REHEARSAL, AND THE CLOWN 75

tied to the text, something one bought not to read but to remember.

The most fascinating example may be the manuscript play of *Sir Thomas More*, in the margins of which Hand B, thought to be that of Thomas Heywood, has added fourteen speeches for a clown (see Figure 4.1).

The speeches are not very good: feeble wordplay, non-sequiturs, failed gags. Facing execution, the clown addresses the hangman: 'I haue a suite to you … that as you haue hangd

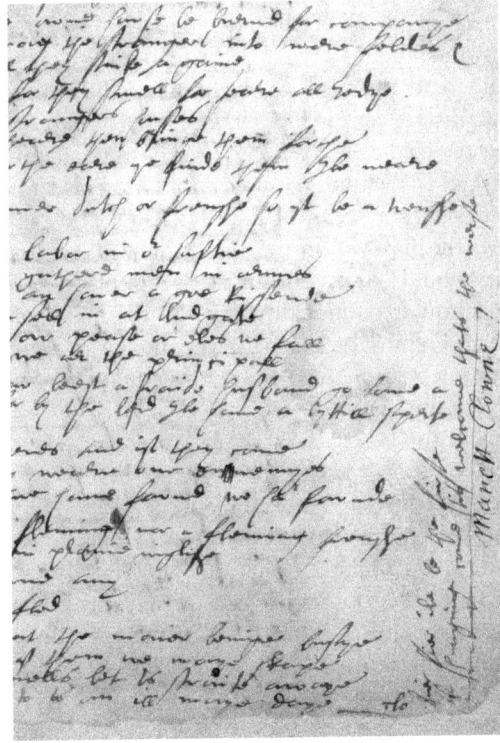

FIGURE 4.1 *The Book of Sir Thomas More*, B.L. MS Harleian 7368, fol. 7r. Showing two lines for the clown and *'Manett Clowne'* in right-hand margin. Used by permission of the British Library.

Lincoln first & will hange hir nexte so you will nott hang me at all' / 'naye . . . you must hang' / 'well then so much for y^t' – hardly a professional-grade revision.[20] This led Eric Rasmussen to suggest that Hand B was *not* creating a new part, but transcribing lines spoken onstage – by Rafe Betts, brother of George Betts, named in the stage directions but never given any lines.[21] If this is correct, here an entire *part* had been left blank for the clown to fill in. We can pity the actors whose cues he stepped on: how ragged must those scenes have been? Though *Sir Thomas More* seems an extreme case, it is also a play-in-process, arrested in transition between performance and re-performance. Might this level of unscriptedness have been widespread?

Clowns, then, could save a performance, but once onstage, they could endanger it as well. Literally: improvisation circumvented state censorship, whose licence was predicated on a play's being acted as written. Yet objections to clowning rarely stress the legal or technical complications it created. *Sir Thomas More* itself stages a scene of improvisation, and depicts it as effortless. In the play-within-the-play, More walks on for Luggins the clown; 'would not my lord make a rare player?', the actors remark, . . . how extemprically he fell to the matter, and spake Lugginses part almost as it is in the very booke set downe'.[22] For Letoy in Brome's *Antipodes* (1638), this adaptiveness makes his clown Byplay the best actor in his company:

> . . . my actors
> Are all in readinesse; and I think all perfect,
> But one, that never will be perfect in a thing
> He studies; yet he makes such shifts extempore,
> (Knowing the purpose what he is to speak to)
> That he moves mirth in me 'bove all the rest . . .
> If he can frible through, and move delight
> In others, I am pleas'd.
>
> (D2v)

Byplay does not degrade the performance; he elevates it. He is prepared, just not 'perfect': some actors memorize, some don't.

It is enough to have the gist of a scene, and 'fribble' – a term that seems to combine frivolity and labour, grace and skill. What 'move[s] delight' is the realization *that* improvisation is occurring, the thrill of watching it teeter between success and failure. Letoy can appreciate it, of course, because he knows the text. But how was this knowledge communicated to audiences?

So far, we have been considering *solo* improvisations, whose guiding principle we assume to be damage control. In group scenes, with their greater complexity, we seem to see the damage that motivated this policy – the chaos clowns introduced. Yet all they motivate is our own assumption: that plays could be 'damaged', and that part-based acting was intended to prevent it. In the 1604 A-text of 1.4 of Marlowe's *Doctor Faustus*, for example, though Wagner's cues for the Clown remain constant, seven cues the Clown gives Wagner differ from those in the 1616 B-text, and the rest arrive late; if the 1604 *Faustus* is a reported text, the Clown's dilatory digressions should have thrown the scene into disarray.[23] But this reading presupposes that the 1616 text represents the scripted version of the scene, and that Wagner is listening for its cues. What if it had no 'scripted version' – just an outline, a plan, a series of keywords and prompts? In this arrangement, as Stephen Purcell notes, Wagner's job is to steer the clown from one joke to the next; he is waiting not for a cue, but for a chance to interrupt.[24] The non-improvising actor must also improvise, that is, provide a framework for the clown's improvisation: in a crucial sense, he runs the scene. Where there is no 'lead' actor, as in 2.2 (featuring two clowns, Rafe and Robin), we find far more variation between 1604 and 1616. So it is not that the A-text documents a performance, and the B-text doesn't. *Both* document performance – of *these* particular scenes, which may have existed fully only in performance.

Like playgoing, plays were not homogeneous substances. They were a patchwork of performance styles, some premeditated and some not – a continuum that allowed the clown to move freely between the play and its satellite forms, and that helps explain the fluctuating, random positions of his scenes in the play itself.[25] Neither was improvisation of a single type: as we have seen, the clown's repertoire depended on the quality of his straight men. Kemp joins the Chamberlain's Men as a solo artist, but by *Romeo and Juliet* there is a visible effort to find him partners; the play shuttles Kemp's Peter to and fro, pairing him with no less than twelve speakers. His scene with the musicians illustrates the urgency. In both Q1 (1597) and Q2 (1599), they merely echo Peter's lines, and he must create all the forward momentum.[26] Yet by *Much Ado About Nothing*, we see a different dynamic: Kemp's Dogberry has dedicated sidekicks, the members of the watch. Dogberry still takes the lead, launching their scenes and capping them, but scenes like 3.3 demonstrate a collaborative process akin to modern improv. Verges makes the opening offer – 'giue them their charge' – and the watch act as collective straight men, priming each joke:

DOGBERY
 . . . You are to bidde any man stand . . .
WATCH
 How if a will not stand?
DOGBERY
 Why then take no note of him . . .

DOGBERY
 . . . bid those that are drunke get them to bed.
WATCH
 How if they will not?
DOGBERY
 Why then let them alone til they are sober . . .

DOGBERY
 If you meete a thiefe . . .
WATCH
 . . . shall we not lay hands on him?
DOGBERY
 . . . let him shew himself what he is, and steale out of your companie.[27]

This could grow stale. But instead, it evolves: on the fourth pass, Verges takes over, adding that 'If you heare a child crie in the night you must call to the nurse and bid her still it.'[28] He addresses the men, but he is talking to Dogberry through them: we know they will reply with 'How if the nurse be asleepe', so he is challenging Kemp to craft the next punchline. And now a complex affective interplay opens up: Verges's pride at helping his superior, when in reality the Verges *actor* has burdened him; a slow burn from Dogberry at being so put upon, before he finds the solution ('Why then ... let the child wake her with crying'); suddenly, we are in a game of 'themes', into whose retaliatory format we have imperceptibly slipped.[29] We cannot know how much was planned, or how many permutations the actors produced before this version was committed to print. But it is clearly an improvisational 'pocket' in the play: Dogberry's exit line 'one word more ... watch about signior Leonatoes door' signals our return to the script. Its payoff, indeed, *relies* on our knowing that the actors are improvising, on the delicate wobble between player and role. They needed no script, only a shared sense of timing, and a willingness to experiment. Scenes like this give them options for variation ('if you hear a dog bark', 'if you meet a fair maid'): the actors could do it differently each day.

Doing it differently may have been the point. A company dependent on playwrights was vulnerable: scripts often arrived late, or in fragments. But if the company were many companies, subdivided into semi-autonomous groups responsible for their own set-pieces, it more efficiently distributed labour and resources. Group rehearsal time was scarce, and its coordination difficult; lead actors met privately to 'instruct' their apprentices – with whom they shared scenes – and clowns may have done so too. The benefit of such a 'pod' system was to delegate phases of composition to performance. Playwrights did not have to deliver whole plays: if there were gaps, they worked themselves out onstage. Scripts could be shorter – and could flex over time, relieving the toll on leads. And as this surplus material grew, the play offered audiences continuous novelty, prolonging its stage life. The Quarto of Greene's *Orlando Furioso* (1594), for instance, may appear 'corrupt' beside Alleyn's manuscript part – the sole extant actor's roll from the Elizabethan stage – but only if our models of playhouse practice do not account for textual drift: comparing the two, we can peel back the layers of growth in a scene. Orlando raves, mad for Angelica; his man Orgalio, desperate to soothe him, vows to fetch her. Alleyn's part suggests Orlando is brought a dummy, for whose silence Orgalio interprets. By the time the full text was printed, however, a live actor has been substituted – a clown in a dress. That change begat another: there is now no need to hurry this 'Angelica' over the stage, because she can talk. The scene thus expands in reverse, adding preliminary jokes to redouble the succeeding ones: the clown's boast of his beauty becomes even funnier if he mentions, at the outset, that he has not shaved his beard.[30] Orlando, meanwhile, is afforded time to breathe after the ten-line speech that closed the previous scene – a speech he can now drop, if he wishes, because it was itself a delay for a mute Angelica. In this way, the clowns incrementally shift labour onto themselves, until an equilibrium is reached. Reinforcing Holger Syme's argument earlier in this volume for the importance of role-length in repertory planning, clowning may have served to mitigate that problem internally, rendering the dramatic ecosystem around them more plastic, dynamic, and adaptable.[31] Clowns were a play's living, connective tissue, fitting texts to the exigencies of performance – and in the process stretching them further, each day giving audiences a little more. Or, sometimes, they simply spawned their own play. The manuscript play *John of Bordeaux* (c. 1591), a sequel to Greene's *Friar Bacon* (c. 1589), does not even bother grafting its clowns to the plot: as in *Doctor Faustus*, they seem to occupy a parallel universe. Pierce, Friar Bacon's assistant, shares only one scene with him; otherwise, he is swindling students, teaching them to dine for free at alehouses, and being chased by the irate proprietors of those alehouses. When he is thrown in jail, we get the direction '*Enter the Iailor and Perce* [for] *the seane of the whiper*', followed by a rule across the page.[32] We have no clue what 'the scene of the whisper/whipper/wiper' was. The clowns knew, and evidently that was enough. Hamlet's advice to the players to 'let ... your clowns speak no more than is set down' may very well have been a laugh-line: audiences would have understood that little, if anything, was 'set down'.

That improvisation was integrated into theatrical practice has profound implications for the nature of early modern performance. If, as Tiffany Stern suggests, 'partial rehearsals of group 'moments' – songs, dances, swordfights, slapstick – were all that it was absolutely *necessary* to rehearse', and if such moments were rehearsed independently, there would have been significant chunks of the play that the company never saw until they were doing it, at the premiere.[33] The premiere was really the first full rehearsal, acted before a paying public; there was no crucial distinction between 'rehearsal' and 'performance'. This partly explains the culture of first performances, always referred to as the play's 'trial', or, indeed, 'rehearsal' – terms that imply the players' test of the play as much as the audience's. Even if approved, plays were understood still to be malleable. Epilogues often invite audiences to 'polish these rude Sceanes', and for this privilege – passing judgement on the play, and participating in its composition – they paid twice the standard admission fee; a premiere, as one of Middleton's gallants puts it, was 'the first cut'.[34] Yet if a set-piece were *intrinsically* improvisational, neither was the second 'cut' final. For these sections of the play, every day was a fresh 'trial'.

If clowning was perpetual rehearsal, rehearsal is the perpetual theme of clowning. We have already seen this pattern without recognizing it – in the anticlimactic 'merriment' of *A Knack to Know a Knave*, for instance, where the clowns spend far longer quarrelling over their petition than actually delivering it. In *Orlando Furioso*, Orlando obsessively repeats the phrase 'Angelica is dead', never satisfied with Orgalio's response:

ORL.   Orgalio.
ORG.
  My Lord.
ORL.

Angelica is dead.

Orgalio cries.

Ah poor slaue, so crie no more now.

ORG.
Nay, I haue quickly done.

ORL.
Orgalio.

ORG.
My Lord.

ORL.
Medors Angelica is dead.

Orgalio cries, and Orlando beats him againe.

ORG.
Why doo ye beate me my Lord?

ORL.
Why slaue, wilt thou weep for Medors Angelica, thou must laugh for her.

ORG.
Laugh? Yes, Ile laugh all day and you will.

ORL.
Orgalio.

ORG.
My Lord.

ORL.
Medors Angelica is dead.

ORG.
Ha ha ha ha.

ORL.
So, tis well now.

ORG.
Nay, this is easier than the other was.[35]

The same illogic drives 3.3 of *Much Ado*, in which the exhaustive elaboration of the Watches' duties replaces their enactment. We are always, it seems, watching the clown *prepare*, or be prepared: he is prompted, drilled, rehearsed – for information, for education, for action – yet always manages an incorrect result. In the absence of a script, paradoxically, the template of improvisation becomes rigid adherence to an imaginary one, which can never be completed; interrogating his suspects, Dogberry insists on compiling a transcript that misrepresents their statements as facts, literally producing a script for the very scene he is in and bungling it at the same time.[36] Deferral and involution are ideal extemporal devices: if comedy spans the gap between theory and execution, improvisation lives in that gap. That gap is also the space of rehearsal – what likewise happens always on the way to something else.

We think of rehearsal and improvisation as mutually exclusive domains, but they are fundamentally intertwined. Yet where we see them most explicitly fused – in depictions of theatrical performance itself – they seem diametrically opposed. Representations of rehearsal invariably devolve into improvisation, simulating the most violent, incendiary forms of it. In Day's *Travels of the Three English Brothers* (1607), Kemp is resurrected to engage some Italian comedians in an 'extemporal meriment'.[37] He (or the actor impersonating him) squanders their rehearsal quibbling over his part, insulting Harlequin's manhood, impugning his wife's virtue, fondling her, and mocking Italians, before following them onstage – whereupon the scene ends, never showing us the play. We have just seen it, in the obnoxious delay tactics that were Kemp's trademark, here memorialized as frustrating even *commedia*. In 2 *Return from Parnassus* (*c.* 1601), two actors audition for Burbage and Kemp; Kemp tells his pupil to 'mark me', spews twenty lines of free-associative nonsense, and then, impossibly, demands that he repeat it *verbatim*.[38] T.W.'s *Thorny-Abbey* (*c.* 1615) stages a more complex improvisation-effect: a fool delivers its prologue, immediately forgets his lines, and forces the prompter to hiss them; he misspeaks even those, and the prompter chases him off.[39] In these highly scripted exchanges, the familiar picture of improvisation starts to emerge: as a skill inimical to theatre, or as lack of skill altogether. The clown's unreadiness becomes a destructive condition, exasperating his fellows and heaping ruin on the performance. Even Letoy in *Antipodes*, who reserved for his clown the highest praise, rebukes him once the play is underway:

> ... you sir are incorrigible, and
> Take license to yourself, to add unto
> Your parts, your own free fancy; and sometimes
> To alter or diminish what the writer
> With care and skill compos'd: and when you are
> To speak to your co-actors in the Scene,
> You hold interloqutions with the Audients.
>
> (D3v)

In Marston's *Histriomastix* (1599), Sir Oliver Owlet's Men are disrupted by their clown's incessant sex jokes: 'this cuckoldly coyle hinders our rehearsal'.[40] In *Love's Labour's Lost*, the clown joins the audience before the play-within-the-play is finished, and starts a fight; the play's performance is its only rehearsal. In *A Midsummer Night's Dream*, even the rehearsal is abandoned.

Whenever theatre documented its own operation, in other words, those documents contradict our inferential evidence of how theatre actually worked. In practice, as we have seen, improvisation happened so rehearsal did not have to; in *representations* of that practice, not only does rehearsal appear centralized, comprehensive, and mandatory, but its purpose is to *prevent* improvisation – failing spectacularly every time. This returns us to where we began: how did the role of improvisation end up marginalized and obscured? Why does theatre give a false account of itself? We have traditionally taken these metatheatrical scenes at face value, when the fact that they dramatize systemic *failure* for comic effect should argue against doing so. Precisely *because* they are scripted, indeed, they exemplify better than anything the appeal of unscriptedness. Despite the extemporality that plays *already* contained, they synthesized *more*, foregrounding it, exaggerating it, sensationalizing it – giving clowns *extra* business, beyond what they assigned themselves.

These scenes form much of the evidence for a hostility to clowning, corroborating the perennial charges against it: the clown is vulgar, self-indulgent, unprofessional, a liability. Yet they are fictional evidence, as may be the narratives they subtend. For dramatists to have enriched and spotlighted improvisation solely to repudiate it suggests that repudiation may not have been the goal. It has looked that way, because to us – heirs of fixed, static texts – theatre is about getting a play 'right'. But these scenes of disorder are not scenes of discipline; there are no consequences to the clown's deviance, except the delight of its onstage and offstage audiences. The *frisson* they generate between performer and script seems an end in itself, not a means to its resolution – and if theatre ever intended to banish clowns, it was remarkably slow to do so, since they – clowns, jigs, 'themes', and the other genres we have surveyed – endured until its closure. If anything, what these scenes document is not the reality of rehearsal, but its invention – what audiences were not supposed to see, a discrete, anxious phase of performance in whose artificial image we have reconstructed a parts system to compensate. Rendering the entire play contingent, accidental, happening always on the way to something else, they instead reiterate the hybridity of early modern theatre, an effort to infuse the drama with the pleasure of the ludic forms around it – a pleasure consisting not in finished products but in process, in watching a thing go wrong and right at once.

Documents regiment theatre into distinct phases and iterable forms, as if we could recover the whole from its parts. At once the most instantaneous mode of performance and the most historically embedded, the most elusive and the most durable, improvisation leaves no trace and yet scatters those traces everywhere, confounding documentation as much by exploding it as resisting it. There is no document to which the clown's activity reduced, so it proliferates into every document: commonplace books, verses, memoirs, eulogies, woodcuts, shop-signs, ballads, jestbooks, drolls, printed 'themes', printed jigs and dances.[41] These too are documents of rehearsal, insofar as they are documents of performance, *and* documents after performance, which become the basis of new performance. Even Hamlet's clown is not quite improvising, for 'gentlemen quotes his jests down / In their tables, before they come to the play': they already know, from prior attendance, what to expect.[42] *Now* he has lines 'set down' for him: do they call for innovation, or repetition? Is he performing, or rehearsing? Are the 'gentlemen' his spectators, his readers, or his prompters? What's the difference? In the radical concentration of his practice to the moment of performance, the clown straddles its infinite elasticity – as well as its circularity, the futility of segmenting theatrical experience into 'before', 'during', or 'after'. So much, then, for feeling out of place: in this book, the clown belongs in every chapter.

Notes

[*] This chapter revises some of the positions I held in my book, *Clowning and Authorship in Early Modern Theatre* (Cambridge: Cambridge University Press, 2014). I am grateful to Tiffany Stern, to my fellow Folger symposium participants, and to Arden for the opportunity to rethink this material.

1 See among many important studies Roslyn Lander Knutson, *The Repertory of Shakespeare's Company, 1594–1613* (Little Rock: University of Arkansas Press, 1991); Tiffany Stern, *Rehearsal from Shakespeare to Sheridan* (Oxford: Clarendon Press, 2000); Evelyn B. Tribble, *Cognition in the Globe: Attention and Memory in Shakespeare's Theatre* (London: Palgrave, 2011).

2 See Simon Palfrey and Tiffany Stern, *Shakespeare in Parts* (Oxford: Oxford University Press, 2007).

3 See James J. Marino, 'Parts and the Playscript: Seven Questions', in the present volume.

4 William Turner, *Turners Dish of Lentten Stuffe* (1612), A1r.

5 For an expanded survey, see Preiss, *Clowning and Authorship*, Ch.2.

6 See Michael J. Hirrel, 'Duration of Performances and Lengths of Plays: How Shall We Beguile the Lazy Time?' *Shakespeare Quarterly* 61.2 (Summer 2010), 159–182.

7 Archie Armstrong, *A Banquet of Jests* (1633), E5r–v.
8 Edmund Gayton, *Pleasant Notes upon Don Quixot* (1654), 271.
9 Anon., *The Pilgrimage to Parnassus*, in J. B. Leishman, ed. *The Three Parnassus Plays (1598–1601)* (London: Nicholson & Watson, 1949), 129–130, ll. 662–677.
10 William Shakespeare, *The tragicall historie of Hamlet Prince of Denmarke* (1603), F2r–v.
11 William Shakespeare, *The tragicall historie of Hamlet, Prince of Denmarke* (1604), G4r.
12 William Shakespeare, *The Two Gentlemen of Verona*, in *Comedies, Histories, and Tragedies* (1623), B8v–C1r; J.[ohn] M.[arston], *Antonio's Revenge* (1602), I2v–I3r; William Shakespeare, *King Lear*, in *Comedies* (1623), 2r2v–2r3r. (The 'Fool's prophecy' is notoriously absent from the 1608 Quarto.)
13 On *ceterae* in printed playbooks, see Laurie Maguire, 'Typographical Embodiment: The Case of *etcetera*', in Valerie Traub, ed., *The Oxford Handbook of Shakespeare and Embodiment: Gender, Sexuality, and Race* (Oxford: Oxford University Press, 2016), 527–548.
14 Anon., *The Famous Victories of Henry the Fifth* (1598), C4r.
15 Palfrey and Stern, *Parts*, 172–175.
16 Then again, the clown here *has* no name, yet is asked to supply one, which may make this an exception.
17 R.[obert?] W.[ilson?], *The Three Ladies of London* (1592), D3v.
18 Anon., *Tarltons Jests* (1612), C2v–C3r.
19 *A Knack to Knowe a Knave* (1594), F1r–v.
20 W. W. Greg, ed., *The Book of Sir Thomas More* (Oxford University Press / Malone Society Reprints, 1911), 23 fol. 11ᵃ, opposite ll. 647ff.
21 Eric Rasmussen, 'Setting Down what the Clown Spoke: Improvisation, Hand B, and *The Book of Sir Thomas More*', *The Library* s.6-13, issue 2 (1991), 126–136.
22 *Sir Thomas More*, 38–39, fol. 17ᵃ, ll. 1150–1153.
23 See Ch.[ristopher] Mar.[lowe], *The Tragicall History of D. Faustus* (1604), B3r–B4r, and Ch.[ristopher] Mar. [Marlowe],

The Tragicall History of the Life and Death of Doctor Faustus (1616), B2v–B3r.

24 Stephen Purcell, 'Editing for Performance or Documenting Performance? Exploring the Relationship Between Early Modern Text and Clowning', *Shakespeare Bulletin* 34.1 (2016), 5–27.

25 There is little difference between 2.2 *Faustus*, which can fall anywhere in the play – after 3.1 in the A-text, after 2.3 in the B-text – and one of Kemp's 'merriments', which might likewise erupt anywhere during the play.

26 See William Shakespeare, *An Excellent Conceited Tragedie of Romeo and Iuliet* (1597), I2v-I3r; *The Most Excellent and Lamentable Tragedie, of Romeo and Iuliet* (1599), K3v–K4r.

27 William Shakespeare, *Much Adoe About Nothing* (1600), E3r–v.

28 Ibid., E3v.

29 Ibid., E4r.

30 Robert Greene, *The Historie of Orlando Furioso* (1594), F1r–v.

31 See Holger Syme, 'A Sharers' Repertory', in the present volume.

32 *John of Bordeaux, or the Second Part of Friar Bacon*, ed. William Renwick (Oxford University Press / Malone Society Reprints, 1935), 43 / fol. 11(34)ᵃ, l. 1059. Fol. 5(27)ᵃ also offers the in-text stage direction, 'Exent Bacon to bring in the shows as you knowe'.

33 Stern, *Rehearsal*, 79.

34 See Tiffany Stern, *Documents of Performance in Early Modern England* (Cambridge: Cambridge University Press, 2009), 89.

35 *Orlando Furioso*, E2v.

36 Shakespeare, *Much Adoe*, G3v–G4v.

37 John Day, *The Travailes of the Three English Brothers* (1607), E4r; the episode runs to F1r.

38 Anon., *The Return From Parnassus, or the Scourge of Simony*, in Leishman, ed., *Parnassus Plays*, 341–342, ll. 1809–1831.

39 T.W., *Thorny-Abbey, or the London Maid*, in R. D., *Gratiae Theatrales, or a choice ternary of English plays* (London: 1662), B2r–v.

40 John Marston, *Histrio-mastix or, the Player Whipt* (1610), E4v.

41 See Preiss, *Clowning and Authorship*, Ch.3.

42 Shakespeare, *Hamlet* (1603), F2r–v.

PART TWO

Documents of Performance

5

Rethinking Prologues and Epilogues on Page and Stage

*Sonia Massai and Heidi Craig**

Our chapter rethinks current notions about early modern prologues and epilogues, by considering, for the first time,[1] how differently these documents functioned on the stage and on the page. These documents are, for example, permanently printed in playbooks (when they were included), even though they were impermanently part of performance; they are permanently not printed in playbooks (when they were not included), even though they were spoken on stage; they were sometimes added to, or written for, the page; and they were sometimes tweaked for readers. This chapter therefore recovers the untold, specifically non-performance-focused story of prologues and epilogues, looking at, but also beyond, their function as theatrical documents spoken in early modern playhouses to consider them as texts that found their way into printed playbooks.

This chapter also offers an overview of the rate of inclusion of prologues and epilogues in early modern printed playbooks. By so doing, it aims to establish whether some types of printed playbooks were more likely than others to include prologues and epilogues, how prologues and epilogues changed over time, and the extent to which printed prologues and epilogues may relate to the prologues and epilogues that were spoken on stage. By focusing on prologues and epilogues as theatrical and print documents, we demonstrate that these texts had functions apart from – and sometimes contrary to – those of their stage counterparts. Printed prologues and epilogues illuminate the complexity of remediation, including the various strategies used to repackage plays existing in the theatrical medium for the medium of print, which is also a central concern of Claire M. L. Bourne's chapter in this volume. While the presence of printed prologues and epilogues may signal a playtext's beginnings on the stage, such paratexts transcend their theatrical origins and take on lives of their own in print.

Out of the 622 plays listed in W. W. Greg's *A Bibliography of the English Printed Drama to the Restoration* up to 1642, 33 per cent include prologues and 26 per cent include epilogues.[2] The rate of inclusion is relatively comparable for prologues and epilogues over time, as shown in Figure 5.1. In most ten-year periods from 1590 to 1642,[3] the numbers of prologues and epilogues rise as the numbers of first editions rise and vice versa, except for the 1590s, when the number of first editions soars, but the number of prologues and epilogues included in first editions plummets. The rate of inclusion of prologues and epilogues continued to rise after the closure of the theatres in 1642. Out of the 191 first editions listed in Greg printed between 1643 and 1660, twenty-two texts have prologues only, eleven have epilogues only, and sixty-eight have both prologues and epilogues; over half of first editions from this period (101 out of 191, or 53 per cent) have therefore either prologues or epilogues.

The drop in the inclusion rate of prologues and epilogues in printed playbooks in the 1590s is extraordinary, and more extraordinary still is the fact that it has not been considered hitherto, given that it challenges received views about the relative popularity of prologues and epilogues in the period. While critics have so far assumed that statements about prologues and

RETHINKING PROLOGUES AND EPILOGUES

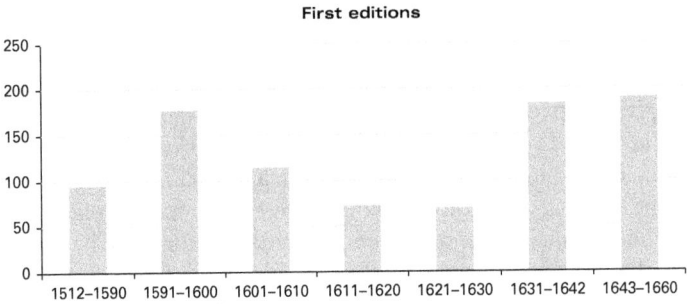

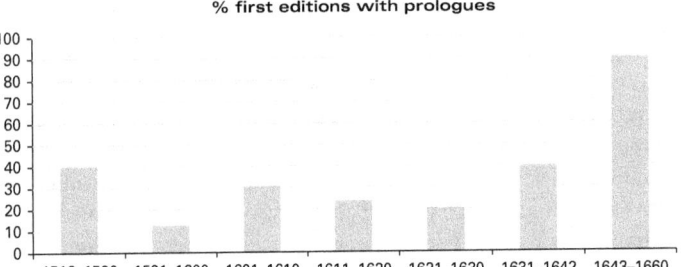

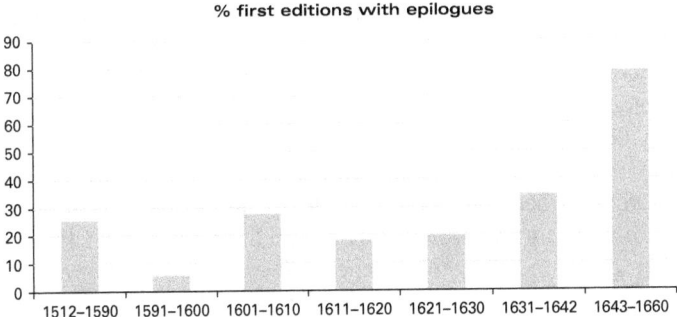

FIGURE 5.1 *Rate of publication and rate of inclusion of Prologues and Epilogues in First Editions.*

epilogues spoken onstage apply equally to their incarnations in print, we reveal the differences between the rates of inclusion of, and attitudes towards, theatrical and printed paratexts. Representative of early scholarship on early modern dramatic paratexts is E. K. Chambers, who states that '[t]he applause was often invited in the closing speech or in a formal epilogue, on the same lines as the prologue, which it seems to have replaced in favour about the end of the sixteenth century'.[4] Chambers reached this conclusion in light of passing references to the relative popularity of prologues and epilogues in the period. One of them comes from *The Birth of Hercules*, a university manuscript play (1597–c. 1600), where the fifth line of the prologue reads 'the epilogue is in fashion; prologues no more'.[5] Chambers is correctly quoting what people said at the time about *performance* – and assumes the same holds true of printed paratexts. The *printing* records, however, tell a different story. The numbers of printed prologues, compared to the numbers of printed epilogues, from 1600 onwards suggest that prologues remained popular, at least for readers, as shown in Figure 5.1. The other two extracts quoted by Chambers, moreover, suggest that only some stage prologues may have gone out of fashion, among them Inductions. According to the prologue that prefaced Beaumont and Fletcher's *The Woman Hater* (London: R. Raworth, 1607), 'Inductions [were by then] out of date, and a Prologue in Verse, [was] as stale as a black Velvet Cloak, and a Bay Garland'.[6]

Other types of prologues and epilogues were, however, just starting to become popular, at least among readers, judging from their survival rate in print. The 'Prologue at Blackfriers' that prefaces Philip Massinger's *The Emperor of the East* (London: J. Waterson, 1632), for example, refers to the practice of speaking a prologue as an 'imperious custome'. Massinger's performed prologue presumably relates to the performance of the text licensed by Henry Herbert in 1631. But what happens when that performance observation is printed for readers? And did the imperious custom of the stage prologue exert a similar pressure on plays in print? The soaring numbers of prologues and epilogues included in printed playbooks in the 1630s suggests that the fashion for speaking prologues was indeed felt in printing houses, such that stationers were expected to print prologues, even when, as here, they were stage-oriented and self-hating. Ironically, such printed prologues, included to replicate fashionable theatrical experience, actually flag up a disconnection between stage and page. *The Emperor of the East* is also representative of the types of playbooks that started to include prologues and epilogues more regularly than others. Figure 5.2 shows the number of first editions that included prologues and epilogues, per type of playbook.

Up to 1590, prologues and epilogues were mostly included in interludes, moralities and miracle plays. After the drop in the inclusion rate of both prologues and epilogues in playbooks published in the 1590s, the most significant rise in the numbers of printed prologues and epilogues occurs in commercial plays originally staged by children's companies in the 1600s and then by adult companies in the 1630s. The 1600s and the 1630s are remarkable for the so-called 'War of the Poets' and the open rivalry between Blackfriars and the Cockpit/Phoenix,[7] but also because they marked two time periods when theatre-making was at its most self-conscious. Prologues and epilogues often focused on the purpose of playwriting, play-going and play-reading; indeed, some are self-conscious about the role of prologues and epilogues, as the example of *The Emperor of the East* indicates. The numbers of prologues and epilogues in printed playbooks during these two time-periods seem therefore to have soared because these paratexts became privileged *page* sites in which playwrights could propose, nuance or criticize different modes of writing, staging, or responding to contemporary drama, either as performed or as reproduced in print. Similarly, the closure of the theatres ushered in a new era of dramatic self-consciousness, when the rise in printed prologues and epilogues reflected a wider increase in dramatic paratexts printed between 1642 and 1660. Interregnum prologues and epilogues could be newly written for the page, reflecting the time of publication, not the moment of performance; these and other

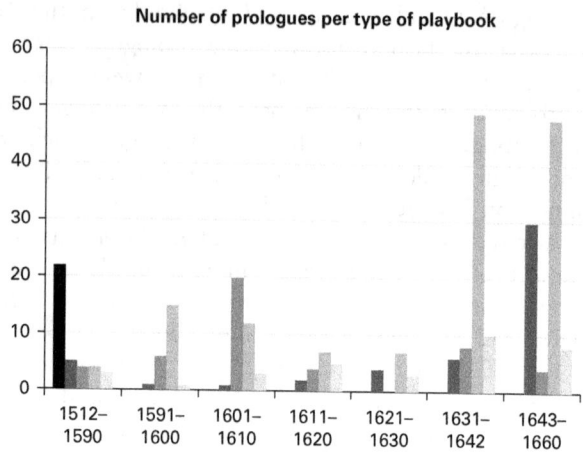
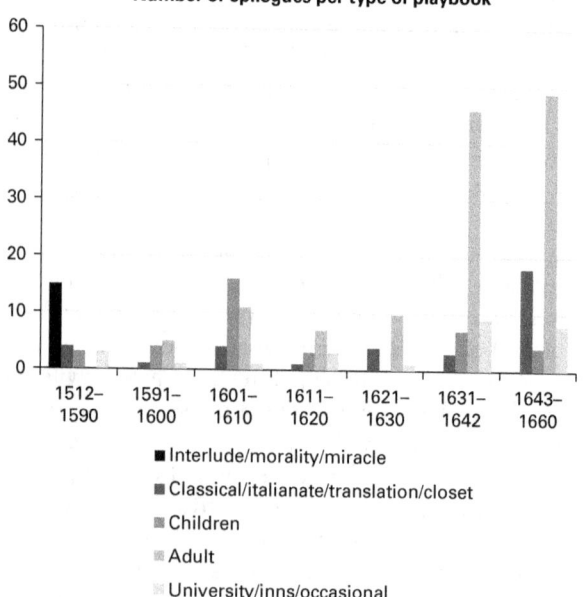

FIGURE 5.2 *First Editions featuring Prologues and Epilogues, per type of play.*

paratexts written during the Interregnum often articulated the value and nature of drama in a moment when the stage was suppressed. At the same time, the effort to recover and publish older stage orations reflected a new appreciation for theatrical documents previously deemed to be expendable.

The drop in the inclusion rate of prologues and epilogues in printed playbooks published in the 1590s seems significant, especially in light of the paratexts' rise in popularity in the 1600s, 1630s, and during the Interregnum. Given that this drop is limited to a single ten-year period, it seems unreasonable to assume that dramatically fewer prologues and epilogues were spoken on stage in the 1590s than from 1600 onwards, even in light of the introduction of benefit performances (special performances for which a share of the revenue would be received by the playwright as part of his payment for writing the play).[8] The introduction of the benefit performance did not simply replace a non-commercial economic model that relied on aristocratic patronage alone. Aristocratic patronage is indeed crucial to an understanding of the old moralities as 'elite great-hall plays', whose pedagogical purposes reflected 'the moral economy of household life'; the prologues and epilogues printed with moralities, emphasising their edifying mixture of learning and mirth, reinforce an understanding of the economic/material conditions of theatrical productions in aristocratic households.[9] However, scholars, including Paul Whitfield White, have shown that the old moralities, whose title pages often included character lists that specified how many actors were needed to perform them, were also regularly performed by professional and amateur companies in public halls and play-performing taverns.[10] Even so, references to public performances in prologues prefaced to the old moralities, which may have functioned to invite applause and remuneration, are extremely rare. An isolated example occurs in Lewis Wager, *The Repentance of Mary Magdalene* (1566):

Hipocrites that wold not haue their fautes reueled
Imagine slaunder our facultie to let,

> Faine wold they haue their wickednes still concealed
> Therfore maliciously against vs they be set,
> O (say they) muche money they doe get.
> Truely I say, whether you geue halfpence or pence,
> Your gayne shalbe double, before you depart hence.
> ...
> Is wisedom no more worth than a peny trow you?
> Scripture calleth the price thereof incomparable.
> Here may you learne godly Sapience now,
> Which to body and soule shall be profitable.[11]

The unusual reference to a paying audience in this prologue suggests that occasional prologues, the 'impermanent' prologues and epilogues that Stern describes in 'Prologues, Epilogues, Interim Entertainment',[12] were not included in printed editions of Tudor interludes as often as the didactic ones that have survived in print. The drop in the number of prologues and epilogues in the 1590s should therefore be ascribed not to a waning of popularity on stage but to what types of prologues and epilogues were deemed to be popular with readers at different times during the entire period under discussion here.

The closure of the theatres in 1642 marked a new phase in the production and transmission of plays in print so the rise in the rate of inclusion of prologues and epilogues after 1642 must be considered more closely: it illuminates not only dramatic attitudes from the era of the theatre ban, but also from the period when the playhouses were open – just. For example, the large numbers of prologues and epilogues included in editions of Beaumont and Fletcher's plays printed after 1642 suggest a significant gap between the number of prologues and epilogues spoken on stage and those transmitted into print before 1642. Out of the eighteen first editions of Beaumont and Fletcher plays printed before 1642, only six (33 per cent) are printed with either a prologue or epilogue.[13] By contrast, out of the thirty-five works first printed in the Beaumont and Fletcher Folio of 1647, twenty-one (60 per cent) are printed with either a prologue or epilogue.[14] If the theatrical paratexts in the 1647 Folio mostly reflect what was actually spoken onstage before 1642, it is unreasonable to assume that the Beaumont and Fletcher plays that happened to be first printed before 1642 were about half as likely to have prologues and epilogues spoken onstage than those that happened to be first printed after 1642. Rather, this increase in inclusion suggests that, after the closure of the theatres, stationers made a concerted effort to reproduce the theatrical experience for reading audiences who could not easily access it. Accordingly, a printer's note in the Beaumont and Fletcher Folio draws attention to the inclusion of theatrical paratexts and the efforts taken to retrieve them, ending with an admission that some were not composed by the dramatists themselves: 'WE forgot to tell the *Reader,* that some *Prologues* and *Epilogues* (here inserted) were not written by the *Authours* of this *Volume;* but made by others on the *Revivall* of severall *Playes*'.[15] This statement raises profound questions about printed prologues and epilogues, asking how many that survive might derive from revivals, not from original performances; it also demonstrates the unprecedented importance accorded to stage orations in print in this later period, when the stage was suppressed.

Although the printing of prologues and epilogues ostensibly forges a connection between a play's staged and textual iterations, ironically, it can also highlight a fundamental disconnection between stage and page. This occurs repeatedly and consistently throughout the period. For example, the prologue attached to *Wily Beguiled* (London: C. Knight, 1606) reveals disparities, rather than continuities, between the two media. The prologue begins with a meta-theatrical joke: upon entering, the Prologue asks a player, 'What play shall wee have here tonight?' The Player answers: 'Sir you may look upon the title.' Looking upon a title-board upon which 'Spectrum' is written (see Matthew Steggle's chapter in this volume for more on the use of stage boards) the Prologue complains, 'What *Spectrum* once again?' A Juggler enters and switches the title-board: a stage direction states that '*Spectrum* is conueied away: and *Wily beguiled* stands in the place of it'.[16] The joke depends on elements of surprise and confusion; in the theatre, the title-board authoritatively announces the title. The impact of this joke is lessened in print: in the play's first edition, 'Wily Beguiled' is what is authoritatively printed on the title page, while 'Spectrum' is only the head title. The Player's instruction to 'look upon the title' generates two different responses: in the theatre, both Prologue and spectator look towards a title-board marked 'Spectrum'; in the playbook, the reader looks to the title page (where one should 'look upon the title') and sees 'Wily Beguiled'. The experiences of the Prologue and spectator are aligned in the theatre but diverge in the context of print. Efforts to reproduce stage effects in print therefore reveal a disconnection between the functions of the theatrical prologue and of its printed iteration; similar such print divisions are addressed by Bourne in this volume.

Another potential disconnection between page and stage emerges when one considers whether printed theatrical paratexts reflect what was actually spoken on stage, either with the particular play with which it was printed, or even at all. Stern notes that prologues and epilogues regularly circulated outside their plays, which led to their regular loss; as she puts it, 'one reason why printed plays often lack prologues or epilogues is that the papers containing them had wandered, not that they never existed'.[17] But, as she also notes, stage orations also 'wandered' into different plays. We know that theatrical paratexts were recycled; the same prologue is prefaced to Dekker's *Wonder of a Kingdom* (London: N. Vavasour, 1636) and Rowley's *All's Lost by Lust* (London; T. Harper, 1633), while the prologue to the 1635 edition of Beaumont's *Knight of the Burning Pestle* is borrowed (with the omission of one line) from Lyly's *Sappho and Phao* (London: T. Cadman, 1584).

The potential disconnection between extant printed theatrical paratexts and what was actually spoken on stage is especially high in plays printed after 1642. During the theatre ban, already-itinerant theatrical documents would have been particularly susceptible to loss – the longer the period between performance and publication, the greater the likelihood that such documents would go missing, while the upheaval that attended the theatrical prohibition threatened dramatic manuscripts of all kinds.[18] In this respect, the increase in printed stage orations after 1642 is particularly remarkable; it suggests perhaps a comparative indifference to them before 1642, when copy texts of stage orations would have been more readily available. It could also be that some of these prologues and epilogues were actually written after the closure of the theatres but presented as pre-1642 documents to bolster the text's ability to conjure the absent theatre. (For further reflection on lost, absent and forged theatrical documents, see Roslyn L. Knutson and David McInnis's chapter in this volume).

Unsurprisingly, given the gap between the interest in and the supply of stage orations after 1642, it appears that post-1642 stationers attached prologues and epilogues to plays in print that may not have had them – or may have had different ones – in performance. In Andrew Crooke and Henry Brome's edition of *Five New Plays* (London: A. Crooke and H. Brome, 1659) by Richard Brome, for instance, the same epilogue appears twice: it is printed after *The Lovesick Court* and then again following *The Weeding of Covent Garden,* where it is the first of two epilogues attached to the play; the latter play also features two prologues. This epilogue may have been spoken aloud with both plays, but Crooke and Brome's inclusive publication of dramatic paratexts in *Five New Plays* suggests otherwise. Matthew Steggle has noted that, along with the two prologues and epilogues, the paratextual matter to *The Weeding of Covent Garden* contain 'three extra, anomalous, items' that have little to do with the play itself: Richard Brome's verse satire 'Upon *Aglaura* printed in Folio', attacking the overly large format of Suckling's play; an eight-line song that has no obvious connection to *Weeding*, but which replicates lines from a song in Brome's comedy *A Jovial Crew;* and Brome's commendatory poem to William Cavendish's *The Variety.*[19] The generic epilogue attached to both *The Lovesick Court* and

The Weeding of Covent Garden could therefore reflect Crooke and Brome's catch-all approach to paratexts, rather than their fidelity to what was actually spoken onstage.

It is especially doubtful that the recycled theatrical paratexts attached to an edition of Beaumont and Fletcher's *Thierry and Theodoret* (Q2b [London: H. Moseley, 1649]) reflect what was actually spoken onstage during the play's performance. Neither of the first two editions of *Thierry* (Q1 [London: T. Walkley, 1621] and the first issue of Q2, from 1648) includes a prologue or epilogue. The second issue of *Thierry* Q2 (1649), features a prologue and epilogue previously attached, respectively, to Beaumont and Fletcher's *The Noble Gentleman* (from F1 1647) and to Shirley's *The Changes, or Love in a Maze* (Q1 1632). The epilogue to *The Noble Gentleman* meanwhile was repurposed for the second issue of the Second Quarto (Q2b) of Beaumont and Fletcher's *The Woman Hater*, published in 1649 by Humphrey Moseley. Critics have characterized these borrowings as indiscriminate: Fredson Bowers described *Thierry* Q2b's theatrical paratexts as 'dramatic flotsam';[20] Tiffany Stern, noting the 'frank plunder' of *The Noble Gentleman*'s stage orations for *Thierry* and *The Woman Hater*, comments that 'it is as though any old Beaumont and Fletcher prologue or epilogue would do for any of their texts'.[21] However, while it is true that *Thierry*'s theatrical paratexts – associated with other plays and only attached to a reprint several years after the closure of theatres – were probably never spoken aloud with that play, the ostensibly indiscriminate recycling of theatrical paratexts seems more careful upon closer inspection. First, why would a stationer (perhaps Humphrey Moseley, the edition's publisher) go to the trouble of sourcing stage orations from two different plays (and one from another dramatist), when he could simply reuse *The Noble Gentleman*'s epilogue along with its prologue? We know the epilogue to *The Noble Gentleman* lent itself to being recycled, since it was reattached it to Q2b of *The Woman Hater*. Moreover, while the theatrical paratexts do not necessarily resonate with *Thierry*, they do resonate with the new context of publication in the late 1640s. *The Changes* epilogue can be read as a poignant commentary on the current moment of theatrical silence:

> If not for what we are, (for alas here
> No Roscius moves to charme your eyes, or eare)
> Yet as you hope hereafter to see Playes,
> Encourage us and give our Poet bayes.[22]

What in 1632 appears to be a highly conventional apology and request for approval becomes in 1649 a pointed reference to theatrical suppression. That there is 'No Roscius' 'to charme your eyes, or eare', is no longer simply an acknowledgment that contemporary actors fail to live up to the standard set by the Roman actor, a paradigm of dramatic excellence. The absence of Roscius instead evokes the regrettable loss of an entire tradition of theatrical performance. Likewise, the straightforward connection between audience approval and continued performances asserted by the epilogue would have been a distant, bittersweet memory by 1649. The epilogue's promise that encouragement will lead to more plays could function as a call for a resumption of performance (a vain one given the tightening restrictions on theatre in the late 1640s);[23] at best it promises that approval will lead to more plays in print.[24] The example reveals that stationers' indifference to printing the performance faithfully did not mean that they indiscriminately printed whatever theatrical documents were at hand. On the contrary: turning away from what was actually spoken onstage gave stationers a wider choice of prologues and epilogues, the selection, reproduction (and perhaps even the composition?) of which could function as form of cultural commentary.

Prologues and epilogues could also be altered for the same play as it moved from performance into print. It is worth highlighting that even when occasional prologues and epilogues were included in a printed playbook, the printed version did not necessarily reflect the version that was spoken on stage.

As the title page in both editions of Richard Edwards' *Damon and Pithias* (1571, second edition 1582) suggests, print publication may lead to the revision of occasional prologues. Having explained that the play was '[n]ewly Imprinted, as the same was shewed be- / fore the Queenes Maiestie, by the Children of her Graces / Chappell', the title page goes on to specify that the prologue was instead 'somewhat al- / tered for the proper vse of them that hereafter / shall haue occasion to plaie it, either in / Priuate, or open Audience'.[25] We have known for a long time that print publication prompted authors like Ben Jonson to omit the work of his collaborators, and that plays often included more lines as printed playbooks than as spoken on stage.[26] But we are less aware of the fact that theatrical paratexts may also have been tweaked and changed in preparation for print publication.

A further disconnection between the stage and the page emerges when the logic for including prologues and epilogues in performance – they were typically spoken, only on first and special performances – is compared to the logic for including them in print. While the presence of a prologue and an epilogue in a playbook suggests a new play 'in its freshest and so most fluid state . . . while a play lacking them appeared to have been audience-tested and approved', once prologues and epilogues *were* included in a printed playbook, they subsequently tended to be reprinted – making exceptions to this rule telling.[27] If any changes occurred in the paratextual materials that accompanied the printed play, these changes were generally incremental additions or a reordering of the sequence in which these materials had originally been printed.

There are, however, a few telling exceptions to the tendency to reprint prologues and epilogues in later editions, which are worth exploring in detail, because they qualify, and therefore clarify and reinforce, the general principle that printed prologues and epilogues denote a stable (and, if anything, a growing) paratextual apparatus, which boosted the readerly status achieved by a play when the latter was reprinted.[28] In some cases, the omission of prologues and/or epilogues from later editions appears to have occurred accidentally. For example, the prologue which appears in Q1 (1597) of *Romeo and Juliet* is dropped from the First Folio; some editors assume the compositor accidentally missed the Prologue printed on A2v because he cast the play off from the head title starting on A3.[29] Similarly, Greg speculates that Q2 1614's omission of the epilogue from Q1 *Wily Beguiled* (London: C. Knight, 1606) stems from 'the use of an imperfect copy'.[30] Whatever the cause, once the epilogue was dropped in Q2 (London: C. Knight, 1614), it was never restored in the subsequent editions of Q3 (London: C. Knight, 1623), Q4 (London: T. Knight, 1630), Q5 (London: T. Knight, 1635), Q6 (London: T. Alchorn, 1638). By contrast, the epilogue in Q1 of *Mercurius Britannicus* (London: 1641; publisher unknown for this edition and all subsequent editions) was probably omitted accidentally from Q2 (also 1641) because it was restored in Q3 (again, 1641), whose title page boasts that the text has been 'reprinted with sundry Additions'.

A further example from John Mason's *The Turk* (London: J. Busby, 1610) suggests that theatrical paratexts could be replaced with more literary ones to bolster the readerly status of the play. The prologue and epilogue that appeared in *The Turk*'s first edition (Q1) were omitted from Q2 (London: F. Faulkner, 1632), while a prose argument was added. The prologue and epilogue in Q1 are generic, while Q2's argument outlines the play's convoluted plot – a series of faked deaths and resurrections, and various configurations of romantic pairings. The omission of the prologue and epilogue and the addition of a new argument would therefore seem to have been deliberate: the replacement of a theatrical paratext with one that is arguably more 'literary' could be seen as an effort to reposition the play primarily as a reading text.

The omission of a prologue and epilogue could also be a part of a wider marketing strategy. For example, Henry Killigrew's *The Conspiracy* (London: A. Crooke, 1638) included a verse prologue and epilogue, which were omitted from the play's single-text Folio edition of 1653, printed under the title

Pallantus and Eudora. In 'The Publisher to the Reader', the stationer John Hardesty characterizes 'the former impression' (Q1) as a '*Corrupted Fragment* or *Foul Draught* of what this Play was intended'. Hardesty states that if 'the Corrections, Expungings, and Additions be consider'd, it is almost the one half otherwise. This hath made me likewise impose a New Name upon it', i.e. *Pallantus and Eudora*.[31] We have long known that reprints could be marketed by denigrating the texts of earlier editions – famously, Heminges and Condell urged readers to buy Shakespeare's First Folio by asserting that its plays already in print were 'diuerse stolne, and surreptitious copies' while F1 offered the plays 'cur'd, and perfect of their limbes'.[32] As *Pallantus and Eudora* demonstrates, however, theatrical paratexts could fall victim to this process of textual 'corruption' and 'correction' – putting pressure on the seemingly clear division between text and paratext.

The fate of the joint prologue attached to the first edition of *The Troublesome Reign of King John* Parts 1 and 2 (Q1 [London: S. Clarke, 1591]) also suggests how the function of stage orations could be undermined if they were transmitted into print, and upheld if they were omitted. The joint prologue to Q1 registers the novelty of the play and the recent popularity of Marlowe's *Tamburlaine*, referring to audiences who 'with friendly grace of smoothed brow / Have entertained the Scythian Tamburlaine, and given applause to an infidel', and entreats them to 'Vouchsafe to welcome ... A warlike Christian and your countryman'.[33] Q2 (London: J. Helme, 1611) omits the joint prologue (but retains Q1's prologue to Part 2), perhaps because the reference to the play's novelty no longer held true, and because the reference to popular plays of the 1590s may have seemed dated by then. Far from making the play seem fresh, retaining such a prologue – with its patently untrue boasts of novelty and time-bound references – would only underscore the play's age. Ironically, the omission of *The Troublesome Reign*'s prologue from Q2 makes the play seem fresher.

To conclude, this chapter has highlighted disconnections between the purpose of stage orations and printed theatrical paratexts. It has therefore reinforced the notion championed by theatre and print historians, such as Stephen Orgel and Janette Dillon, that, if the play is a book, it is not a play.[34] These scholars have stressed the distance between text and performance, between what we can reasonably assume happened on stage and what was eventually reproduced on the page. We have similarly suggested that extant printed theatrical paratexts cannot always be taken to represent what was spoken on stage. The transmission from stage to page often marked a change in the purpose, phrasing, and collocation of these texts, which were not simply reproduced or omitted when stage plays reached the press, but were instead often radically transformed.

Notes

* Craig gratefully acknowledges the support of the Huntington Library, where she completed her portion of this chapter as a short-term fellow.

1 Earlier studies have considered prologues and epilogues as dramatic, political or bibliographical devices: see, for example, Douglas Bruster and Robert Weimann, *Prologues to Shakespeare's Theatre: Performance and Liminality in Early Modern Drama* (London and New York: Routledge, 2004), or David M. Bergeron, *Textual Patronage in English Drama: 1570–1640* (Aldershot: Ashgate, 2006). We instead focus on prologues and epilogues as textual artifacts and on their transmission from stage to page.

2 Our use of the term 'prologue' is inclusive of all varieties of prologic materials, ranging from choric introductions and choruses that introduce the play and then reappear throughout (as, for example, in *Henry V*), inductions, as well as prologues that introduce the play as performed and readerly prologues written for print.

3 Given the slow rise of a reading market for printed playbooks in the sixteenth century, we have included all first editions published between 1512 and 1590 in a single period-group; the 1630s have been rounded up to 1642.

4 E. K. Chambers, *The Elizabethan Stage*, 4 vols (Oxford: Clarendon Press, 1923), 2: 550.

5 Chambers, 2: 547n.

6 Chambers, 2: 547n.

7 For more details, see, for example, J. P. Bednarz, *Shakespeare and the Poets' War* (New York: Columbia University Press, 2001); Andrew Gurr, *The Shakespearian Playing Companies* (Oxford: Oxford University Press, 1996); Andrew Gurr, *The Shakespearean Stage 1574–1642*, 4th edn (Cambridge: Cambridge University Press, 2009); or Martin Butler, *Theatre and Crisis 1632–1642* (Cambridge: Cambridge University Press, 1984).

8 See, for example, Tiffany Stern, *Documents of Performance in Early Modern England* (Cambridge: Cambridge University Press, 2009), esp. 81–82 and 93–96. Stern establishes that 'benefits were eased into the theatrical process, existing for some authors on some days in some theatres before 1600 or so, and existing for most authors in most theatres (and largely on the second day) only from the late 1620s' (93).

9 G. Walker, *The Politics of Performance in Early Renaissance Drama* (Cambridge: Cambridge University Press, 1998), 52.

10 Paul Whitfield White, *Theatre and Reformation: Protestantism, Patronage and Playing in Tudor England* (Cambridge: Cambridge University Press, 1993).

11 Lewis Wager, *The Repentance of Mary Magdalene* (1566), A2v.

12 Stern, *Documents*, 81–119.

13 It is worth noting that some Beaumont and Fletcher plays include prologues and epilogues in second-plus editions printed before 1642, but not in first editions, such as the second edition of *The Knight of the Burning Pestle* (1635), and the third edition of *The Maid's Tragedy* (1630). These editions confirm both the accretive nature of printed prologues and epilogues, as well as the revived interest in printing stage orations in the 1630s.

14 This higher rate of inclusion does not simply reflect the folio format; the relative paucity of stage orations in Shakespeare's First Folio [and of course there's the fact that the prologue to *Troilus* only entered really late and only because of contingencies in the playhouse] indicates that, while a large format could accommodate inclusion of prologues and epilogues, it did not guarantee it.

15 Francis Beaumont and John Fletcher, *Comedies and Tragedies* (London: H. Moseley and H. Robinson, 1647), g2r.
16 *Wily Beguiled* (London: C. Knight, 1606, 1614), A2r–v.
17 Stern, *Documents*, 100.
18 For example, because dramatic manuscripts were often housed in playhouses, unprinted plays and stage orations must have been lost forever when the theatres were pulled down. Gary Taylor, *Thomas Middleton: The Collected Works* (Oxford: Oxford University Press, 2007), 51–52.
19 Matthew Steggle, 'Brome, Covent Garden, and 1641,' *Renaissance Forum* 5 (2001), Retrieved from http://web.archive.org/web/20051219211148/http://www.hull.ac.uk/renforum/v5no2/steggle.htm
20 Fredson Bowers, general ed., *The Dramatic Works in the Beaumont and Fletcher Canon*, 10 vols (Cambridge: Cambridge University Press, 1976), 3: 373.
21 Stern, *Documents*, 106.
22 James Shirley, *Changes, or Love in a Maze* (London: W. Cooke, 1632), A1v.
23 Parliament renewed the ordinance against playing four times, on 16 July 1647, 11 August 1647, 22 October 1647, and 9 February 1648, each time increasing the severity of the penalties for actors and spectators who contravened the law. Authorities also cracked down on surreptitious performance during and immediately following the trial and execution of Charles I, conducting destructive theatrical raids in January 1649 and pulling down the Fortune, Cockpit and Salisbury Court theatres in March 1649.
24 Although Greg, Bowers and Stern point out that *Thierry* reprints *The Changes* epilogue, a single word change seems to have gone unnoticed. In *Changes*, the prologue promises 'if this Play / Proceed more fortunate, wee shall *blesse* the day'; in *Thierry* this line has becomes, 'if this Play / Proceed more fortunate, wee shall *crown* the day.' (our emphasis) The change in wording from 'bless' to 'crown' seems significant in the context of the year of publication.
25 Richard Edwards, *Damon and Pithias* (1571), A1r.

26 The title page of Ben Jonson's *Every Many Out of His Humour* (London: W. Holme, 1600), for example, states that the printed text of the play '[c]ontain[s] more than hath been Publickely spo- / ken or Acted' (A2r). In 'To the Reader', his preface to *Sejanus his Fall* (London: T. Thorpe, 1605), Jonson once again provides one of the best-known accounts of how print publication occasioned the removal of lines by a collaborator: 'Lastly I would informe you, that this Booke, in all nū- / bers, is not the same with that which was acted on the / publike Stage, wherein a second Pen had good share: in / place of which I haue rather chosen, to put weaker (and / no doubt lesse pleasing) of mine own, then to defraud so / happy a *Genius* of his right, by my lothed vsurpation' (¶2v).

27 Stern, *Documents*, 82; exceptions are discussed on 101.

28 Reprints of playbooks denote exceptional levels of popularity among early readers, given that, on average, only one in six plays reached publication in the period, and less than half were ever reprinted, let alone reprinted more than twice. For more details, see, for example, Peter W. M. Blayney, 'The Publication of Playbooks', in J. D. Cox and D. S. Kastan, eds, *A New History of Early English Drama* (New York: Columbia University Press, 1997), 387.

29 Stanley Wells, Gary Taylor, John Jowett, and W. Montgomery, eds, *The Oxford Shakespeare: A Textual Companion* (Oxford: Oxford University Press, 1987), 290.

30 W. W. Greg, *A Bibliography of the English Printed Drama to the Restoration*, 4 vols (London: Printed for the Bibliographical Society at the University Press, Oxford, 1939–59), 1: 234b.

31 H. Killigrew, *Pallantus and Eudora*, London: J. Hardesty. 1653), A2r.

32 Heminges in William Shakespeare, *Comedies, Histories and Tragedies* (London: E. Blount, J. Smethwick, I. Jaggard, W. Aspley, 1623), πA3r.

33 *Tamberlaine* (A2r).

34 Stephen Orgel, 'The Book of the Play', in P. Holland and S. Orgel, eds, *From Performance to Print in Shakespeare's England* (Basingstoke: Palgrave Macmillan, 2006), 13–54; Janette Dillon, 'Is There a Performance in this Text?', *Shakespeare Quarterly*, 45 (1994), 74–86.

6

Title- and Scene-Boards

The Largest, Shortest Documents

Matthew Steggle

This piece argues that early modern theatre made routine use of both title-boards and scene-boards: painted signs bearing, respectively, the title of the play being acted and the location of the action. In particular, it draws on examples from the stage directions of the amateur dramatist William Percy, who seems to envisage almost a hierarchy of different information contained within written signs around the playing area. It also looks to visual evidence. These signs, I will argue, made a considerable difference to the experience of early modern theatre. What is more, their status as written texts, generated by playwriting, means they are members of the family of 'documents of performance' that constitute the text of a play. Explicitly setting out an interpretive frame for the play's theatre audiences, these title- and scene-boards must be considered afresh, because they are part of the problem of the play *qua* textual object.

Physical objects

It has long been recognized that early modern theatre seems sometimes to have made use of boards on which was written the title of the play. The principal evidence for this takes the form of metadramatic allusions within plays, as can be illustrated by a few representative examples. In the Induction of Ben Jonson's *Cynthia's Revels*, the title appears to be visible to the audience, presumably on a signboard, since one of the characters comments: 'the title of his play is *Cynthia's Revels*, as any man that hath hope to be saved by his book can witness'.[1] The comedy *Wily Beguiled* begins with a 'title' on stage saying 'Spectrum', which is changed during the Induction to the correct title: '*Spectrum* is conueied away: and *Wily beguiled*, stands in the place of it'.[2] Another title-board seems to be described in the opening of Beaumont's *The Knight of the Burning Pestle*, where the Citizen refers to it while complaining to the actor: 'you call your play, *The London Marchant*. Downe with your Title boy, downe with your Title'.[3] Richard Brome's Caroline comedy *The City Wit* seems to have a title-board carried in by a Prologue-character, who describes himself as 'I, that bear its Title'.[4] Conversely, there are also several references to the use of signs to indicate location. One might mention Sidney's *Defence of Poetry*, alluding to the practice as normal even as early as 1579: 'What childe is there, that coming to a Play, and seeing Thebes written in great Letters vpon an olde doore, doth beleeue that it is Thebes?'[5] Examples could be multiplied, many times over, but the basic principle seems clear.[6]

And yet theatre historians of the later twentieth century were reluctant to embrace the idea that these conventions were at all usual, seeing them as 'cumbersome' and unsophisticated, a value judgement that may have clouded their assessment of the evidence. They preferred instead to see them as exceptions which were commented upon when used: early features which 'occasionally' persisted in some drama, perhaps particularly in the private theatres.[7] This orthodoxy was comprehensively demolished in 2007 by Tiffany Stern, who offered many hitherto unnoticed primary citations from across early modern drama, and in particular through the Caroline period, which appear to allude to the practice. Stern argued instead that both title-boards, and their near-relatives 'scene' (or 'location')-boards, were widespread across time and across theatrical context, and that seeing them was one of the expectations that people would have brought to drama of all sorts in the period. In the decade since it was published no-one, as far as I am aware, has come up with a riposte to Stern's heavily documented argument. My further thinking here about what title- and scene-boards are, and what effect they have, is only made possible by Stern's pre-existing demonstration of just how much evidence there is for their widespread use. So, starting from this new position, what can one say about title- and scene-boards?

First, such boards are documents, of a sort. They can in fact be thought of as fringe members of the extended family of the 'documents of performance' of the early modern theatre, a category whose more normal members include scripts, letters, songs, prologues, and arguments, as well as the manuscripts and printed texts discussed in other chapters of this book. Tiffany Stern (again) writes about how one might conceptualize this flotilla of textual fragments:

> Together, the fragments that the playhouse made, in conjunction with the fragments that play-writing had produced, and the additional fragments brought about for advertising and explaining the play, were the documents that amounted to 'the play' in its first performance.... Thus, each separate document that made up a play has its own story, its own attachment to the other documents, its own rate of loss and survival. And, as any fragment could be separately written aside from the playscript, so it could easily and at any subsequent time be updated or freshly composed or added to by someone else.[8]

Title- and scene-boards fit well with this definition. They are texts generated in the playwriting process; linked to the other documents within the set they belong to; and yet capable of being swapped, at various points in a play's life-cycle, by various agents. There are several early modern plays whose titles seem negotiable, and at least some early modern plays whose intradiegetic locations were changed when the play was revised: such plays will have required, as well as their other textual changes, a fresh set of scene-boards.[9]

And yet title- and scene-boards are particularly paradoxical members of the larger family to which they belong. They will have been by far the biggest and heaviest physical objects in that category, and yet in terms of text, they were by far the briefest, only a word or two long. They also had a larger direct readership than any of their cousins except the playbill. For sure, all the other types of document underpinned the performance as delivered, and some were read out on stage. But *qua* documents, these other forms were only directly read by a handful of people, unless and until they appeared in print. Everyone literate who attended the play, though, would have had to engage with the title-board. And they are exceptional in one more respect, in being the most elusive members of their family. Not a single material example is extant, although hundreds must have been made. The status of these boards as lost texts, of a kind, makes them the province not just of theatre historians but also of textual editors.

Second, both title- and scene-boards matter because, if they were indeed routinely used, their use would have had significant effects upon their plays. A scene-board, like a location caption in a modern film, changes the nature of the exposition by spelling out the intradiegetic location omnisciently, unambiguously, and immediately, and in a way that remains legible and prominent throughout the action. And title-boards put on stage the play's title, or to be strictly accurate one of its titles. Titles have been described as 'the briefest, the most primitive, and often the most densely meaningful member of the loose family of textual forms that together make up an early modern play'.[10] Title-boards, instantiating those densely meaningful titles in particularly terse form and putting them before the audience's eyes throughout the performance, are putting on stage a headline by which continually to judge the action of the play.

Third, and cautiously, one can start to collate references to these boards' physical form and location. One type of evidence is provided by the remarkably problematic playtexts of William Percy (1570–1648), aristocrat and amateur dramatist, who seems to have written his six surviving plays around 1601–05, and then recopied those plays much later in his life into the various manuscripts through which they survive. Percy frequently refers in his manuscripts to the possibility of performance of these plays by a children's company at Pauls or elsewhere, although there is, as Matthew Dimmock warns, 'no evidence that any of the plays were performed on the professional stage'.[11]

Percy's particular taste is for very detailed descriptions of the costuming and of the initial stage setting, of a kind without exact parallel in any other extant dramatic texts of the period. The nearest analogy, perhaps, lies in early modern descriptions of civic entries and the like, where, interestingly, written signs are also frequently mentioned as part of the tableaux.[12] Debate continues as to whether Percy's texts may be taken as witnesses of actual practice in early modern theatre, or whether the staging conventions they use are entirely products of an impractical and book-learned imagination.[13] Nonetheless, and with that caveat, Percy consistently wants his plays to use both title-boards and scene-boards. *The Faery Pastorall* has a particularly detailed opening instruction:

> Highest, aloft, and on the Top of the Musick Tree the Title *The Faery Pastorall*, Beneath him pind on Post of the Tree *The Scene Eluida Forrest*. Lowest off all ouer the Canopie [ΝΑΠΑΙΤΒΟΔΑΙΟΝ] or *Faery Chappell*.[14]

That is, Percy imagines a title-board at the top of the stage, on the music tree or music-house; below it, and offset to one side of the midline since it is on one of the supporting posts, a scene-board; and further down still and centred on the canopy, a scene-board which represents a subset of that second

FIGURE 6.1 Signs imagined by William Percy, superimposed onto an image of the Blackfriars Playhouse, Staunton, Virginia. By permission of the American Shakespeare Center's Blackfriars Playhouse

location, since in the play the Fairy Chapel is within the forest. The relationship between these signs is made clear by their spatial arrangement.

Another Percy play uses its space slightly differently: *The Cuckqueans and Cuckolds Errants* is to display that title – all thirty characters of it – 'highest and aloft'. Further down the stage are a series of locations that are not subsets of one another: 'Harwich'; 'Colchester'; 'The Raungers Lodge'; and 'Maldon'. As P. C. Kincaid has discussed, the way that Percy lays these words out in the manuscript, in noticeably larger handwriting than the rest of the text, seems to imply that they are to be written on signboards above the respective doors.[15] This obviously recalls a Terentian convention where different doors depict different locations; while it has sometimes been argued that Percy's practice is therefore Terentian rather than belonging to contemporary English drama, we do not in fact know that that convention was *not* used on the English stage as well. (A particularly relevant comparison here is *The Comedy of Errors*, which appears to use signboards of the Centaur and Porcupine to follow a similar 'Terentian' convention.)[16]

A third Percy play combines title-and scene-board into one, while also considering an alternative scheme as well: 'The Title aloft and about being both Title and Scene A COUNTRY TRAGOEDYE IN VACUNIUM or CUPIDS SACRIFICE one of the two, The first in regard of propertie of Scene . . .'.[17] That very vagueness is of course a sign of Percy's amateurism, but it is interesting that Percy thinks that a sign-board can do duty for both title and scene at once. Perhaps the most complex example lies in the three manuscripts of *Mahomet and His Heaven*, which between them offer a bewildering array of options for signs made meaningful in their relationship to one another. Percy starts by specifying 'The Scene and Title aloft MAHOMET AND HIS HEAVEN', but in another manuscript Percy imagines the title-board to read ARABIA SITIENS, again combining title and location in one board. Furthermore, Percy seems to imagine other scene-boards on the stage, including 'MEDINA TALNABI next MELCHIT', 'AMPHIPOLIS OF THE DESERTS', and 'THE PORTERS LODGE'. It is not entirely specified that these names are written on signs, but Percy's use of capitals suggests it, particularly since he does also specify a written sign to identify one of the props: 'an old and homely Tankard of gold on a shelf, with Cock or Tap at foote, written under THE TANKARD OF TRYALL'. Again, this may be Percy's amateurism, an overly literal approach to representation that recalls the mechanicals of *A Midsummer Night's Dream*: but nonetheless, it is what he specifies.[18] *The Faery Pastorall* has a related but different use of onstage signs associated with props: Percy requests several large onstage properties including 'A Kiln of Brick', but adds that if the stage is too crowded, they may be omitted and replaced only with signs 'with their Nuncupations onely in Text Letters'. Thus, an audience member in Percy's hypothetical theatre would be faced with multiple different signs to read, at different heights, some on the midline of the stage and others offset, with their relative location giving information as to how to interrelate them. In particular, for Percy, 'aloft' is where the main title of the play is put.

The stumbling-block, of course, remains that Percy's dramas are not necessarily guides to the practice of the theatres in which he seems to have hoped they might be performed. But what can be seen in Percy, around 1601–5, is consistent with a quite different, and equally problematic, type of material: visual representations of the English stage.

Pictures, of course, are of dubious value in theatre history, for three main reasons. First, evidence of any kind is very thinly spread, leading one to argue about (as it may be) the Globe in 1605 based on pictures that are not of the Globe, and are mostly not from 1605. Second, any occasion being recorded is untypical, by virtue of the very fact that it is being recorded. Third, any image that has been made is not a casual smartphone photo, indexical and unguarded, but rather a labour-intensive object enmeshed in many cultural codes. So the visual evidence must be treated with a healthy sense of danger: it is more an idealization of what a theatre *might* look like than a snapshot of what actually happened in a particular theatre on a particular day. Nonetheless, and with these caveats, some images of early modern English theatres seem to contain further evidence for written boards on stage.

What is generally regarded as the most important and relevant picture of the interior of an English theatre, the copy of De Witt's sketch of the Swan playhouse, depicts a stage covered with words thanks to its captions, but no explicitly depicted signboard. But in 1619, the polymath Robert Fludd published a picture of a theatre including a stage containing, part way up its rear wall, a projecting structure with a tiled roof and two windows. That building bears a rectangular framed signboard which is of considerable size, being almost the same width as the pair of double doors directly beneath it on the midline of the stage. On the board is written 'THEATR / VM · ORBI ·', the theatre of the world.[19] Debate continues about whether the picture is based on Fludd's memories of the

Globe, as Frances Yates argued; or of the Blackfriars, I. A. Shapiro's interpretation; or on neither, as Herbert Berry has argued, being instead a fanciful idealization of a theatre. But whichever interpretation one chooses, that large framed sign, high up on the midline, describing – in effect – the location of the action, is a valid point of reference in considering the horizon of expectations around signboards in early modern theatres.[20]

A little later still, Inigo Jones's drawings contain evidence for title-boards. Jones's sketch for the main stage of Montagu's *The Shepherd's Paradise* (1633) includes a frontispiece running along the top, with what appears to be a large swag of fabric at its centre, in which are written the words 'The Shep< >', and while the rest of the inscription is illegible, it is clearly intended to read 'The Shepherd's Paradise'. Given that the gap between the pilasters is around thirty feet, the swag appears to be about five feet across.[21] Similarly, Jones's sketch for the standing scene of another court entertainment, 'Florimène' (1635), includes a frontispiece which runs over the top of the stage. At its midpoint, two cherubs carry a shield on which is written the single word 'Florimen', and this feature again is large, as large as the gap between the two sets of stairs at the front of the stage.[22] A third Jones sketch, dated 1639 and entitled, rather ambiguously, 'for ye cockpit', pictures a blank cartouche in the centre of the arch across the top of the stage, which also accords with a reference in William Davenant's admittedly later *The Siege of Rhodes* (1656), which had 'RHODES' written upon the frieze that encompassed the scene. Similarly, the set for Davenant's *Cruelty of the Spaniards in Peru* (perf. 1658) includes 'An Arch. . . rais'd upon stone of Rustick work; upon the top of which is written, in an Antique Shield, PERU. . .'.[23]

Suggestive, too, in this connection, are the two frontispieces from early modern English drama, which are often analysed for their sketchy representations of an early modern stage: William Alabaster's *Roxana* (1635) and Nathaniel Richards' *Messalina* (1640).[24] In both cases, the bottom centre panel of the title page contains a small and truncated sketch of an early modern stage, seen slightly from above, extending from the front rails to the junction with the back of the stage, and including about the first storey of the back of the stage before being cut off by the panel above it. What we are interested in here is not the detail on the drawing itself, but the way it is spatially related to the main title, which in both cases appears in the panel above it, centred over the stage like a giant title-board.

All of this evidence, of course, can individually be written off as atypical: the printed images are too fantastic, Jones is an importer of new foreign fashions into England, the Davenant references are too late. But that they all tell a story that is in common with William Percy's earlier expectations suggests that title-boards, large, central, and aloft, were indeed a feature of the English stage.

And with this as a frame, one can turn to a commercial-theatre play from this date which seems to trade on the problems of interpretation presented by a hierarchy of written signs, meaningful in their spatial relationship to one another. This is Jonson's *Poetaster*, as it is generally known, a play which, as we shall see, seems to have been performed under the title *The Arraignment*.[25] In the Induction to this play, a comically myopic Envy 'arises' from below, to inspect the stage before the play starts. First, she reads the title – from, as we might now suppose, a title-board visible centrally and high up on the stage:

> Whats here? *Th'arraignment?* I: This, this is it,
> That our sunke eyes haue wak't for, all this while:
> Here will be subiect for my Snakes and me.

Turning to the audience, she is dazzled by 'the shine / Of this assembly', and it is some time before she resumes reading, moving down to the scene-board (or boards, since she seems to see three separate ones):

> Marke, how I will begin: The Scene is, ha?
> *Rome? Rome?* and *Rome?* Cracke eystrings, and your balls
> Drop into earth; let me be euer blind.[26]

Envy expects that the scene-boards will read 'London', and that the play can therefore be badged as topical and scandalous: she is disappointed by the boards, which modify her expectations gained from the title-board, and all three of which say the same thing. This passage, which has always seemed puzzling on the page, seems to match what we see in Percy's plays in terms of a hierarchical set of information displayed on boards.

Indeed, it is fascinating to think how Jonson's play would work in performance with the word 'Rome' visible on stage and the words *The Arraignment* looming above the stage throughout. 'Rome', perhaps, speaks for itself: Jonson's play is obviously interrogating different ideas of Romanness, and the place-name and its cognates already run like a motif through the speeches of the play, so that the word's presence on stage reinforces what we can see already from the dialogue. The title, though, is more interesting. For most of the action, Jonson's drama appears to be working up to the arraignment of Horace by his enemies. It pivots on the moment in the courtroom when the tables are turned and the accusers find they are the ones on trial, so that the title above the stage reveals its second, true, meaning. Lurking behind these two literal arraignments are the more indirect ones: of Ovid for his sexual indiscretion, handled by Augustus somewhat extra-judicially; of Augustus himself for his autocracy and neglect; of Jonson by his enemies and of those enemies by Jonson. If *Poetaster*, as a title for a play, invites consideration of individuals and of poetic taste, *The Arraignment* foregrounds legal and judicial processes in action. Displayed on stage throughout, it would make the play we think of as *Poetaster* into a much more obviously political theatre experience, for all that the scene-boards insist that the location is Rome.

We are moving towards a vision of the early modern stage space as containing multiple written signs, at different heights, meaningful in their spatial relationship to one another. A crude analogy might be with contemporary news television, as seen – as it may be – with the sound off in an airport. To anyone who has never seen the conventions before, the welter of text on screen is confusing: a station identification in one corner; captions on screen that supply the name of this particular news programme, or the location that the reporter is reporting from, or the news headline, or an expansion of that news headline. This is to say nothing of news streams, subtitles, and other features. We are so used to the spatial conventions that underlie these devices that we rarely notice the work we are doing in distinguishing them and discerning their relationship, nor the way that they set the frame within which we interpret the story being told. The early modern stage is less dynamically changing in its use of onstage writing, but the point about information literacy stands.

There are some practical implications that can only be gestured at. Henslowe, for instance, refers several times to employing a painter, and several times to the purchase of boards. Most of those are, almost certainly, for building projects rather than signboard-making, and yet the preparation of title-boards, like the preparation of playbills, would need to be considered among the now largely invisible backroom labour and expenses of the playhouse. Certainly, the Revels accounts include some expenses for painting signboards. And was there in the theatre a standing stock of title-boards and scene-boards, requiring storage space somewhere? No such stock is obviously visible in the most detailed records we have, Henslowe's inventories.[27]

Furthermore, not all forms of theatre environment are equal. Jones's designs, with a seemingly permanent place for a title at the front of the stage, point the way to a proscenium arch theatre, with the title shield forming, in effect, part of the embryonic fourth wall between stage and audience. By contrast, a title-board high up at the back of the playing area, so that the actors play to the audience in front of it and not on the other side of it, changes the dynamic of the stage space.

This chapter has developed its idea mainly through references in William Percy and early Jonson – neither of them the most canonical of authors – and yet the implications are far wider. These now largely invisible title- and scene-boards should be of great concern to literary critics.[28]

More or less any early modern play gains an interesting twist if its title is visible on stage, throughout, in a prominent position of authority. One thinks of *Measure for Measure*, the scriptural title of which would start off as a comment on the plotting and counter-plotting, while beneath it both the Duke and Angelo try to take upon themselves the role of the voice of the recorded law. As the play goes on, though, the words above the stage would modulate into a reminder of the inevitability of a moral reckoning, anticipating their appearance in the dialogue in the last scenes. Another example, one where the title is interestingly at odds with the action, is John Ford's *'Tis Pity She's a Whore*. In Ford's tragic masterpiece, Annabella is generally regarded as a sympathetic character whose desire to be good is sincere, and whose epitaph in the last line of the play – 'Who could not say, *'Tis pitty shee's a Whoore?*' – is a catachresis, a deliberately crass effect by the dramatist.[29] If, in the scenes where Annabella looks up to heaven and attempts to pray, that epitaph is already written in the heavens above her, it adds to an audience's sense that there is something unfair about the state of the universe. Other early modern plays will gain yet different effects from their title being written on top of the performance.

Mutatis mutandis, the same is true of scene-boards. In *Troilus and Cressida*, for instance, there is an obvious connection between the doomed hero Troilus and his doomed city Troy, but matching boards would make that more obvious. Another interesting example would be *Coriolanus*, in which the main title again has a relationship of a sort with a scene-board. What other effects can be created by boards which make the geographical location literally legible?

A particularly interesting subset within this problem is the group of plays whose title takes the form, 'The [person(s)] of [place]', since this form of title contains an intrinsic location. When watching *The Jew of Malta*, for instance, would an audience see a title-board reading simply 'The Jew', and a scene-board reading 'Malta'? Certainly, Henslowe sometimes refers to the play merely as *The Jew*.[30] Similarly, as Gerald Baker has shown, early references to the play we call *Othello* tend to refer to it as *The Moor of Venice*, its subtitle in print, while references to Othello the character tend to call him 'The Moor'.[31] Again, we might speculate that an early audience could see a titleboard reading simply 'The Moor', and, to begin with at least, a scene-board indicating 'Venice', a paradoxical state of affairs that encapsulates, in the tension between those two signs, Othello's impossible position. And every invocation of 'Moor' in the play resonates with the word already written above the stage as if a divine judgement on him. Again, readers may explore for themselves extensions of this argument to different plays, but the idea that title and location may be in dialogue with each other can be widely extended.

To pursue this idea further, one could do with more information about these putative boards showing title and location; the usual forms of wording that might appear upon them; and the exceptions. It would be good to have more systematic data on the lengths of text on known examples, and any information that could bear on the question of how double titles might be handled (since one reference to the practice, in Shirley's *Rosania*, seems to imply that both titles are visible at once).[32] One might look for evidence from other more theatrical traditions from the continent and the later English stage, and invoke the tools of what has been called the 'spatial turn' in early modern drama studies. What I aim to have shown here is that such research expeditions are warranted, because there is evidence of the practice from the early modern English stage narrowly defined, and because it makes a considerable difference to the play as performed. In having the status of 'document of performance', these title- and scene- boards are part of the problem of the play *qua* textual object.

Notes

1   Ben Jonson, *Cynthia's Revels,* ed. Eric Rasmussen and Matthew Steggle, in *The Cambridge Works of Ben Jonson*, 7 vols, eds. Martin Butler, David Bevington and Ian Donaldson (Cambridge:

Cambridge University Press, 2012), 1.432, Prologue 33. In the 1616 Folio, it is called '*Cynthia's Revels, or the Fountain of Self-Love*'.

2 *A Pleasant Comedie, Called Wily Beguilde* (1606), 3.

3 Francis Beaumont, *The Knight of the Burning Pestle* (1613), B1r.

4 Richard Brome, *The City Wit*, Prologue, cited from the edition of Elizabeth Schafer, *Richard Brome Online*, http://www.hrionline.ac.uk/brome/

5 Sidney, *An Apologie for Poetrie* (1595), H1r.

6 For copious further examples see G. F. Reynolds, 'Some Principles of Elizabethan Staging', *Modern Philology*, 2.4 (1905), 581–614; W. J. Lawrence, 'Title and Locality Boards on the Pre-Restoration Stage' in *Elizabethan Stage Studies* (Philadelphia: J. P. Lippincott, 1912), 41–72; and Tiffany Stern, 'Watching as Reading: The Audience and Written Text in Shakespeare's Playhouse,' in Laurie Maguire, ed., *How to Do Things with Shakespeare: New Approaches, New Essays* (Oxford: Blackwell, 2007), 136–159.

7 Quotations from Andrew Gurr, *The Shakespearean Stage 1574–1642*, 3rd edn (Cambridge: Cambridge University Press, 1994), 172, 180, 193; also M. C. Bradbrook, *Themes and Conventions of Elizabethan Tragedy*, 2nd edn (Cambridge: Cambridge University Press, 1980), 11.

8 Tiffany Stern, *Documents of Performance in Early Modern England* (Cambridge: Cambridge University Press, 2009), 4.

9 For the detachability and mutability of titles, see Gerald Baker, 'The Name of Othello Is Not the Name of *Othello*', *Review of English Studies*, 67 (2016), 62–78; relocated plays include Massinger's *Believe as You List*, moved from Western Europe to the Near East; Jonson's *Every Man In His Humour*, relocated on revision from Florence to London; and, indeed, allegedly, Shakespeare's *Measure for Measure*.

10 Matthew Steggle, *Digital Humanities and the Lost Drama of Early Modern England: Ten Case Studies* (Aldershot: Ashgate, 2015), 19.

11 Matthew Dimmock, 'Introduction' to William Percy, *William Percy's Mahomet and His Heaven: A Critical Edition* (Aldershot:

Ashgate, 2006), quotation from 56; Reavley Gair, 'Percy, William (1574–1648)', *Oxford DNB*.

12 A representative example is Dekker's *The Magnificent Entertainment* (1604); see also the vivid illustrations in *La ioyeuse [et] magnifique entrée de monseigneur Francoys ... en sa tres-renomée ville d'Anvers* (Antwerp, 1582), in colour online reproduction at the British Library *Renaissance Festival Books* website [accessed 1 August 2018].

13 See Dimmock, 'Introduction', 52.

14 Percy, quotation from Robert Denzel Fenn, 'William Percy's *Faery Pastorall*: An Old Spelling Edition', PhD thesis, University of British Columbia, 1997.

15 P. C. Kincaid, 'A critical edition of William Percy's *The Cuckqueans and Cuckolds Errants*' (PhD thesis, University of Birmingham, 2000), Introduction 62. The play is cited from this edition.

16 See Arthur F. Kinney, 'Shakespeare's *Comedy of Errors* and the Nature of Kinds', in Robert Miola, ed., *The Comedy of Errors: Critical Essays* (London: Routledge, 1997), 155–182.

17 Percy, cited in Stern, 'Watching as Reading', 152.

18 All quotations from Percy, *Mahomet and His Heaven,* ed. Dimmock, 61–62, and apparatus.

19 Robert Fludd, 'Theatrum orbi[s terrarum]', in *De anime memorativae Scientia, quae vulgo ars memoriae vocatur. Ars Memoriae*, in *Opera*, 17 vols in 7 ([Oppenheim: J.T. de Bry], 1617–1638), ii. 55, cited from the online reproduction at the University of Cambridge, https://exhibitions.lib.cam.ac.uk/reformation/artifacts/a-memory-theatre/ [accessed 1 August 2018].

20 The debate, with earlier references, is summarized by Ernest L. Rhodes, *Henslowe's Rose: The Stage and Staging* (Lexington: University Press of Kentucky, 1976).

21 Reproduced in John Orrell, 'The Paved Court Theatre at Somerset House', *British Library Journal*, 3 (1977), 13–19.

22 See Karen Britland, '"Florimène": The Author and the Occasion', *Review of English Studies,* 53 (2002), 475–483.

23 Cited from John Orrell, *The Theatres of Inigo Jones and John Webb* (Cambridge: Cambridge University Press, 1985); Orrell

also discusses the 1639 sketch and casts doubt on whether it is for the Cockpit-at-Court, or actually the Cockpit. For Rhodes, see Stern, 'Watching as Reading'.

24 Discussed by John H. Astington, 'The Origins of the *Roxana* and *Messalina* Illustrations', *Shakespeare Survey*, 43 (1991), 149–169; Stern, 'Watching as Reading', has leads towards other possibly relevant visual representations.

25 See the textual essay on *Poetaster* in the *Cambridge Works of Ben Jonson*, online at https://universitypublishingonline.org/cambridge/benjonson/k/essays/Poetaster_textual_essay/ – the play is called, on its first printing, *Poetaster, or The Arraignment* [accessed 1 August 2018].

26 Ben Jonson, *Poetaster or The arraignment* (1602), all quotations from A2r. The word "Poetaster" is not mentioned by Envy at all, although it does appear five times in the dialogue. It is not clear that the play in its original performance used that word as any form of title. Compare *Cynthia's Revels*, whose licensing record calls it *Narcissus, The Fountain of Self-Love* – reflecting perhaps a bookseller's sense of the vendibility of the mythological elements rather than the play's title in performance, which clearly read *Cynthia's Revels*.

27 R. A. Foakes, ed., *Henslowe's Diary*, 2nd edn (Cambridge: Cambridge University Press, 2002), 6, 7, 11, 13, 93, 218; see Reynolds, 'Some Principles of Elizabethan Staging', 581–614, for the Revels Accounts.

28 Indeed, Stern, 'Watching as Reading', already suggests this, with different examples; my work builds here upon hers.

29 John Ford, *'Tis pitty shee's a whore* (1633), K4r.

30 For references to the play as *The Jew*, see Foakes, ed., *Henslowe's Diary*, 19, 22, 321.

31 Baker, 'The Name of Othello Is Not the Name of *Othello*'.

32 The *Rosania* reference is discussed by Stern, 'Watching as Reading'.

7

What Is a Staged Book? Books as 'Actors' in the Early Modern English Theatre

Sarah Wall-Randell

In his widely used textbook of theatrical props design, Thurston James begins the chapter on book-props with a brief comic scene:

ACTOR
   On my entrance, I'm to be carrying a Bible. Do you have it ready?
PROP CREW HEAD
   Sure, it's there on the prop table.
ACTOR *(Walking to the table, searching)*
   You mean—this dictionary?
PROP CREW HEAD
   You and I know it's a dictionary. But you're an actor. You can make the audience think it's a Bible.
[. . .]

ACTOR
Here, look what this idiot is giving me to use for a Bible.
STAGE MANAGER
It looks like a dictionary.
PROP CREW HEAD
Aw, a book's a book.[1]

In this vignette, James contrasts the stereotype of the oversensitive, demanding actor with the utility-minded, quick-and-dirty technician. The actor's view here, that a dictionary would be miscast in the role of a Bible onstage, turns out to be shared not only by the stage manager, but by the author as well, for the rest of James's chapter offers detailed and painstaking instructions for sourcing, adapting, or constructing, using wood, leather, twine, and various papers, what James calls 'character books', or books playing specific parts, whose identities must be made legible to the audience.[2] Certainly, for the skilled designer as well as the actor and the discerning audience member, James implies, it is far from true that 'a book's a book'.

What exactly are book-props, then, once we have granted that they are not uniform and interchangeable objects? Props overall are an especially significant element in the early modern theatre because, in a stagecraft without illusionistic sets, the objects actors hold take on greater prominence. Tiffany Stern has noted the duality in the mimetic expression of early modern props: their 'heavy realism', in contrast to the more suggestive or sketched-in quality of scenery, and, on the other hand, the symbolic or metonymic way in which they are used. The nimbler, more efficient medium of the prop, such as a crown or throne, can stand for what cannot, practically, be brought onstage, such as a castle.[3] The way that props enact theatrical representation, the relationship they effect between the object and what it represents, is variable. Some props are only approximations of, or stand-ins for, the objects they 'play' onstage, when the real thing would be too dangerous or too precious: a stage dagger is made of wood, or is blunted; a stage crown is made of base metal painted gold. Other, more quotidian objects, like cups or ropes, may straightforwardly play themselves. Books might be said to make up a distinct, third category of prop: at once a stand-in and the thing itself. When a book is required for a play, the precise title named in the text is not required; an existing book, of the right size and appearance, may be appropriated.[4] But all books have a specific identity, whether or not an observer can see it from the outside; even if the actor in Thurston James' imaginary drama convinces the audience that the dictionary is a Bible, it is still a dictionary. What is the ontological status of a prop book, when it is, and when it isn't, the book that the play says it is?

The nature and provenance of book-props is a pressing question for the study of early modern drama, since late-sixteenth and early-seventeenth-century plays commonly require them. Alan Dessen and Leslie Thomson count 130 examples of books and table-books called for in the stage directions they tabulate in printed plays from 1580 to 1642.[5] Martin Wiggins and Catherine Richardson, in their monumental *British Drama 1533–1642: A Catalogue*, survey not only props specified in stage directions, but also props whose use is indicated or implied in characters' lines. Using Wiggins' and Richardson's prop lists, limiting my count to plays performed in the public theatres, and not including letters, scrolls, or other documents, but only books that may be presumed to be codices, such as Bibles, prayer-books, law-books, school-books, magic books, and specific works like Ovid, Virgil, and Seneca, I find 128 plays recorded by Wiggins between 1580 and 1623, first performed by over a dozen different companies, that include books as props.[6] Many plays call for one book; more than a few, like Marlowe's *Doctor Faustus*, Munday et al.'s *Sir John Oldcastle*, and Marston's *What You Will*, call for a small library.

So the early modern stage was a space regularly inhabited by books. Books on shelves or in stacks evoke scenes of study; in an actor's hand, they offer an image of privacy or pretext for solitude (for instance, the book that Polonius presses on

Ophelia in *Hamlet*, 'that show of such an exercise may colour / Your loneliness' [3.1.44–45]); they give verisimilitude to the swearing of oaths.[7] Yet an assessment and analysis of book-props has lagged behind other exciting recent work both in the field of early modern theatre history and in studies of the material book. In their landmark collection *Staged Properties in Early Modern England*, Jonathan Gil Harris and Natasha Korda and their contributors define and advance the critical conversation about histories and theories of early modern stage-props, but the essays do not address books.[8] Early modern histories of books and reading, meanwhile, have tended to focus on the many ways in which books, including play-books, were conceived, produced, circulated, and used in ordinary life, to the neglect of those exceptional, spectacular appearances of books onstage.

In considering prop-books, we must grapple with lacunae in the record. Even as they are graspable and portable by actors onstage, props are ephemeral within the archive, leaving only partial traces in stage-directions and references within play-texts. As scholars of early modern playing practices have made clear, surviving documentation of props – which includes Philip Henslowe's famous inventory of costumes and properties owned by the Lord Admiral's men in 1598 (as it survives in the transcription made by Edmond Malone for his 1790 edition), as well as some other documents of theatrical accounting and a handful of 'plots', or backstage outlines of entrances and exits – are, on the one hand, vivid evocations of the staging of plays both extant and lost, and on the other, incomplete documents (Knutson and McInnis have more to say on this in their chapter) that offer only a partial picture of early modern prop-use. Douglas Bruster notes that Henslowe's inventory seems to select for 'special things, objects related to particular characters and plays', as well as inherently valuable or hard-to-replace objects, while passing over less 'special' items necessary for staging the plays in the Admiral's Men's repertory, such as cups, plates, bottles, letters, and books.[9] Marlowe's *Doctor Faustus*, for instance, is specifically accommodated in the inventory by the 'Hell mought' and 'j dragon in fostes', but the multiple books called for by the play – at least four volumes, representing Aristotle, Galen, Justinian, and the Vulgate Bible, are required in Act 1, Scene 1 alone – are unaccounted for. Were these books held among the Admiral's Men's stock along with the hell-mouth and dragon, but left unmentioned, or did they come from somewhere else? Peter Thomson conjectures that actors could have made their own properties, while Neil Carson suggests that actors may have supplied small props out of their personal belongings.[10] Korda has proposed that Henslowe, who also operated as a pawnbroker, may have sold or rented to the players, for use as props, items that borrowers had pawned and failed to redeem.[11] In the surviving pawn accounts, the goods Henslowe accepted as collateral are mostly clothing, but on at least one occasion, he received a book in pawn, when, on 16 September 1594, he loaned ten shillings to a Goody Haryson 'vpon a bybell & x peces of lynen'.[12] The accounts are partial; perhaps there were other, unrecorded books among Henslowe's stock of pawned property, which could have supplied the multiple books needed in the opening scene of *Doctor Faustus* and in other plays.

Tiffany Stern has suggested another theory of a source for book-props, besides the actors' own possessions and items forfeited from Henslowe's pawn business: a potential 'company library', a collection of reference books, such as the Bible, Holinshed's *Chronicle*, Plutarch's *Lives*, Ovid's *Metamorphoses*, Painter's *Palace of Pleasure*, and other key texts, that could have been owned by a playing company and made available to playwrights to mine as sources in the writing process.[13] (See Munro's chapter in this volume for records of one playwright, Robert Daborne, borrowing books from Henslowe in what may be precisely this way.) In *Tamburlaine*, as Ethel Seaton showed in 1924, Marlowe draws the list of Tamburlaine's conquests not from a general idea of world geography, but specifically from Ortelius's 1570 *Theatrum Orbis Terrarum*; Ortelius's atlas could well have been another of those reference works in the company library.[14]

Moreover, the books in the 'company library' could have done double duty as props, either emerging onto the stage meta-theatrically, 'as themselves' – Ovid in *Titus Andronicus*, Seneca in Middleton and Dekker's *The Honest Whore*, the Bible in many plays – or by playing the parts of other books as needed.[15] (See Stern's essay in this volume for further discussion of printed materials, in this case ballads, appearing as props and perhaps 'playing themselves'.) Andrew Sofer has suggested that, through re-use, props can bring their own kind of intertextuality to early modern plays and to repertories. The King's Men performed both Jonson's *Alchemist* and Shakespeare's *Tempest*; what if the cittern played by Doll in *The Alchemist*, Sofer asks, was the same instrument played by Ariel in *The Tempest*?[16] Book-props, as they too moved between plays, might carry extra resonances from their previous appearances. Was the Bible that Sir Hugh Evans reads while he waits to duel with Caius in *The Merry Wives of Windsor* 3.1 the same prop as the poisoned Bible Julia kisses in Act 4, Scene 2 of Webster's *Duchess of Malfi*, a play first performed by the same company about fifteen years later, in 1612–13? *Merry Wives* was presumably still in the King's Men's repertory in the sixteen-teens, since it was issued in a 1619 Quarto; if the same Bible appeared in a comic context in *Merry Wives*, does that heighten the ghoulish absurdity of Julia's death? A Bible appears again in another King's Men play of about 1620, Middleton's British history *The Mayor of Queenborough* (or *Hengist, King of Kent*); the virtuous Queen Castiza takes an oath of her fidelity on a Bible in Act 4, Scene 2. If an audience member saw *The Duchess of Malfi* after *The Mayor of Queenborough*, would the memory of Middleton's innocent noblewoman swearing on the Bible make the abuse of the holy book by Webster's Cardinal, killing his lover Julia by forcing her to swear on the same Bible and then seal her oath with a kiss, all the more blackly odious? All these prior or simultaneous 'lives' of objects – props' origins in the households of pawn customers or of the elite patrons of playing companies, their service in other plays – become part of the associations they bring with them for playwrights, actors, and audiences, and thus part of the meaning that these props make within their plays. We already acknowledge that the creative process was collaborative among playwrights, plotters, managers, and actors in the sixteenth- and early seventeenth-century theatre. The human resources and reputation of a particular company certainly shaped the plays that writers like Shakespeare and Marlowe produced; perhaps the same is true for their resources of books, props, and book-props. Perhaps, that is, the presence of a particular book in a company library inspired a playwright to write another part for that book, or shaped how author or company conceptualized or realized a book that was a 'character' within the play.

In what follows I will examine two plays that make spectacular use of a book-prop. Marlowe's *Tamburlaine, Part II*, calls for a holy book, the 'Alcoran' (Qur'an) to be desecrated, while Thomas Heywood's *If You Know Not Me, You Know Nobody Part I*, requires a different holy book, a venerated English Bible. In these plays, then, we have two of what James calls 'character-books', props that must represent specific books and communicate their identities to the audience. These two books present different, but very material, problems of representation for an early modern playing company. The Qur'an could not draw upon familiar associations, could not be recognized, and thus would have to be envisaged, materialized onstage, anew; the physical attributes of the Bible, conversely, would have been intimately recognizable to the audience, so much so that details of its form, particularly its size, would have carried historical, doctrinal, and political import.

Tamburlaine, Part II is not the first English play to present a Qur'an onstage – one had appeared briefly in Robert Wilson's *The Three Ladies of London* (c. 1581) – but it is certainly the most spectacular.[17] Late in the play, after vanquishing Persia, Turkey, and Africa, Marlowe's Scythian conqueror makes his next target the supremacy of God Himself. Tamburlaine calls for a copy of the Qur'an to be brought onstage, and commands that 'the Turkish Alcaron, / And all the heapes of supersticious bookes, / Found in the Temples of that *Mahomet*, / Whom I have thought a God ... be burnt' (STC 17425, K5r). 'My sword hath sent millions of Turks to Hell ... And yet I live untoucht by Mahomet', Tamburlaine brags, and, following the medieval and early modern Christian misconception that Muslims consider Mohammed a god, he dares the Prophet to avenge, if he can, this ultimate affront, sacrilege against the holy book. The heavens remain silent as the book goes up in flames, and Tamburlaine exults in his debunking of religion:

Wel souldiers, *Mahomet* remaines in hell;
He cannot heare the voice of *Tamburlain*,
Seeke out another Godhead to adore,
The God that sits in heaven, if any God
For he is God alone, and none but he.

(K5r)

This is a showstopping moment of stagecraft that retains the power to shock even in the present.[18] It is the last great gesture of Tamburlaine's will, and his death from illness shortly afterward may, it is suggested, be the result. What, though, did audiences see when they looked at Tamburlaine's Qur'an? Given the great unlikelihood that any member of the Admiral's Men or of their audience would have seen an actual Qur'an, how might the company have represented it? In a large or small format, slim or thick? With Arabic or explanatory English characters on its spine or fore-edge? What might it mean, in this context, for an English book to represent the sacred book of another faith, one seen as deeply foreign, in such a moment of blasphemy and iconoclasm?

The work of Nabil Matar, Daniel Vitkus, Linda McJannet, Bernadette Andrea, and others has opened up to us the huge presence of the Islamic world in the fears and imaginations of the early modern English, and has examined how English knowledge of Islam was shaped through the reports of captives and travellers in the wide reaches of the Ottoman Empire who had 'turned Turk'. But copies of the Qur'an, either in manuscript, the medium used by believers until the nineteenth century, or in print, as studied by academic theologians, did not circulate in England in the sixteenth century outside the most specialized academic communities. In 1630, Abraham Wheelock, soon to be appointed the first Professor of Arabic at Cambridge, wrote to the Arabist William Bedwell, seeking to obtain a Qur'an in the original language for the University Library; Bedwell agreed to donate his own manuscript, since he could find no other source for an additional copy.[19] The Qur'an was finally printed in English in 1649, translated from the French by Alexander Ross, but before then it was not readily available in Britain in either English or Arabic.

If English audiences had not seen the Qur'an, they were nevertheless accustomed to its invocation as a byword for false or pretended religious views. As Matthew Dimmock has shown, both Catholic and Protestant writers had sought to identify the errors of the other with 'Mahometanism'.[20] Both sides too co-opted the idea of the Qur'an specifically to dismiss writings across the confessional divide: *The Alcaron of the Barefote Friers*, a translation of the German humanist Erasmus Alberus's parody of the Rule of St Francis, appeared in London in 1550, while *Luthers Alcoran* (1642) was the English title of an attack on Protestantism by the French Cardinal Jacques Davy du Peron.[21] The idea of the Qur'an as the epitome of error, and also specifically as a book, was a powerful one.

Some hint as to what Marlowe or his audience might have imagined a Qur'an to look like is provided by a visual representation of Mohammed contemporaneous with *Tamburlaine* that Dimmock cites as a late-sixteenth-century example of the long tradition of using the figure of the Prophet as the opposite of Faith in allegorical depictions of the virtues and vices. In one of a series of embroidered wall hangings on this theme commissioned *circa* 1580 by Bess of Hardwick, and still hanging in Hardwick Hall, a woman in Tudor dress, herself labelled *Fides* and holding a small book marked *Faith*, stands over the recumbent figure of a man in a turban. The man is propped on his elbow atop another book, marked

Acaron.[22] The similarity of the books is striking; the need for labels indicates their potential interchangeability. Possibly created in response to the 1580 treaty between Elizabeth I and the Sultan Murad III (as part of the negotiations, Elizabeth affirmed to the Sultan in a letter their common monotheism and joint opposition to idolatry[23]), the hanging shows one 'religion of the book' conquering another.

The parallel centrality of the English Bible to Reformation Christianity and the Qur'an to Islam, as shown in the Hardwick Hall hanging, is also an acknowledgement of an undeniable symmetry between the two faiths and their two books, and suggests other resonances that the burning of the Qur'an onstage in *Tamburlaine* may have had for an English audience. The scene, in which Tamburlaine seems at once to embrace scepticism ('if any God'), monotheism ('For he is God alone and none but he'), and megalomania, has long been read as either a celebration of iconoclasm or an excoriation of atheism.[24] Just a generation before, Marian authorities had used public burnings of books, including English Bibles, as a strategy for enforcing religious orthodoxy (instances are documented in Foxe's *Actes and Monuments*). Elizabethan censors did not generally employ such spectacles, however, so Tamburlaine's action resurrects a violence against books that had been submerged in memory. The Protestant insistence on the truest access to God being located in the word of God makes the burning of sacred texts, if we posit the Qur'an as standing in metaphorically for the previously endangered English Bible, especially fraught.

Indeed, it seems not unlikely that, in the absence of a widely accepted iconography for the Qu'ran, a Bible, after all the most widely distributed book in early modern England, would have played its part here. Might it be disturbing, or seem blasphemous, to a Christian audience to imagine a Bible standing in for a Qur'an? If we return to the idea of props shared across plays enabling certain intertextual in-jokes and resonances, we might imagine the Admiral's Men using the same book or books for its performances of *Tamburlaine* and

Doctor Faustus. If Tamburlaine's prop Qur'an doubled for Faustus's 'Jerome's Bible', is it possible that an audience who saw both plays could have recognized the book in the two roles? Even if such a doubling would be invisible to the audience, the interchangeability of these books speaks to the iconic power of books in Marlowe's imagination and on the stage, and to the unique category they occupy of text and object. As their material textuality both sits within and intersects with the text of the play, book props both are and are not the roles they play.

From the sweeping Eastern travelogue of *Tamburlaine* to a play that depicts locations just outside the playhouse: another starring role for the Bible, and for a Bible, appears in Heywood's *If You Know Not Me, You Know Nobody, Part 1*. First performed by the Queen's Men at the Red Bull theatre in 1604 or 1605, and first printed in quarto in 1605, the play is a bio-drama celebrating Queen Elizabeth as a Protestant heroine, focusing especially on her virtue and courage when imprisoned during Mary's reign, and culminating in her accession. The events of the play draw from the laudatory account of Elizabeth's princesshood in Foxe's *Actes and Monuments*, as well as from reports of the pageants and ceremonies surrounding her coronation entry into London in January 1559. In the closing moments of the play, the newly crowned queen graciously accepts from the Lord Mayor twin tributes from the citizens of London: a purse and a Bible.

ELIZABETH
> We thanke you all, but first this booke I kisse,
> Thou art the way to honor; thou to blisse,
> An English Bible, thankes my good Lord Maior,
> You of our bodie and our soule have care,
> This is the Jewell that we still love best,
> This was our solace when we were distrest,
> This booke that hath so long conceald it selfe,
> So long shut up, so long hid; now Lords see,
> We here unclaspe, for ever it is free:

Who lookes for joy, let him this booke adore,
This is true foode for rich men and for poore,
Who drinkes of this, is certaine nere to perish,
This will the soule with heavenly virtue cherish,
Lay hand upon this Anchor every soule,
Your names shalbe in an eternal scrowle;
Who buildes on this, dwel's in a happy state,
This is the fountaine clear immaculate,
That happy yssue that shall us succeed,
And in our populous Kingdome this booke read:
For them as for our owne selves we humbly pray,
They may live long and blest; so lead the way.
   FINIS.

(ll. 1578–98)[25]

In formally rhymed couplets, and in repetitive, plain phrasing – 'this booke' (l. 1578) 'This is' (l. 1582), 'This was' (l. 1583), 'This booke' (l. 1584), 'this booke' (l. 1587), 'This is' (l. 1588), 'This will' (l. 1590), 'this Anchor' (l. 1591), 'This is' (l. 1594), 'this booke' (l. 1596) – the Queen iteratively demands that the audience notice the book, returning their eyes again and again to the object in her hands. Displaying the English Bible, suppressed by Mary's bishops, Elizabeth makes it wear a succession of different metaphorical costumes: jewel, food, drink, anchor, groundplot, and fountain.

Elizabeth casts the English Bible as a smaller version of herself, another Marian captive, 'So long shut up, so long hid', now 'for ever . . . free' (l. 1585–86). The scene's source is in a pageant staged at the Little Conduit in Cheapside created for Elizabeth's coronation procession in February 1559, an account of which was immediately published in a pamphlet, and is included in Stow's *Survey of London* (1598, reprinted 1603). In the pageant, an old man with a scythe representing Time emerged from the locked door of a cave, leading a young woman dressed in white silk with a headdress labelled 'in Latin and English, *Temporis filia*, the Daughter of Time'. As the Daughter approached Elizabeth, it became clear that 'on her breast was written her proper name, which was *Veritas*, Truth who held a book in her hand upon the which was written *Verbum veritatis*, the Word of Truth'.[26] Truth handed the book to one of the Queen's attendants, who passed it to her: an English Bible. Time brings Truth out of captivity; Truth is Elizabeth, the Reformed Church, and the English Bible, all newly free. As Heywood faithfully records in *If You Know Not Me*, the Queen kissed the Bible and held it aloft.

The connection between pageant and play is deepened and complicated because the Bible in the pageant refers to (and perhaps was) a specific, identifiable edition. As David Daniell has pointed out, not only did the 1559 coronation entry inspire Heywood's closing scene in 1604, but the pageant itself took its visual language from the title page of the 1557 Geneva New Testament (STC 2871), the first English Bible text to be printed since the Great Bible of 1539.[27] In a woodcut emblem on the title page, Time, with a scythe and hourglass, leads a nude woman, wearing a tiara, out of a cave. Text running up and down the sides of the emblem reads 'God by tyme restoreth truth / And maketh her victorious.' Here, truth is the Word of God freed from the old translation, the Catholic-establishment Vulgate, and brought directly from the original Greek into the language of the people, with explanatory notes on every page to liberate the meaning of hard passages for the individual believer. The pageant is a living tableau of the woodcut, and might be seen as a joint celebration of Elizabeth's ascension and of the publication of the Geneva New Testament; it would then make sense that the book that Truth gave Elizabeth was, in fact, a Geneva New Testament.

What, then, of the book extolled by Elizabeth onstage in Heywood's play? Considering that the Bible was the most commonly owned book in early modern England, and that the Geneva New Testament was printed over a dozen times between 1557 and 1604, the staged book could easily have been the real thing. What would have struck viewers about the Bible in this scene, though, whatever book 'played' it, was its size. In the sixteenth century, the size of an English Bible was a

FIGURE 7.1 *The Geneva New Testament* (1557), B.L.C.17.a.15. By permission of the British Library.

contentious and political matter. Reformers passionately held that the individual believer must have direct access to the Word, unmediated through clergy gatekeepers; the small size of a Bible clearly communicated the fact that it was meant for private contemplation and home use. The 1557 Geneva New Testament was an octavo, and although subsequent printings included at least one quarto (1583), it was far more often published as an octavo, duodecimo, or thirty-two-mo. The complete Geneva Bible (1560) was also a relatively small book, first and most often printed in quarto. By contrast, the Bishops' Bible of 1568, the product of an effort undertaken by Elizabeth's bishops to produce a new, official English translation that would replace the outmoded Great Bible and re-take control of Bible interpretation from the popular, but also populist, unauthorized, and foreign-made Geneva, was first and most often printed in folio. Its size showed its intended function, to be read aloud in church, and to serve, in that communal space, as a visible symbol of the Word. The Bishops' Bible, its title-page bearing an image of Elizabeth herself, remained the approved translation, going through many editions, until the appearance of the royally sanctioned version of 1611.

In 1604, then, the book carried by Heywood's Elizabeth could have represented either the official, public Bishops' Bible, associated with the Anglican middle way, or the private, unofficial, more nonconformist Geneva Bible; its size, large or small, would have signalled significant doctrinal difference. One might expect the book-prop in this final scene of Heywood's play to be monumental, since the book is made the focus of so much attention and the outdoor theatre was large; the milieu is not unlike a reading from the pulpit. The play as a whole works to confirm Elizabeth's legacy as a great and triumphant queen; this scene could be read in an accordingly conservative way, reaffirming the triumph of 'her' Bible, the Bishops' version, as the centre of the nation's religious devotion. Yet the practicalities of stage-use must be considered: the Bible has to be held by the Bishop concurrently with a purse, and handed to Elizabeth, who speaks over it before kissing it and raising it aloft. The use of a smaller book-prop that could have been comfortably held in one hand by the actor playing Elizabeth, and thus signalling the Geneva Bible, would have had a more radical function, affirming the continued importance in the Reformed church of private, independent Bible reading for all, ranking above the legacy of any monarch. By investing it with polemic meaning, Heywood makes the book-prop speak.

This final scene is not the only time in the play in which a book did so. In an earlier episode not found in Foxe, the Princess Elizabeth is held under house arrest, guarded by Queen Mary's dangerous advisors including Sir Henry Beningfield and Bishop Gardiner. Elizabeth is installed in a room containing books including the Bible. The princess asks for writing materials to send a letter to Mary, and while she works on her message, Beningfield goes through her property, muttering horrified asides:

> BENINGFEILD *takes a booke and lookes into it.*
> BENINGFEILD
> What has she written here? (*He reads.*)
> Much suspected by me, nothing prov'd can be,
> *Finis quoth Elizabeth* the prisoner,
>
> Pray god it prove so, soft what book's this,
> Marry a God, whats here an English bible?
> *Sanctum Maria* pardon this prophanation of my hart,
> Water *Barwick*, water, Ile meddle with't no more.
> (ll. 1034–41)

Incorporating Elizabeth's famous prison couplet into this scene, Heywood has changed it both circumstantially and materially. Traditionally, Elizabeth is supposed to have scratched the lines 'Much suspected by me, / Nothing proved can be. / *Quod* Elizabeth the prisoner' into the window of her room at Woodstock, using a diamond.[28] Imagining Elizabeth's inscription not on a window but in a book, Heywood turns Elizabeth's protest graffiti into a mimesis of the 'bookish' practices of annotation and marks of ownership through which many early modern readers really interacted with their books, especially with Bibles, and in which they expressed devotional thoughts and interpretive opinions of their own.

'Weary of writinge, sleepy on the sodaine' (1043), Elizabeth dismisses Beningfield and goes to bed, upon which a dumbshow begins, following the traditional style of the staging of dreams on the early modern stage.

> *A dumb show.*
>
>> *Enter* WINCHESTER, CONSTABLE, BARWICK, *and* FRYARS: *at the other dore* 2. ANGELS: *the* FRYAR *steps to her, offering to kill her: the* ANGELS *drives them back. Exeunt. The* ANGEL *opens the Bible, and puts it in her hand as she sleepes, Exeunt* ANGELS, *she wakes.*
>
>> (ll. 1048–53)

Finding the Bible in her hand when she awakes, Elizabeth realizes that the book has travelled across the room on its own:

> Then 'twas by inspiration, heaven I trust
> With his eternall hand, will guide the just.
> What chapter's this? *Whoso putteth his trust in the Lord, Shall not be confounded:*
> My savior thankes, on thee my hope I build,
> Thou lov'st poore Innocents, and art their shield.
>
>> (ll. 1062–67)

Is this Bible the same book-prop that features in the final scene, and can we deduce anything further about its format from the context here? A 500-page folio seems unlikely to fit 'in' Elizabeth's hand, and to bring physical pain rather than spiritual comfort; this bedroom Bible seems even more certainly than the presentation Bible in the finale to be a small-format book and thus to signal the Geneva translation. Yet confusingly, the line Elizabeth reads, from Isaiah 49.23, is closest to the language of the English Bibles of the 1530s, which combined William Tyndale's English translation of the Pentateuch and New Testament with Myles Coverdale's translation of the remaining books: the Coverdale Bible (1535), the 'Matthew' Bible (1537), and finally the 'Great' Bible (1539), the first royally authorized version. Aside from accidental variations in spelling and punctuation, Coverdale's wording of the Isaiah passage is the same in all these 1530s versions: 'thou mayst knowe howe that I am the Lord. And who so putteth hys trust in me, shall not be confounded.'[29] Notably, Coverdale has the singular 'his trust', as in Heywood, rather than the generic plural 'their trust' that appears in the later, revised Bishops' Bible of 1568: 'thou mayst knowe howe that I am the Lorde, and that who so putteth there trust in me shall not be confounded.'[30] The Bishops' Bible was the official English Bible for church use in Heywood's own time, and is the text we would imagine as his default source. It is entirely possible, though, that Heywood was transcribing from a 1530s edition such as the Great Bible rather than from the newer Bishops' Bible when he wrote this scene in 1604; old books do hang around, and perhaps the Bible available to him, his own or one that the Queen's Men held in a 'company library', was a Coverdale, Matthew, or Great Bible. And, of course, the 1530s Bible would be more historically appropriate than the 1568 one to a scene taking place during Mary's reign in the mid-1550s. The evidence here, the single word 'his' versus 'their', seems too slight to make a firm case, but one thing is clear: the edition that seemed most likely to be the 'character' book in the final scene of *If You Know Not Me*, the Geneva Bible, is the least likely here, as the Geneva wording is markedly different: 'thou shalt knowe that I am the Lord: for they shal not be ashamed y^t waite for me.'[31] Perhaps the Queen's Men had two prop Bibles, or perhaps the prop-book in this scene is a Geneva Bible 'playing' a Great Bible.

The text that the actor playing Elizabeth reads, of course, properly comes from Heywood's play, not from the book-prop. We see that Heywood was not troubled by editing the Bible passage for brevity, turning 'I am the Lord, and . . . whoso putteth his trust in me' into 'whoso putteth his trust in the Lord'. The prop is not exactly the Bible, even if an actual Bible is used, and the action performed by the player is not exactly reading.[32] This document onstage, although it has a speaking role, is not playing itself.

What does it mean for Heywood's players to use, or not use, real Bibles as prop Bibles, to 'cast' a secular book as a Bible, or to use one kind of Bible as a prop for another that had very different doctrinal associations? In this play about very recent English history, it is meaningful as well as convenient for the real books daily viewed and handled by English Protestants to appear onstage. Yet the books' very recognizability, as glimpses of the form and words of specific Bibles seem to appear between the lines of Heywood's play, creates representational tension as well. The slippage between new and old translations, between format and content, forces them to be analysed as objects too: they compel reflection on what sacred properties a book may have, on what devotional choices are encoded and made visible in size. By allowing the language and materiality of real books to interpenetrate the language of the play, books are both subsumed into the play and stand apart from it, evoking not the spectacular elsewhere of a Hell-mouth or a dragon, but the recent past of Elizabeth's reign, the here and almost-now.

In exploring the ontological status of a book onstage, and asking whether and how books can 'play' themselves, this essay has contrasted what was almost certainly not a Qur'an, with what is likely to have been an English Bible, though not necessarily the one it purports to be. Both raise questions about religion and text. Tamburlaine rejects the 'superstitious' nature of the 'Alcoran', but Marlowe is intending the book to represent all religions, and may have enjoyed the blasphemy of having the text of another religion 'played' by a book with the correct 'look', a Bible. If so, the play equates Christianity with Islam. Somewhat similarly, Heywood's play equates two bibles, conflating the Bishop's and Geneva Bibles as though the differences between them and the forms of Protestantism they represent are negligible. Both plays thus deepen, question and ironize their fictional observations about faith by the physical books they stage. Through books, as sources, as actors, and as visual statements, the plays use the materiality of props to affirm, undercut or query the dialogue. What does this say for other books in other plays? Books onstage are both literally 'page' and literally 'stage', and if they are really the texts they play or sources for the play in which they feature, they are part of the fiction that is also part of the fact; while, if they are not, they are facts that are fictionalized. Whatever books onstage are, they represent a moment when the real interpenetrates the fiction, raising questions about the traditional opposition between 'page' and 'stage' and asking us to think in a wholly new way about early modern theatrical mimesis.

Notes

1 Thurston James, *The Theater Props Handbook: A Comprehensive Guide to Theater Properties, Materials, and Construction* (Studio City: Players Press, 2000), 35.
2 James, *Theater Props*, 40.
3 Tiffany Stern, *Making Shakespeare: From Stage to Page* (Abingdon: Routledge, 2004), 94.
4 Given the relatively high cost of paper in the sixteenth and early seventeenth centuries, it seems unlikely that a playing company would go to the expense of constructing a faux book by having a block of blank paper bound, rather than using a real book; I therefore assume that any book-prop onstage is an 'actual' book.
5 Alan C. Dessen and Leslie Thomson, *A Dictionary of Stage Directions in Early Modern Drama, 1580–1642* (Cambridge: Cambridge University Press, 1999), 34–35.

6 Martin Wiggins in association with Catherine Richardson, *British Drama 1533–1642: A Catalogue*, 8 vols (Oxford: Oxford University Press, 2012–2018). (Since I am interested in props owned by playing companies, I did not count books called for in masques, civic pageants, or university plays.) Frances Teague has also done important work in cataloguing props in Shakespeare's plays; she combines letters and books in the category of 'documents'. Teague finds 'documents' occurring in Shakespeare's plays with a frequency ranging from 1 per play (*Comedy of Errors*, *The Tempest*) to 15 (*Love's Labour's Lost*), with an average of 6.3 documents required per play. See Teague, *Shakespeare's Speaking Properties* (Lewisburg: Bucknell University Press, 1991), 195–196.

7 Charlotte Scott has surveyed the uses of books, both as props and in metaphors, in Shakespeare's dramatic canon. See Charlotte Scott, *Shakespeare and the Idea of the Book* (Oxford: Oxford University Press, 2007).

8 Jonathan Gil Harris and Natasha Korda, eds, *Staged Properties in Early Modern English Drama* (Cambridge: Cambridge University Press, 2002).

9 Douglas Bruster, 'The Dramatic Life of Objects in the Early Modern Theatre,' in Harris and Korda, eds, *Staged Properties*, 72–73.

10 Peter Thomson, *Shakespeare's Theatre* (London: Routledge and Kegan Paul, 1983), 31; Neil Carson, *A Companion to Henslowe's Diary* (Cambridge: Cambridge University Press, 1988), 53.

11 Natasha Korda, 'Household Property/Stage Property: Henslowe as Pawnbroker', *Theatre Journal* 48, no. 2 (1996), 194–195. Since the majority of the pawn customers were women, Korda reads the movement of these items from women's household property to stage property as an overlooked way in which women contributed to early modern theatrical making. The pawn accounts appear in R. A. Foakes, ed., *Henslowe's Diary*, 2nd edn (Cambridge: Cambridge University Press, 2002), 107–118, 142–162, and 253–261.

12 Foakes, ed., *Henslowe's Diary*, 156.

13 Stern, comment during Folger Shakespeare Library symposium 'Shakespeare's Theatrical Documents,' Washington, DC, 18–19 March 2016.

14 Ethel Seaton, 'Marlowe's Map,' *Essays and Studies* 10 (1924), 13–35.

15 As Zachary Lesser and Holger Schott Syme commented during the Folger 'Shakespeare's Theatrical Documents' symposium (ibid.), one might begin to reconstruct the catalogue of such a 'company library' by tracking the influence of particular sources across a company's repertory, and to trace the circulation of books between playing companies and playwrights through notable appearances of books onstage.

16 Andrew Sofer, 'Properties,' in *The Oxford Handbook of Early Modern Theatre*, ed. Richard Dutton (Oxford: Oxford University Press, 2009), 567–570. For a theoretical perspective on re-use in the theatre (of narratives, actors, music, and materials, including props), see Marvin Carlson, *The Haunted Stage: The Theater as Memory Machine* (Ann Arbor: University of Michigan Press, 2001). I am indebted to Richard Preiss for this reference.

17 Kyd's *Soliman and Perseda*, from *c.* 1589–92, slightly after *Tamburlaine*, also calls for a Qur'an. The Qur'ans in Wilson's and Kyd's plays are deployed differently from the Qur'an in *Tamburlaine*. There they are used for swearing false witness, and are thus a stereotype of the doctrinally errant, including Catholics as well as Turks, who turned holy books into material talismans by which to swear. On Kyd's Qur'an, see Elizabeth Williamson, *The Materiality of Religion in Early Modern English Drama* (Abingdon: Ashgate, 2009), Chapter 4.

18 Some contemporary productions of *Tamburlaine*, such as at the Bristol Old Vic in 2005, have chosen to make Tamburlaine's blasphemy against all religions rather than against Islam, by leaving the Qur'an unnamed among a heap of books (see Dalya Alberge, 'Marlowe's Koran-burning hero is censored to avoid Muslim anger,' *The Times*, 24 November 2005, 3). At the Royal Shakespeare Company in 2018, in a production directed by Michael Boyd that played interestingly with graphic versus symbolic representations of violence, the reference to the Qur'an was retained, but the books were tossed into a pit in which fire was suggested with flickering lights, rather than being unequivocally, visibly burnt. Scorched sheets of paper then fell from above, perhaps in an echo of the mass of documents and

office papers scattered over the streets of lower Manhattan after the 9/11 attack on the World Trade Center.

19 See Nabil Matar, *Islam in Britain 1558–1685* (Cambridge: Cambridge University Press, 1998), 74–75. A Latin text of the Qur'an had been printed in Basel in 1543, and copies survive in English academic libraries, but the heavy interspersal of analysis and refutation with the text makes this book more a work of Christian theology than a copy of the Qu'ran *per se*; see Matthew Dimmock, *Mythologies of the Prophet Muhammad in Early Modern English Culture* (Cambridge: Cambridge University Press, 2013), 83–84.

20 Dimmock, *Mythologies*, 64–100.

21 *The Alcaron of the Barefote Friers, that is to say, an heape or number of the blasphemous and trifling doctrines of the wounded Idole Saint Frances taken out of the boke of his rules...* (London, 1550; STC 2nd edn 11313); *Luthers Alcoran, Being a Treatise first written in French by the Learned Cardinal Peron, of famous memory, against the Hugenots of France* (London, 1642; Wing D2638).

22 The image is reproduced and discussed in Dimmock, *Mythologies*, 74–76.

23 The letter was published in Haklyut's 1589 *Principall Navigations*. See Daniel Vitkus, *Turning Turk: English Theatre and the Multicultural Mediterranean, 1570–1630* (New York: Palgrave Macmillan, 2003), 51.

24 See Joel Slotkin, '"Seeke out another Godhead": Religious Epistemology and Representations of Islam in *Tamburlaine*,' *Modern Philology* 111, no. 3 (2014), 408–436, for a survey of critical responses to *Tamburlaine*'s Qur'an-burning.

25 Thomas Heywood, *If You Know Not Me You Know Nobody Part I*, ed. Madeline Doran (London: Malone Society, 1935).

26 Richard Mulcaster, *The Queen's Majesty's Passage through the City of London to Westminster the Day before Her Coronation* (1559), quoted in Hester Lees-Jeffries, 'Location as Metaphor in Queen Elizabeth's Coronation Entry (1559): *Veritas Temporis Filia*,' in *The Progresses, Pageants, and Entertainments of Queen Elizabeth I*, ed. Jayne Elisabeth Archer, Elizabeth Goldring, and Sarah Knight (Oxford: Oxford University Press, 2007), 77.

27 David Daniell, *The Bible in English: Its History and Influence* (New Haven: Yale University Press, 2003), 276–277.

28 Leah S. Marcus, Janel Mueller, and Mary Beth Rose, eds, *Elizabeth I: Collected Works* (Chicago: University of Chicago Press, 2000), pp. 45–46

29 *The Byble in Englyshe that is to saye the content of all the holy scrypture, both of ye olde and newe testament* . . . (Paris, 1539; STC 2nd edn 2068), Hh1v.

30 *The. Holie. Bible conteyning the olde Testament and the newe* (London, 1568; STC 2nd edn 2099), M(6)r (fol. xciii).

31 *The Bible and Holy Scriptures Conteyned in the Olde and Newe Testament* . . . (Geneva, 1560; STC 2nd edn 2093), Eee3r.

32 In the present-day theatre, it is typical for prop books and documents to contain a *lorem ipsum*-style dummy text, to avoid breaking the concentration of the actor, who recites from memory the lines that are supposed to be 'read'. See James, 40.

PART THREE

Documents After Performance

8

'Flowers for English Speaking'

Play Extracts and Conversation

András Kiséry

Scholars interested in the reception of Shakespeare have long been searching for traces left by early modern readers of plays. In addition to the very limited amount of marginalia and discursive commentary, they have identified phrases, lines, and passages copied into printed and manuscript miscellanies, anthologies and commonplace books, which are also discussed by Laura Estill in the present volume.

While early modern readers obviously valued plays not only for their 'lines' but also for their 'plots' and 'passages' (the latter usually meant things that come to pass: events, exciting turns of the plot),[1] their marking and note-taking was focused on phrases, lines, and segments of the dramatic dialogue that can be marked or copied. The conclusions we can draw from the passages they collected are limited: as Lois Potter warned, play extracts show 'what was thought quotable, but not necessarily what was most read or what had been most theatrically successful'.[2] Yet careful study of such extracts also reveals the uses to which readers put their playbooks, and through these uses, something about the playtexts themselves.

Critics have often used the evidence from traces of active reading and from note-taking to address questions about the place and prestige of drama in the textual and literary culture of the period. They have suggested that early modern readers who excerpted and copied passages from plays subjected them to some version of the practice of 'commonplacing', a process that was crucial to humanist education and early modern literary culture. Commonplacing readers rendered classical texts into shorter passages, organizing them under headings to make them reusable in written composition. The very act of commonplacing a play would therefore have included it in the canon of texts to which such treatment was appropriate: the texts of classical authors. Historians of the book, too, have seen the use of italics or the use of double inverted commas in the margin to highlight sententious lines or passages in vernacular play books as pre-selecting them for future extraction and manipulation. Such typographical marking would then not only be a reflection of humanistic manuscript practices, but also a way early modern publishers advertised their plays as deserving academic treatment appropriate to classical texts.[3]

These important suggestions have been integrated into larger narratives about how commercial plays, Shakespeare's in particular, rose from sub-literary to literary status in the early modern period. Whether 'the literary' is meant in the more ambitious modern sense that is constrained to textual works of art, or in the broader early modern sense of learning, and what such elevation of plays might mean for a notion of 'the literary' itself, is usually left unexplored and unexplained; social cachet and cultural classification, high status and literariness, are in good bourgeois manner considered to be coterminous.[4] While scholarship is clearly divided on this issue, it is unified in its concern with writing, with the production and enjoyment of written composition, and with poetic or humanist authorship on a classical model (whether of the dramatist, of the commonplacing author-to-be, or both).[5]

Through considering some specific play extracts in their contexts, this chapter will highlight additional reasons for note-taking from plays in the early modern period, up to the somewhat arbitrary divide of the Restoration. Without denying the embeddedness of drama in the textual culture of the period, it will focus on the crucial relationship between dramatic texts and colloquial interaction. The conversation-oriented use of playtexts registers the distinctiveness of drama and traces a cultural-historical narrative in which drama is not a marginal entity in need of being elevated into the mainstream, but a key factor.

Viral forms

Sententious extracts were gathered from plays into notebooks that were later to be consulted and used. If readers entered them under a topic heading in a commonplace book, they hardly ever recorded the source of the extracted fragment. If they wrote them *seriatim*, i.e. in the order they found them in the playtext, they may have copied them under the title of the play, but when they used these notes later on, the passages were put in circulation without indication of their origins in the work of a particular playwright or drama.

Traces of the circulation of the following couplet around the turn of the century can serve as an illustration.

'Offer no love-rites, but let wives still seeke them,
'For when they come unsought, they seldom like them.[6]

The 1600 Quarto of *Every Man out of His Humour* was among the first commercial plays equipped with gnomic pointing, that is, with inverted commas in the margins, and this couplet is among the lines thus marked.[7] Whether or not one agrees with the enthusiastic reaction by the speaker's interlocutor, 'this is Gospel', the couplet was deemed suitable for inclusion in *England's Parnassus*, the 1600 anthology of extracts from English poems and plays organized under commonplace headings, where it appears under the heading 'Marriage', and is attributed to 'B. Iohnson'.[8] Sometime between 1600 and 1613, a Derbyshire gentleman called Edward Pudsey also copied the couplet along with several other extracts from the play into his notebook; in this case, as on occasion elsewhere in the manuscript, he used italic hand to reflect the gnomic points in the margin of the play quarto.[9]

Soon after the play's appearance, the lines also found their way into the notebook-diary of John Manningham, a law student at the Middle Temple. Manningham's record of a performance of *Twelfth Night*, and his anecdote about Burbage announcing himself at a lady's door as 'Richard III' only to be told that 'William the Conqueror', i.e. Shakespeare has been there before him, have made him well-known to Shakespeare scholars. This couplet, however, is unrelated to Manningham's interest in plays, players, and playwrights, as it appears among a number of sentences he derived not from a play, but from a sermon which Robert Scott, the junior dean of Trinity College, Cambridge, delivered in 1601. While Scott may have thought that the couplet was indeed like Gospel when he cited it in his sermon, there is no trace of either Scott's or Manningham's awareness of its origin in a play.[10] What was happening to the couplet here can hardly be considered an effect of 'playreading'; Manningham's note is only a play extract or a post-performance document in a fetishistic sense. Rather, this is the story of an epigrammatic couplet passing through all the major public textual media of the period: stage, print – both in a playbook and in an anthology – and pulpit, transmitted from one to the other, through memory, conversation, or manuscript notes.

Lines or couplets in such circulation do not necessarily originate in a play at all.[11] When a character in John Marston's

The Malcontent rehearses the closing couplet of an epigram by Thomas Bastard, she immediately ascribes it to 'an honest priest' – which Bastard, a well-known author of epigrams, had indeed become by the time the play was written. The dialogue makes a point of the pre-play attribution, but when the couplet is picked up in *Bel-vedére* it is – like the rest of the materials in this printed commonplace book of single lines and couplets – not attributed at all.[12] Not only did plays rehearse a vast amount of proverbial material, but also playwrights like Webster or Marston – who raided Montaigne for his *Dutch Courtezan*[13] – depended on extensive borrowing of commonplace materials in constructing their dialogues. Pointed, aphoristic, sententious lines, as well as striking phrases, puns, and jokes that appear in plays, rather than originating in the surviving dramatic work, may very well have been captured by the dramatist from written or oral sources, without our realizing their intricate prehistories.

A much more elaborate example of the passage of a passage from notebook to notebook is provided by Laura Estill, who follows the circulation of a proverb that appears in *Love's Labours Lost*. The lines 'Fat paunches have lean pates, and dainty bits / Make rich the ribs but bankrupt quite the wits'[14] rework a proverb already in wide circulation by the time Shakespeare quoted them, which continued to be copied and re-copied in Shakespeare's phrasing, and then, in modified form, was copied again as a proverb with no awareness that at one stage it had passed through Shakespeare's comedy.[15] What Estill's spectacular reconstruction of the circulation of this proverb shows is that Shakespeare's play is only one node, and not even the most important one, in the network of the phrase's labyrinthine transmission.

The careful and imaginative research of Tiffany Stern and others has shown songs to be literally and materially detachable from early modern play scripts, separate pieces of paper that moved in and out of plays, which also came to be copied as songs in their own right.[16] Though epigrams, proverbs, aphoristic observations, and jests did not have the same kind of physical independence from the dramatic dialogue, they resemble these separate pieces of paper in that they are readily detachable self-contained short forms, held up in scripted dialogue as objects to be taken away. Rather than understanding them as pieces created by extraction from something larger, it might be more productive to see them as viral utterances passing through bulkier, baggier host materials, already dissociated from their context as they replicate themselves in another. Plays are particularly good hosts, breeding grounds and transmitters of such viral infection – but the logic of this metaphor for their circulation invites us to make the virus, not the host organism, the unit of our analysis.

When *sententiae*, songs, or jests[17] are lifted from a play, they become indistinguishable from similar materials sourced from elsewhere. They enter the buzz of those anonymous or anonymized short forms that are, like drama itself, amphibious. As our examples indicate, these forms are as strongly associated with orality and conversation as they are with textuality and inscription, and move briskly between media. Of course, almost anything extracted from the text of a play would by definition have been extracted from scripted conversation, but unlike a description that might be copied for its poetic qualities, *sententiae* are dramatized and isolated by the play through their use on stage. The delivery of a *sententia* by a stage character, who rehearses it as a quotation, holds it up as a textual object deserving our consideration, models its dissemination even as it makes it available for further circulation among the play's audience.

Describing the *sententia* as an oral form goes counter to the literary emphases of current scholarship. Play readers collecting *sententiae* in their notebooks with an eye to using them in conversation is a practice that does not so much assimilate drama to literature, as distinguish the dramatic medium as a form of exemplary orality. In this model, readers' notes are not preparatory work for written composition, but supporting material for oral performance. Such a model makes better sense of some well-known instances of early-seventeenth-century dramatic extracts, and also reveals how often plays were read for details that were conversational or otherwise markedly oral in character.

Edward Pudsey's manuscript notebook, where the couplet from *Every Man Out* quoted earlier appears in a set of passages taken from Jonson's play, illustrates this tendency. The manuscript includes about 18 pages of notes extracted from 26 early-seventeenth-century plays. Although Pudsey also copies full lines, couplets, and occasionally brief passages from plays, many of his extracts are shorter than a pentameter line, whereas the passages he copies from historical and other sources in the rest of his notebook are usually considerably longer. From sentences through phrases to individual words, Pudsey's play extracts record the verbal, linguistic innovations of early modern drama. He often tags his extracts by noting their topic in the margin, but many do not fit any thematic heading. Much of what he takes from plays are expressions he must have found apt, surprising, or novel – Jonson's *Every Man Out* yields him such remarks as 'ffollowing the fashion afarr of like a spye', expressions like 'well parted', 'dazeled & distasted iudgme*n*t', 'pursue no favor', or 'wyld in her affections'. On occasion he even copies individual words – like 'Discompanyed' and 'discloakt' from *Cynthia's Revels*, or the verb 'exist' from Marston's *Antonio's Revenge*. So rather than imagining Pudsey as a critic or commentator on plays, his play-reading is best understood as driven by a desire to acquire and appropriate the verbal competence traded on the stage and in playbooks.

Listening to plays for turns of phrase, and for 'good words, very good words' – as one hapless stage character enthuses as he is writing down the very words with which his interlocutors mock him[18] – was of course a frequent subject of satire. When referred to in plays, it reassured play-goers of their own superior wit, while also reminding them to appreciate the theatre as 'the *Mint* that daily coyns new *words*', and to recognize it as the cultural institution in charge of the circulation and distribution of linguistic capital generally.[19] As Pudsey well understands, such capital consists of much more than a good vocabulary and a storehouse of proverbial wisdom with which to pepper one's utterances. His notes clearly show that he is interested not only in sententiae and aphorisms, words and phrases, but also in the give and take of conversational performance: forms of address, and situationally defined remarks.[20] He learns from *Every Man Out* to ask someone 'to house your head' (i.e. to put your hat back on), and from *Cynthia's Revels* to say 'your phrase was without mee' in order to express incomprehension. From Jonson he also copies elaborate pleasantries like 'Yow forgiue the humor of my ey in obseruing it', 'Your desert & indeuors are plentifull', 'I must entreat yow to exchange knowledg with this gent'. and 'ffashion me an excuse to &c'. From Marston he learns to ask someone to 'hony me with fluent speech' or to shut them up by telling them to 'Keele your mouth it runs ouer'. From Shakespeare he takes examples of witty repartee, copying Benedict's response in *Much Ado* to Beatrice's 'Will yow not eat your woard. *Res[ponse]*. with no sause that can be deuised to it', and from *Hamlet*, 'Ile take my leaue. *Respon[se]*. Yow cannot take from me any thing that I will not more willingly part withall except my life', as well as Hamlet's answer to Ophelia's 'Yow are keen my L. *respon[se]*. yt wil cost yow a groaning to take of my edge.'[21] Pudsey's book registers an interest in the blueprints for improvisation and thinking on one's feet that are provided by play scripts. This conversational interest has such compulsive force that it defines Pudsey's attention not only to comedies, but also to politically fraught texts, which he mines for expressions rather than substance or argument: Pudsey was reading politics and history largely for witty talk.[22] In his practice, it is not drama that is incorporated in a canon of classical or political literature, but such literature that is occasionally assimilated to texts that modelled conversation, namely, playbooks.

Plays and colloquies

The fact that drama, as scripted conversation, reflects and shapes actual conversations that take place among its publics may almost seem a trivial observation. We know this from epigrams and plays that show less-than-sophisticated figures wooing with phrases stolen from other plays. A character in Thomas Tomkis's *Albumazar*, for example, woos 'with compliments drawn from the plays I see at the Fortune and Red Bull, where I learn all the words I speak and understand not'.[23] Yet the dominantly literary focus of the study of early modern play-reading has made it difficult to integrate the colloquial use of plays into a larger cultural-historical narrative. Humanist pedagogy is central to our understanding of the habits and practices of play-reading. The study of the technologies of textual production, commonplace books, note-taking, written translation, and composition, has resulted in a 'solitary and scribal model' of humanist education and book use.[24] This approach, determined by the written evidence available, also de-emphasizes the spoken word, which was also central to the humanist understanding of language, to education in the arts of language, and, of course, to drama.

The period between the late fifteenth and early seventeenth century saw not only the invention of the mechanical reproduction of the written word, but also the discovery of the distinction and particularity of the spoken word – an effect of the way swift, informal cursive script permeated all areas of life from record-keeping to correspondence. The interest is registered by theories of conversation (initially in the larger sense of sociability) from Castiglione to Guazzo, and by the demand for a technology to record the spoken word resulting in a wide variety of systems of shorthand. By the early seventeenth century, plays and sermons were taken down in shorthand, and people took notes of oral transactions on their tablets or 'tables' – the spoken word could now be recorded before it flew away.[25] The emphasis on orality in humanist education was thus part of the larger phenomenon of the codification, textual embodiment and authorization of orality in the period – a development that amounted to the Renaissance invention of orality, and of colloquial speech in particular, through the medium of writing.

For the humanists, Latin was a living language, which they wanted not only to read, but also to write and speak. And as with any vernacular, the logic and structure of good Latin was modelled on the usage of native speakers, and specifically, the Romans of the Republic and the early Empire. Speech was both the theoretical base and the goal of Latin instruction.[26]

The colloquial language of Roman comedy, and of Terence in particular, was the cornerstone of the teaching of spontaneous everyday Latin oral communication, as it provided direct access to the colloquial language of the Romans. According to Erasmus, 'a true ability to speak correctly is best fostered . . . by conversing and consorting with those who speak correctly . . . among Latin writers who is more useful for speaking than Terence? He is pure, concise, and closest to everyday speech.' Erasmus formulates the key paradox of humanist education when he says Terence is 'the best [master of speech], which is why one should be always turning his pages'.[27]

At early modern schools, Terence's plays were not only read but also performed, in part as classroom exercises, and in full as staged school theatricals.[28] His six comedies remained a key feature of the curriculum, supplemented by colloquial dialogues by Erasmus, Vives, or Cordier (that were themselves informed by Terentian comedy) and by vernacular translations and phrasebooks that were used as study-aids.

'Study-aid' phrasebooks, indeed, made up the first collections of play extracts in print circulation. The earliest in English was the 1483 *Vulgaria quedam abs Terencio in Anglicam Linguam Traducta*, which was published to accompany John Ankwyll's school grammar, and had been reprinted a further six times by 1529. In 1534, it was superseded by Nicholas Udall's *Floures for Latine Spekynge Selected and Gathered Oute of Terence, and the Same Translated in to Englysshe*, reprinted seven times by 1581 – its title a vernacularized term for the genre of such a collection of excerpts: the words *anthology* and *florilegium* both mean 'collection of flowers'. In 1598, precisely around the time when vernacular playbooks started appearing in larger numbers and were first equipped with gnomic pointing for *sententiae*, Richard Bernard's *Terence in English* appeared, which provides after each scene an English prose translation, followed by the moral lesson that can be drawn from the scene, a list of *formulae loquendi* (in two languages) and a Latin-only list of *sententiae*. These books, like their numerous continental counterparts, provide one or several vernacular equivalents for each Latin phrase and expression extracted, creating a bilingual phrasebook or conversation manual. And, since the phrases are printed in the order in which they appear in the comedy, an index usually aids in finding the apt phrase or expression.

While these phrasebooks are to help with spoken Latin, the vernacular equivalents they offer are colloquial English expressions, not word-for-word translations in the style of interlinear glosses, and the effort to provide apt equivalents sometimes seems intended to serve the need of those looking for a good *English* expression too. This is how Udall renders some of the Latin phrases from the first scene of the *Andria* in the 1540 edition of his *Flowers for Latin speaking*:

Paucis te volo. I would speake a woorde or two with you.
. . .
Excessit ex ephoebis, He is past childhoode, or, he waxeth a man, or, he groweth well towardes mans state.
. . .
Captus est, He is taken, or, he is in the snare, or, he is in the lashe. And prouerbially, he is in for a byrde, or he is in by the weke.
. . .
Dic sodes, Tell me I pray you, tell on a good felowship, Tell me if thou be a good feloe.[29]

Many of Udall's English phrases also turn up in his own comedy *Ralph Roister Doister*: of the expressions above, scene 2 of the play has 'He is in by the weke' and 'I muste needes speake with thee a worde or twaine', for example. Udall shows the formative influence of Terence on the language of English comedy, and the interdependence of comedy and phrase books in the transmission of polished colloquial expressions in the vernacular. Familiarity with the textual technologies for learning colloquial Latin prepared the audiences of English commercial plays to consider them as conversational resources too. Likewise, the awareness of a distinct colloquial register of a language, and the grammar-school training in scripting conversations in this register, contributed to the polyphony of English dramatic writing.

In the classical canon, comedy came closest to recording everyday conversation – in addition to Terence, and to a lesser degree Plautus, Aristophanes was also understood in sixteenth century commentary to be 'rooted in contemporary speech'.[30] Comic dialogue can model the language of familiar discourse, partly because – as sixteenth century poetics regularly noted – it is written in a stylistic register that sets it apart from the formal, elevated diction and vocabulary of tragedy, but also because it is characterized by quicker exchanges, more direct interaction among a larger number of characters, and utterances more enmeshed in the immediate context, than tragic discourse.[31] Tragedies written for the English commercial theatre in the late-sixteenth and especially early-seventeenth centuries are remarkable not only for deploying scenes with a comic conversational texture – think of Iago's banter with Emilia and Desdemona in *Othello* 2.1, or Hamlet's exchanges with Rosencrantz and Guildenstern – but also for using, even in some of the darkest tragic scenes, a language that resembles the flexible, spontaneous-sounding back-and-forth of Terentian conversation rather than Senecan declamation or stichomythia.[32] The note-taking attention to dramatic dialogue was thus extended to all dramatic genres: phrases and expressions selected out of Shakespeare and his contemporaries were gathered as 'flowers' for English speaking, much as Udall's Terentian collection offered 'flowers for Latin speaking'.

John Cotgrave's well-known *The English Treasury of Wit and Language Collected out of the Most, and Best of Our English Drammatick Poems* is often described as the 'first English drama anthology'.[33] Critics have discussed the compiler

John Cotgrave's literary preferences as reflected by the plays he selected for excerpting, but a comparison of *The English Treasury* with *Wits Labyrinth*, a small quarto booklet of phrases and sentences described in the preface as the print version of its author J. S.'s notes from his readings, suggests that the choice of plays is not always the most distinctive feature of such an anthology.[34] Although *Wits Labyrinth* does not advertise or even indicate its dramatic origins, all of its passages that I have been able to trace to an earlier printed source were taken from plays. Cotgrave's book contains 1,700 play extracts, which is comparable to the *c.* 1,400 entries in *Wits Labyrinth*. But while *The English Treasury* offers 311 pages of thematically organized passages of varying, and often considerable length (the longest being 60 lines), few of which are sententious expressions, and none colloquial formulas, *Wits Labyrinth* is a 53-page list of single-line *sententiae* and phrases. These two anthologies belong to two different genres, their compilers taking notes from plays for different ends.

In a way that resembles many collections of Terentian extracts, *Wits Labyrinth* is divided into a sententious and a colloquial part: the first section consists 'of most witty, Ingenious, wise, and learned sentences and phrases', which are general, context-independent statements, and the second of 'Most pithy, facetious, and patheticall complementall expressions', which are mostly phatic or emotive phrases intended to engage an interlocutor. As the following short set of lines from *Albumazar* shows, the book's tendency to take extracts from the same source *seriatim* can blur the distinction between the two parts of the collection:

> The worlds a theatre of theft, great rivers rob the smaller
>   brooks, and them the Ocean.
> Close as a Usurers purse.
> Let reason cleer your sight.[35]

While the first two of these lines are instances of sententious generalizations, the last one would seem to belong with the pithy, facetious, complementall expressions, like the longer set of phrases from S.S.'s *The Honest Lawyer* which begins:

> Your example steeres mee.
> Our moderators are our swords.
> I burst, if I containe my passion.
> I'le be a just executor, of your will.[36]

J. S. takes 'My hopes are prevalent', and 'Why are you cloath'd in teares or sorrow' from John Day's *Law-trickes*; 'You seeme to tread on aire', 'Let me enjoy my longings' and 'Tis now about the noone of night' from Jonson's *Sejanus*; 'You are full of faire desert' and 'You are a man most deare in my regard' from Heywood's *A Woman Killed with Kindness*. Each of these plays are represented by many other lines, and no sample can represent the hundreds of lines in the book.[37] What can be said, however, is that there is nothing literary or dramatic about most of these phrases: the interest in their aptness or originality that this anthology registers is use-oriented. In functional terms, *Wits Labyrinth* is related to such miscellanies as the 1640 *Academy of Complements*, a pragmatic courtesy manual consisting of forms of address, sample letters, model dialogues, phrases, that concludes in a list of difficult, Latinate words with their more familiar synonyms.

Wits Labyrinth is not the only instance of the use of plays in a miscellany providing instruction in the art of conversation and compliment. As well as publishing the *English Treasury*, which he considered the 'quintessence' of hundreds of 'drammatic poems',[38] John Cotgrave also published another miscellany. *Wits Interpreter* (1655) offers itself as a guide '*in the most acceptable qualifications of discourse, or writing,*' in which the '*whole mystery of those pleasing witchcrafts of eloquence and love are made easie*'.[39] The second section of this manual is called 'Theatre of Courtship, Accurate Complements'. It consists of 51 dialogues, each of them about a page or two, and each excerpted and, where necessary, slightly adapted from plays.[40] They are scenes of wooing, in various registers and with various outcomes: a manual of amorous conversation. Whether they were consulted by anxious solitary readers in preparation for such encounters, or enjoyed in sociable reading or in private theatricals, as John Astington suggests,[41] these familiar colloquies, in a book that also contains model letters and various entertaining curiosities, serve to inspire and aid polite social intercourse.

Like the words, phrases, colloquial expressions, and proverbs extracted from plays, these longer extracts represent yet another textual form that mediated between dramatic works and everyday conversation. They participate in the process I have been tracing here, in which the public stage and the publication of playbooks created, shaped, stylized, and to some degree also standardized the private, colloquial use of language. *Wits Labyrinth* carried the Horatian promise 'Aut prodesse, aut delectare potest' (i.e. it can profit as well as delight) on its title page, and in terms of the profit readers could expect to reap, conversational proficiency was one of the most important – if now least appreciated – uses of drama in the early modern period. Since the practice was developed and disseminated through humanist education, and since it both presupposed a written text and required writing and note-taking, it can certainly be called a literary use of drama, in the early modern sense of having to do with learning and writing. But unlike mining plays for materials to be used in written composition, using them to learn how to talk aptly and respond sharply did not assimilate drama to a pre-existing canon of non-dramatic literary texts. Such use depended on a feature specific to drama, namely, its representation of informal, improvisational conversation in social interaction. Whether this is evidence of vernacular drama being 'literature', or whether it designates play scripts as literary drama, is a different question, and not even necessarily the most interesting one.

Notes

1 See the brief notes of appreciation appended after a series of extracts from each play in Abraham Wright's book, BL MS Add 22608; the comments are reprinted in Arthur C. Kirsch, 'A Caroline Commentary on the Drama', *Modern Philology*, 66 (1969), 256–261.

2 Lois Potter, *Secret Rites and Secret Writing: Royalist Literature, 1641–1660* (Cambridge: Cambridge University Press, 1989), 118.

3 Roger Chartier and Peter Stallybrass, 'Reading and Authorship: The Circulation of Shakespeare 1590–1619', in Andrew Murphy, ed., *A Concise Companion to Shakespeare and the Text* (Oxford: Blackwell, 2007), 35–56; Zachary Lesser and Peter Stallybrass, 'The First Literary *Hamlet* and the Commonplacing of Professional Plays', *Shakespeare Quarterly*, 59 (2008), 371–420. Charles Whitney's wide-ranging *Early Responses to Renaissance Drama* (Cambridge: Cambridge University Press, 2006) reveals the variety of uses and reactions plays were subject to, and while its primary focus is not on textual culture, it gives a sense of the rich array of what evidence we have of the responses to plays, and also highlights the tensions between dramatic character and the anonymity of the commonplace (see esp. 82–91).

4 For an example of the slippage, see Lukas Erne, *Shakespeare as Literary Dramatist*, 2nd edn (Cambridge: Cambridge University Press, 2013), 95. Erne seeks to correct the claim that 'plays were not regarded as "literature" but as relatively ephemeral entertainment reading on no higher plane than, say, a novel made from the script of a popular moving picture' not by revising or critically considering the blatantly ahistorical terminology, but by asserting the literariness of drama in precisely those terms, as something on that 'higher plane' – see esp. 98–99. Erne is quoting the claim as formulated by Fredson Bowers, 'The Publication of English Renaissance Plays', in Fredson Bowers, ed., *Elizabethan Dramatists*, Dictionary of Literary Biography 62 (Detroit: Gale Research Company, 1987), 406–16. The problem is pointed out by Adam G. Hooks, who seeks to establish what was distinctive about the publication of

plays, rather than use the elasticity of the term 'literary' to squeeze plays into the category, see *Selling Shakespeare: Biography, Bibliography and the Book Trade* (Cambridge: Cambridge University Press, 2016), 28–30.

5 In addition to work already cited, see also Lukas Erne, *Shakespeare and the Book Trade* (Cambridge: Cambridge University Press, 2013), 186–232.

6 Ben Jonson, *Every Man out of his Humor* (1600), F3v. Here, and throughout, i/j and u/v have been regularized.

7 On the use of gnomic pointing in English drama, see G. K. Hunter, 'The Marking of Sententiae in Elizabethan Printed Plays, Poems, and Romances', *The Library 5th ser.*, 6 (1951), 171–188; Lesser and Stallybrass, 'The First Literary *Hamlet*'.

8 Robert Allott, *Englands Parnassus: or The Choysest Flowers of our Moderne Poets, with their Poeticall comparisons* (1600), O4v.

9 Bodleian MS Eng. Poet. d. 3., fol. 39v.

10 BL MS Harleian 5353 fol. 9r, and Robert Parker Sorlien, ed., *The Diary of John Manningham of the Middle Temple, 1602–1603: Newly Edited in Complete and Unexpurgated Form from the Original Manuscript in the British Museum* (Hanover: University Press of New England, 1976), 41.

11 Mary Bly, 'Defining the Proper Members of the Renaissance Theatrical Community', *Renaissance Drama,* 40 (2012), 113–123, is valuable for correcting the assumption that when the same joke appears in more than one play, it was the canonical author who came up with it, but her model still limits the scope of such circulation to the theatre.

12 *Bel-vedére or The Garden of the Muses* (1600), Q1v.

13 Charles Crawford, *Collectanea, Second Series* (Stratford-on-Avon: The Shakespeare Head Press, 1907), 1–48.

14 *Love's Labour's Lost*, ed. John Kerrigan (Harmondsworth: Penguin, 1982), 1.1.26–27.

15 Laura Estill, *Dramatic Extracts in Seventeenth-Century English Manuscripts: Watching, Reading, Changing Plays* (Newark: University of Delaware Press, 2015), 201–223.

16 Tiffany Stern, *Documents of Performance in Early Modern England* (Cambridge: Cambridge University Press, 2009),

120–173. Letters could be similarly detachable, but were unlikely to show up in other plays or contexts. Paradoxically, letters don't travel: see Alan Stewart, *Shakespeare's Letters* (Oxford: Oxford University Press, 2008), 25–34. On the independent circulation of prologues and epilogues, see the chapter by Craig and Massai in this volume.

17 Lucy Munro, 'Reading Printed Comedy: Edward Sharpham's *the Fleer*', in *The Book of the Play: Playwrights, Stationers, and Readers in Early Modern England*, ed. Marta Straznicky (Amherst and Boston: University of Massachusetts Press, 2006), 47–50, 54–55.

18 John Marston, *Antonio's Revenge*, ed. W. Reavley Gair (Manchester: Manchester University Press, 1978), 1.3.22.

19 Richard Flecknoe, *Miscellania* (1653), 103–104. On newly coined words as a commodity in the 'knowledge marketplace' of the theatre, see Robert N. Watson, 'Coining Words on the Elizabethan and Jacobean Stage', *Philological Quarterly*, 88 (2009), 49–75, and 'Shakespeare's New Words', *Shakespeare Survey*, 65 (2012), 358–377.

20 Jean-Christophe Mayer, 'Les spectateurs de Shakespeare: à la découverte des lettres et carnets de ses contemporains', in *Shakespeare et ses contemporains: Actes du colloque 2002 de la Société Française Shakespeare*, ed. Patricia Dorval (Paris: Société Française Shakespeare, 2003), 149; Fred Schurink, 'Manuscript Commonplace Books, Literature, and Reading in Early Modern England', *Huntington Library Quarterly*, 73 (2010), 468.

21 Stratford ER/82/1/21 ff. 1v, 2r, 2v.

22 András Kiséry, *Hamlet's Moment: Drama and Political Knowledge in Early Modern England* (Oxford: Oxford University Press, 2016), 274–280.

23 Of course poetry can also circulate in this 'non-poetic' way – witness how much of Shakespeare's *Lucrece* crops up as sententious material: Sasha Roberts, *Reading Shakespeare's Poems in Early Modern England* (New York: Palgrave Macmillan, 2003), 129–137.

24 Lynn Enterline, *Shakespeare's Schoolroom: Rhetoric, Discipline, Emotion* (Philadelphia: University of Pennsylvania Press, 2012), 43.

25 Tiffany Stern, 'Sermons, Plays and Note-Takers: *Hamlet* Q1 as a "Noted" Text', *Shakespeare Survey*, 66 (2013), 1–23.

26 Martin Elsky, *Authorizing Words: Speech, Writing, and Print in the English Renaissance* (Ithaca: Cornell University Press, 1989), 35–69.

27 *De Ratione Studii*, translated by Brian McGregor, in Craig R. Thompson, ed., *Literary and Educational Writings* 2, *Collected Works of Erasmus* vol. 24 (Toronto, Buffalo, London: University of Toronto Press, 1978), 669; *De Copia*, translated by Betty I. Knott, ibid., 416; translations modified.

28 Ursula Potter, 'Performing Arts in the Tudor Classroom', in Lloyd Kermode, Jason Scott-Warren, and Martine Van Elk, eds, *Tudor Drama before Shakespeare 1485–1590* (New York: Palgrave Macmillan, 2004), 143–165; Enterline, *Shakespeare's Schoolroom*, esp. 33–61.

29 *Floures for Latine Speakyng Selected and Gathered oute of Terence, and the Same Translated into Englyshe . . . : Compiled by Nicolas Udall* (1540), A1r–A2r.

30 Tanya Pollard, 'Greek Playbooks and Dramatic Forms in Early Modern England', in Allison K. Deutermann and András Kiséry, eds, *Formal Matters: Reading the Materials of English Renaissance Literature* (Manchester: Manchester University Press, 2013), 105.

31 The critical potential of making linguistic distinctions among genres is shown by Jonathan Hope, *Shakespeare and Language: Reason, Eloquence and Artifice in the Renaissance* (London: Arden Shakespeare, 2010), 187ff.

32 Jonathan Hope and Michael Witmore, 'The Hundredth Psalm to the Tune of "Green Sleeves": Digital Approaches to Shakespeare's Language of Genre', *Shakespeare Quarterly*, 61 (2010), 374–382.

33 Jeremy Lopez, *Constructing the Canon of Early Modern Drama* (Cambridge: Cambridge University Press, 2014), 47. On *The English Treasury*, see G. E. Bentley, 'John Cotgrave's *English Treasury of Wit and Language* and the Elizabethan Drama', *Studies in Philology*, 40 (1943), 186–203; Potter, *Secret Rites*, 17–19; Estill, *Dramatic Extracts*, 88–94, and Joshua J. McEvilla, with contributions from Sean M. Winslow, *An Online Reader of*

>   *John Cotgrave's The English Treasury of Wit and Language*,
>   https://shakespeareauthorship.com/cotgrave/index.htm.

34 *VVits Labyrinth. Or, A Briefe and Compendious Abstract of Most Witty, Ingenious, Wise, and Learned Sentences and Phrases. Together with Some Hundreds of Most Pithy, Facetious, and Patheticall, Complementall Expressions. Collected, Compiled, and Set forth for the Benefit, Pleasure, or Delight of All, but Principally the English Nobility and Gentry. By J. S., Gent.* (1648).

35 *VVits Labyrinth*, B2v.

36 *VVits Labyrinth*, G1r.

37 Some of the lines from Shakespeare are listed in *The Shakspere Allusion-Book*, ed. John Munro (London: Oxford University Press, 1932), 1:515; but cf. Furnivall's note, 1:514.

38 *The English Treasury of Wit and Language Collected out of the Most, and Best of Our English Drammatick Poems; Methodically Digested into Iommon Places for Generall Use. By John Cotgrave, Gent.* (1655), π3r.

39 *Wits Interpreter, the English Parnassus. or, a Sure Guide to Those Admirable Accomplishments that Compleat our English Gentry, in the Most Acceptable Qualifications of Discourse, or Writing. . . . By I. C.* (1655).

40 John H. Astington, 'Dramatic Extracts in the Interregnum', *Review of English Studies*, 54 (2003), 601–614.

41 Astington, 'Dramatic Extracts' 609.

9

Shakespearean Extracts, Manuscript Cataloguing, and the Misrepresentation of the Archive

*Laura Estill**

As Leah Marcus has explored, scholars have often imagined what would come of finding more documents handwritten by Shakespeare.[1] This chapter suggests Shakespeare's canonical status colours not just how we value what manuscript evidence we find, but what we can find in the first place. This chapter highlights the worth of non-Shakespearean manuscripts and argues that we need to rethink the canon-focused biases inherent in our cataloguing and research practices in order to better apprehend early modern dramatic texts and their afterlives.

Early modern English plays were conglomerations of separate parts, as Tiffany Stern has shown: songs, prologues, plots, and other elements of plays were not always written by the playwright. Instead of imagining a playwright as someone who has wrought an entire text, Stern encourages us to consider playwrights as play-patchers.[2] Rather than focusing on a dramatic text in its composition or during performance, however, this chapter instead focuses on afterlives: the pieces of plays that were removed from their original context after publication. These selections from plays, also called dramatic extracts, offer valuable evidence about early responses to plays, yet they are often overlooked or taken out of context by researchers. András Kiséry's chapter in this volume, for instance, draws on print and manuscript extracts to suggest that drama's 'representation of informal, improvisational conversation in social interaction' is why readers and playgoers copied selections from plays.[3] This chapter demonstrates the need to reappraise how early modern plays and extracts were and are catalogued and made findable.

From all catalogued accounts of pre-1600 manuscripts, extracts from Shakespeare apparently outnumber those of other dramatists. This figure, however, is not because of Shakespeare's popularity in the Elizabethan period and is, furthermore, not necessarily accurate: it is because of later centuries' habits of Shakespeare-centric cataloguing and scholarship. A reception history focused on Shakespeare elides the bulk of the archive, and, as such, the majority of evidence about responses to early English drama. Roslyn L. Knutson and David McInnis posit a 'continuum of "lostness"' when it comes to lost plays;[4] I suggest that 'unfindable' could be considered part of this continuum.

Library catalogues and canon

There are certainly manuscripts with selections by plays from Shakespeare and his contemporaries yet to be found: that is, catalogued, digitized, and discussed. The bulk of *known* early modern dramatic extracts, however, are known because they appear in libraries and archives that have been catalogued. Most major library catalogues such as those from the Bodleian Library at Oxford University were compiled by librarians and archivists before digital workflows; they were manuscript or printed catalogues, designed to be consulted as codices or cards. Digital library catalogues that make manuscripts searchable are modelled on earlier catalogues: often, the content remains the same, even if the mode of access is different.

The pre-digital origins of library catalogues might not seem worth stating, however, it is precisely because these finding aids were created before easily searchable texts that they cemented our notions of the canon. Archivists who catalogued manuscripts could only identify those sources that were labelled with a title or author in the manuscript or that they could recall from memory. And in the eighteenth, nineteenth, and twentieth centuries, Shakespeare's plays were more recognizable, and therefore more likely to be catalogued, than those of lesser-known playwrights such as Lording Barry or George Wilkins. Library cataloguing, then, acts as a self-reinforcing cycle: known elements are catalogued, which makes them more readily findable, which makes them more known to scholars and cataloguers. When it comes to those selections from plays that early playgoers and readers copied, Shakespeare, specifically, is over-represented both in our catalogues and our scholarship.

Not only would Shakespeare's plays have been more easily identifiable to early cataloguers, his position at the centre of the nineteenth-century literary and theatrical canon means that selections from his works were thought worth identifying in even the shortest library catalogue descriptions, whereas those from lesser-known playwrights might not have been identifiable, or thought worth mentioning. Manuscript catalogue entries vary greatly in length, from one- to two-sentence descriptions to pages-long lists of complete manuscript contents. Particularly with shorter descriptions, it is only the most important writers who are named.

The catalogue entry for Bodleian Rawlinson MS D. 952 offers an example of how Shakespearean extracts are often privileged over the other contents of a manuscript. The description runs:

> A common-place book of sentences out of plays, under heads in alphabetical order.
>
> On the first leaf is a list of twenty-four comedies and tragedies (by Davenant, Massinger, &c.) printed between 1607 and 1632, 'read of me', and of ten others (by Ben Jonson, &c.) up to the year 1633, described as 'comedyes not yet learned'.
>
> The only Shakespearean play in the former list is Pericles.[5]

Although this manuscript contains only two Shakespearean extracts amidst pages of other dramatic content,[6] the catalogue entry's final sentence singles out those few lines. Library catalogues announce what a cataloguer can determine about a manuscript; furthermore, they are often crafted around expectations of what will be most useful to scholars, which highlights certain elements and can give a biased or inaccurate description of a volume's contents.

When authors are listed, cataloguing practices have historically privileged Shakespeare over even those authors we think of as canonical. The British Library Catalogue entry for Additional MS 27406, an aggregation of seventeenth- and eighteenth-century texts, lists only five names: Simon Patrick, the Bishop of Chichester; Prudentius, the Roman poet; John Bence, a merchant; P[eter] Le Neve, the antiquarian; and Shakespeare.[7] This manuscript, however, also includes poems by Ben Jonson, Thomas Dekker, Walter Raleigh, Francis Beaumont, and even four lines from Sir Philip Sidney's *Arcadia*, none of which are mentioned in the catalogue entry. The manuscript includes a complete copy of Thomas Randolph's dramatic monologue, 'The Conceited Pedlar' (f. 121r–27v), that is similarly omitted from the description.[8] BL Add MS 27406 is a composite volume, that is, a gathering of many different pages, 'in several hands and paper sizes': as the *Catalogue of English Literary Manuscripts* (*CELM*) explains, Le Neve gathered many of these pages together.[9] As a composite volume, the different items are clearly differentiated for a reader or cataloguer handling the artifact: new handwriting

and new paper signals separate items. Yet the British Library
Catalogue mentions only three items of the dozens gathered
together here: the first item (ff. 1–18, Patrick's translation of
Prudentius), the Shakespearean content (selections from *The
Rape of Lucrece*, f. 74), and a letter from Bence to Le Neve, the
person responsible for gathering this manuscript (f. 116). But
Le Neve, and the others who compiled this manuscript by
copying and gathering its contents (it was later bound in the
nineteenth century), did not signal the Shakespearean extracts
as more important than the others: they are buried mid-volume
and not highlighted in any way in the manuscript itself. It is
library cataloguing that has elevated Shakespeare to a level of
prominence above other poets and playwrights of his day, such
as Jonson, Dekker, Beaumont, Sidney, and Randolph.

Beyond the many short works in BL Add MS 27406, this
composite volume also includes a 'separate' (a short manuscript
intended to circulate alone) that contains the entire text of
Thomas Randolph's *Conceited Pedlar,* titled and attributed
'Tho: Randolphs Pedlar' (ff. 121r–127v). Jill Levenson draws
attention to 'Randolph's great popularity during his lifetime
and for a generation after', which is confirmed by this full-
text manuscript copy of this 'satirical monologue in verse
and prose'[10] – one of three full-text manuscripts known – and
multiple early editions.[11] This handwritten copy gives
information about the first performance, a piece of information
absent from early modern print sources: 'All S^{ts}: 1627', that is,
All Saints' Day (1 November 1627). As one of only three full-
text manuscript copies of a work by a formerly lauded author,
this copy has been a known scholarly commodity for decades,
but it is still not in the manuscript's official library catalogue
description. As is all too often the case, this manuscript's value
to scholarship is not represented by its catalogue entry.

British Literary Manuscripts Online (*BLMO*) includes a
facsimile of BL Add MS 27406, including Randolph's
Conceited Pedlar. As with all of their metadata, *BLMO*
replicates library catalogues, rather than writing new, detailed
descriptions. Similarly, *BLMO*'s facsimiles, including BL Add

MS 27406, have all been created by digitizing existing microfilm collections – its core is drawn from the 'Britain's Literary Heritage' microfilms by Harvester.[12] In this case, however, the cataloguing metadata is even less substantial than that provided in the British Library's Online 'Manuscripts and Archives' catalogue: *BLMO* simply includes the description of BL Add MS 27406–27408 as a group of three manuscripts, 'POETICAL pieces: the collections of Oliver and Peter Le Neve and Thomas Martin, of Palgrave, comprising religious, political, lyrical, and other compositions'.[13] *BLMO* users wanting to find dramatic or literary works, even by Shakespeare, who do not miraculously stumble upon the search term 'poetical' or 'lyrical', will find no results: instead, they will need to turn to the bibliographic resources beyond library catalogues that underpin archival research on early modern drama.

The catalogues that describe manuscripts have been written (and, at times, re-written) over centuries: it can be difficult to trace who wrote each individual entry. Each library has been catalogued to different standards, and sometimes the descriptions vary widely between collections within a given library. For instance, a catalogue description of a manuscript in the British Library's Harleian Collection can run to a dozen pages, whereas a description of a manuscript in the British Library's Additional Collection is often just a few sentences long. The guides for how to catalogue manuscripts are long and detailed;[14] even these, however, make assumptions about the material being catalogued and suggest that literary manuscripts be catalogued at the item level. Cataloguing 'literary' manuscripts as one object assumes that one manuscript contains a single or few identifiable literary work(s), which, in the case of a composite volume or miscellany, is not accurate. Further scholarship in this area will necessitate collaboration between archivists and scholars not only to improve catalogue entries (a monumental task itself) but also to write the history of the catalogues that have been and continue to be created.

Beyond the library catalogue

Scholars interested in studying early modern dramatic texts can supplement library catalogues and search across archives by turning to more specialized bibliographic resources. As Gregory A. Pass notes, 'As an undifferentiated group of materials, manuscripts rest uneasily or not at all in the library catalog. Manuscript descriptions reside more often in finding aids that stand apart from the main library catalog'.[15] First-line indices were one of the earliest resources that materialized to fill the needs of literary researchers for whom traditional manuscript cataloguing was inadequate.

The earliest first-line index was the British Museum's unpublished 'First-line index to English (and some French and Latin) poetry', which was compiled in the 1880s and continues to be expanded on.[16] Published, and later, online first-line indices emerged in the twentieth century, with important contributions indexing major archives such as those by Margaret Crum (Bodleian Library) and Peter Seng (Houghton Library, Harvard)[17] as well as indices on particular topics, such as Steven W. May and William Ringler's *Elizabeth Verse* and Harold Love's index of 'English Clandestine Satire 1660–1702'.[18] These sources, and more, were consolidated, put online, and made searchable in the Folger Shakespeare Library's *Union First-Line Index of English Verse* (firstlines.folger.edu). First-line indices were and are an important part of democratizing the archive so that the contents of manuscripts are accurately represented without a bias towards canonical authors.

First-line indices, however, are by their nature restricted to poetry, which means that of the wealth of early modern manuscript miscellanies they cover, only the poems are listed. As a result, songs and speeches from plays only fall within the purview of a first-line index when they are written in verse. The other contents of manuscript miscellanies can be difficult to categorize and catalogue – such as prose letters, recipes ('receipts'), pen trials, and so on – to the point where our very name for these manuscripts, miscellanies, is derived from their heterogeneity and miscellaneity. When dramatic extracts appear in these volumes, particularly when they are not signalled by title or author, they are often overlooked by cataloguers.

Perhaps the most important finding aid for literary manuscripts is Peter Beal's monumental *Catalogue of English Literary Manuscripts* (*CELM*), which arose to meet the needs of scholars that were not being fulfilled by library catalogues and first-line indices.[19] *CELM* expanded on the information available in library catalogues and first-line indices by describing manuscript contents beyond poetry. Although *CELM* has broadened our understanding of the literary canon (particularly by increasing its coverage of women writers from the early printed volumes), it is still predicated on the author. So far, the online instantiation of *CELM* has attempted to cover only one anonymous work, *Leicester's Commonwealth*. That means that dramatic materials by lesser-known or unknown authors are not included in *CELM* – even when they appear alongside dramatic material by canonical authors.[20]

For instance, BL MS Egerton 1994 contains fourteen full-text plays and a masque, but *CELM* lists only five of its dramatic works: *The Elder Brother* by Beaumont and Fletcher; three plays by Thomas Heywood; and *Loves Changelings Change*, adapted from Sidney's *The Old Arcadia*. *CELM*'s focus on canon neglects more than half of the manuscript, which includes handwritten and sometimes unique copies of important plays such as the anonymous *Thomas of Woodstock, Edmund Ironside*, and *Nero*. This manuscript is so well-known it even has its own *Wikipedia* page, which currently does a better job of listing its dramatic contents than *CELM* (though even the *Wikipedia* entry does not, at present, mention the selections from Sidney).[21] The British Library catalogue entry for Egerton 1994 lists the dramatic contents, but not always in a way that is easily searchable by scholars: for instance, it lists *Thomas of Woodstock* as 'King Richard the Second; a tragedy'.[22] And while, indeed, this play has been published as *Richard II, Part 1* (and sometimes attributed to Shakespeare), most scholars know it by the title *Thomas of Woodstock*, which is not to be found in the catalogue entry. Similarly, the ascription of *The Lady Mother* to Henry Glapthorne 'has never seriously been challenged',[23] yet Glapthorne's name is omitted from the library catalogue page for BL MS Egerton 1994, the only known manuscript copy of this work. Catalogue entries for manuscript plays are especially important for works by lesser-known playwrights that are not included in *CELM*, such as Glapthorne's *The Lady Mother* or Walter Monfort's *The Launching of the Mary* (also in BL MS Egerton 1994), because the unpublished nature of their work means it is also beyond the scope of print-focused databases to which scholars turn every day, such as the *Database of Early English Playbooks* (*DEEP*) and the *English Short-Title Catalogue* (*ESTC*).[24]

Although we can imagine a happy time where *CELM* is expanded to include all literary works, even by anonymous authors, realistically, the project has to be bounded so that it can have in-depth coverage. It would take years (the work of digitizing and broadening *CELM* to its current state spanned from 2005–2013[25]) and much funding to develop this project further: and it can be a challenge to convince funding agencies that we need expansion to help us research authors who are ignored in BL MS Egerton 1994 like Glapthorne or Robert Daborne.[26] Matteo Pangallo's work-in-progress, a *Database of English Manuscript Drama* (*DEMand*), will offer a searchable database of full-text manuscript plays.[27] Similarly, the online edition of Martin Wiggins's *British Drama 1533–1642: A Catalogue*, to be undertaken by Catherine Richardson and Mark Merry, will be an invaluable resource.[28] The *British Drama* print volumes mention many, but not all, known dramatic extracts. The *Lost Plays Database*, discussed by Knutson and McInnis in this volume, is a welcome addition to these resources, as it provides all known evidence about plays for which we no longer have complete texts.[29] There is much work to be done for bibliographers, cataloguers, archivists, and other researchers to expand our understanding of early modern textual and dramatic culture.

Overlooked evidence of play-reading

Even when a manuscript or author makes it into a particular bibliographic resource or catalogue, dramatic extracts, and particularly non-Shakespearean dramatic extracts, can still be ignored. For instance, two songs from plays by Thomas Otway that appear in BL Add. MS 27406 are missing from all the bibliographical resources in which scholars would expect to find them (see Figure 9.1). Despite Otway's being an author included in *CELM*, the songs are omitted from Beal's database; similarly, they are not found in the short British Library catalogue description discussed earlier. The Folger *First Line Index* lists the poems' first and last lines, and even the appended date listed in the manuscript (1714), but does not note that these songs appeared in Otway's plays.

The first song, 'Princes that rule, & Empires Sway', appeared in Otway's *Alcibiades* (first published in 1675). It is followed by 'How blessd he appears' from Otway's *Friendship in Fashion* (first published in 1672). Martin probably copied these selections from the one-volume *Works of Mr Thomas Otway* (1692), where *Alcibiades* and *Friendship in Fashion* are the first and second plays, respectively. It is not an overstatement to say that had these songs been published in a Shakespeare play, they would have been discussed by scholars at length. Songs from plays by Otway, however, provide no less insight into the reception of drama and early textual cultures.

Linking a manuscript copy of song to a play can help scholars better understand 'documents of performance', as Stern puts it: that is, researchers can find and analyse songs that have been incorporated into a play by a playwright/ play-patcher. Similarly, identifying a song *from* a play can help us understand a work's reception history and how it was read and understood. Yet these two songs from Otway's plays are

> Princes that rule, & Empires sway,
>   How transitory is their State!
> Sorrows the Glories do allay,
>   And richest Crowns have greatest weight.
>
> **II.**
>
> The mighty Monarch treasons fears,
>   Ambitious thoughts within him rave;
> His life all Discontent and Cares,
>   And he at last is but a Slave.
>
> **III:**
>
> Vainly we think with fond delight,
>   To ease ye Burden of our Cares;
> Each grief a second does invite,
>   And Sorrows are each others Heirs.
>
> **IV.**
>
> For me, my honour ile maintain
>   Bee gallant Generous and Brave
> And when I quietude would gain
>   At least I find it in ye Grave.
>
> **I**
>
> How blest he appears
> That revels, and loves out his happy years
> That feircely spurs on till he finish his race
> And knowing life's short, Chuses living apace
> To Cares we were born, twere a folly to doubt it
> Then love and rejoyce ther's no living without it.
>
> **II.**
>
> Each Day we grow older
> But as fate approaches, ye Brave still are bolder
> The joys of love with our Youth slide away.
> But yet there are pleasures yt never decay
> When Beauty grows Dull, & our passions grow Cold,
> Wine still keeps it Charms, & we drink when w'are ol[d]
>
> Tho: Martin. 1711

FIGURE 9.1 'Songs from Otway's Plays', BL Add MS 27406, f. 114 v. © The British Library Board.

not findable by scholars. And because they are extracts from a Restoration play copied in the early eighteenth century, it seems likely that they will remain under-catalogued (when mentioned at all) in bibliographic resources for the foreseeable future, even though they appear in a volume where Shakespearean extracts are well-documented.

The need to be able to find and identify extracts from Otway's plays will be readily apparent to scholars of Restoration theatre. This should be, however, also important to scholars who work on English theatre from before the closure of the theatres in 1642, and, indeed, even for those who work on non-dramatic early modern literatures. Harold Love's convincing argument on this point (with its reference to D. F. McKenzie) is worth quoting at length:

> Within a broad sociology of the scribal text, the identification of scribal communities and the analysis of their intellectual affiliations, political allegiances, and relationships to patronage networks is one of the most rewarding tasks facing manuscript studies. The first goal of such inquiries should be to explain how certain works rather than others should have been brought together between a given pair of covers over a given span of time. For a few celebrated collections this question has been answered, but most continue to be treated merely as quarries for editions of individual writers with no attention given to accompanying parliamentary speeches, medical remedies, antiquarian documents, or prophecies, whose patterns of circulation are often just as intricate and culturally revealing.[30]

As Love points out, it is important to think about entire manuscripts as evidence of reception: each manuscript can be considered as evidence of a text's 'sociology'. McKenzie notes that 'we must . . . consider carefully the expressive functions of the text's modes of transmission, and account for its reception by an audience or readership'.[31] The questions we ask of manuscripts shape our understanding of an entire textual culture: changing our focus from authors to copyists and readers can be a powerful corrective.

Finding and identifying dramatic extracts today

Without improved cataloguing or indexing, it will be impossible to make quantitative claims about the reception history of early modern drama. Scholarly claims about a play or playwright's relative popularity based on manuscript extracts must begin with many caveats: the high loss rate for unbound volumes; the large number of manuscripts not-yet-catalogued; and, as this chapter has demonstrated, the over-representation of Shakespeare in catalogues, bibliographies, and scholarship.

The full-text transcription of manuscripts offers one potential way to break the cycle of canon-centred cataloguing and scholarship. The Folger Shakespeare Library's *Early Modern Manuscripts Online* (*EMMO*, in beta) holds great promise in this regard:[32] if the Folger transcribes all of its early modern manuscripts, new dramatic extracts will surely turn up. Paired with an algorithm that can find similarities in other digitized text (such that developed by *Commonplace Cultures*[33]), full-text manuscript transcriptions can allow us to see what plays early readers were actually reading, even if they are now largely forgotten.

The expense of manuscript transcription and digital project design and maintenance, however, means that for the foreseeable future many dramatic extracts will remain uncatalogued. My own *DEx: A Database of Dramatic Extracts* is a still-growing site that fills this gap somewhat by indexing extracts from plays performed and published before 1642 that are found in manuscripts written before 1700.[34] *DEx* allows users to search across archives and includes material that is outside the author-bound purview of *CELM* or the poetry-based scope of the Folger's *First Line Index*. While *DEx*, which is still being updated, can lead researchers to new evidence about the reception of early modern plays, it too is limited by scope: users interested in thinking about a manuscript as a complete unit will still have to turn elsewhere for codicological information and non-dramatic contents.[35] *DEx*, then, is just one tool available to researchers of early modern drama and the archive; and like all other catalogues and bibliographic resources, *DEx* encourages particular research questions. There are many dramatic extracts still to be catalogued in *DEx*. Similarly, there are also dramatic extracts that are simply beyond the scope of the project, like Otway's Restoration songs in Figure 9.1 as well as numerous selections that survive in manuscripts from the eighteenth century and beyond.

While some manuscripts will undoubtedly continue to be valued because of their Shakespeare content, improved cataloguing and finding aids will allow scholars to move beyond author-centric and, specifically, Shakespeare-centric questions. Where we have previously only been able to conjecture about early readers or point to selective manuscripts as evidence, we are on the cusp of being able to search and analyse more comprehensive and quantifiable evidence of the early reception of plays. The chapters in this collection are a testament to the varied and rich kinds of conclusions we can draw from archival evidence – increased findability of this evidence, including dramatic extracts, can only lead to improved research and further compelling interpretations. When we seek and document only Shakespearean extracts, however, we misrepresent the wealth of material evidence on readership, reception, and literary and dramatic culture that the archive has to offer.

Notes

* I would like to thank Tamara Atkin, Beatrice Montedoro, Kailin Wright, and Tiffany Stern for their thoughtful feedback on this chapter.

1 For more on this (misplaced) scholarly longing for Shakespeare's manuscripts, see Leah Marcus, 'The Veil of Manuscript', *Renaissance Drama*, 30 (1999–2001), 115–131.

2 Tiffany Stern, *Documents of Performance in Early Modern England* (Cambridge: Cambridge University Press, 2009).

3 András Kiséry, '"Flowers for English Speaking": Play Extracts and Conversation', in this volume (169).

4 Roslyn L. Knutson and David McInnis, 'Lost Documents, Absent Documents, Forged Documents', in this volume (241).

5 [William Macray], *Catalogi Codicum Manuscriptorum Bibliothecae Bodleianae Partis Quitae Facsiculus Quartus* (Oxford: Clarendon, 1898), 216.

6 For more on the contents of this manuscript, see Beatrice Montedoro, 'Comedies and Tragedies "read of me" and "not yet learned": Dramatic Extracting in a Newly Re-discovered Manuscript', in *Early British Drama in Manuscript*, ed. Laura Estill and Tamara Atkin (Turnhout, Belgium: Brepols, 2019).

7 http://searcharchives.bl.uk/IAMS_VU2:IAMS040-002030841 [accessed 15 July 2018].

8 Scholars have, however, long known of its presence. See, for instance, Bernard M. Wagner, 'Thomas Randolph's *The Conceited Pedlar*', *Times Literary Supplement* (9 April 1931), 288.

9 Beal, *CELM*, http://www.celm-ms.org.uk/repositories/british-library-additional-25000.html [accessed 10 July 2018].

10 Jill L. Levenson, 'Thomas Randolph (June 1605-March 1635)' in *Jacobean and Caroline Dramatists*, ed. Fredson Bowers, Dictionary of Literary Biography 58 (Detroit: Gale, 1987), 232.

11 For a bibliography of early editions, see *CELM* and the *Database of Early English Playbooks*, deep.sas.upenn.edu [accessed 10 July 2018].

12 *BLMO*, homepage [paywalled resource, accessed 15 July 2018] and 'source microfilm collections'. For more on the challenges and affordances of *BLMO*, see Laura Estill and Andie Silva, 'Storing and Accessing Knowledge: Digital Tools for the Study of

Early Modern Drama', in *Shakespeare's Language in Digital Media*, ed. Janelle Jenstad, Mark Kaethler, and Jennifer Roberts-Smith (London and New York: Routledge, 2018), 131–143.

13 This description first appeared, without differentiating the three manuscripts, in the 1877 *Catalogue of Additions to the Manuscripts in the British Museum in the Years MDCCCLIV-MDCCCLXXV*, 2 vols (London, 1877), 2: 316.

14 Important guides include *Descriptive Cataloging of Rare Materials (Manuscripts)* (Chicago: Rare Books and Manuscripts Section of the Association of College and Research Libraries, 2016) and Kathleen D. Roe, *Arranging and Describing Archives and Manuscripts* (Chicago: Society of American Archivists, 2005).

15 Gregory A. Pass, *Descriptive Cataloguing of Ancient, Medieval, Renaissance, and Early Modern Manuscripts* (Chicago: Rare Books and Manuscripts Section of the Association of College and Research Libraries, 2003), xi.

16 James Woolley, 'Finding English Verse: First-Line Indexes and Searchable Electronic Texts', *Bibliographical Society of America* (2013), bibsocamer.org/BibSite/Woolley/index.pdf, 1 [accessed 21 August 2018].

17 Margaret Crum, *First-Line Index of English Poetry, 1500–1800, in Manuscripts of the Bodleian Library, Oxford*, 2 vols (Oxford: Clarendon Press, 1969); Peter J. Seng, *English-Language Manuscript Verse in the Houghton Library: First-Line Index*, 1987, hollisarchives.lib.harvard.edu/repositories/24/resources/6760 [accessed 21 August 2018].

18 Steven W. May and William A. Ringler, Jr., *Elizabethan Poetry: A Bibliography and First-Line Index of English Verse, 1559–1603* (London and New York: Thoemmes Continuum, 2004); Harold Love, 'First-Line Index to Selected Anthologies of Clandestine Satire', in *English Clandestine Satire, 1660–1702* (Oxford: Oxford University Press, 2004), which used to be online at Monash University and can now be accessed through the Wayback Machine.

19 *CELM* began in print as the *Index of English Literary Manuscripts*, which originally appeared in 4 volumes (9 parts) (London and New York: Mansell, 1980–1993).

20 For more on the importance of turning to anonymous works, see Arthur Marotti, 'The Verse Nobody Knows: Rare or Unique Poems in Early Modern Manuscripts', *Huntington Library Quarterly* 80, no. 2 (2017), 201–221. See also Marcy North on how pivotal anonymity was to early modern literary culture in *The Anonymous Renaissance: Cultures of Discretion in Tudor-Stuart England* (Chicago: University of Chicago Press, 2003).

21 http://en.wikipedia.org/wiki/British_Library,_MS_Egerton_1994 [accessed 17 August 2018].

22 http://searcharchives.bl.uk/IAMS_VU2:IAMS032-001982918 [accessed 17 August 2018].

23 Julie Sanders, 'Glapthorne, Henry', *Oxford Dictionary of National Biography* (2004): doi.org/10.1093/ref:odnb/10796 [accessed 17 August 2018]. See also Charles L. Squier, 'Henry Glapthorne (July 1610–1643?)', *Jacobean and Caroline Dramatists*, ed. Fredson Bowers, Dictionary of Literary Biography 58 (Detroit: Gale, 1987), 107–114.

24 Alan B. Farmer and Zachary Lesser, *DEEP* (University of Pennsylvania), deep.sas.upenn.edu; *ESTC* (British Library), estc.bl.uk.

25 Beal, *CELM*, 'About'.

26 Jamie 'Skye' Bianco explains that 'digital humanities is directly linked to the institutional funding that privileges canonical literary and historiographic objects and narratives'. See Bianco, 'This Digital Humanities Which Is Not One' in *Debates in the Digital Humanities*, ed. Matthew K. Gold (Minneapolis: University of Minnesota Press, 2012): dhdebates.gc.cuny.edu/debates/text/9 [accessed 19 December 2018]. For more on the canon-replicating tendencies of digital projects, specifically with regards to Shakespeare, see Estill, 'Digital Humanities' Shakespeare Problem', *Humanities* 8, no. 1 (2019), article 45, doi.org/10.3390/h8010045 [accessed 25 March 2019].

27 I would like to thank Pangallo for sharing his *DEMand* prospectus.

28 Martin Wiggins, *British Drama 1533–1642: A Catalogue*, vol. 1: 1533–1566 (Oxford: Oxford University Press, 2012), viii.

29 Knutson and McInnis, 'Lost Documents, Absent Documents, Forged Documents', throughout.

30 Love, 'The Work in Transmission and its Recovery', *Shakespeare Studies,* 32 (2004), 73–80; 74.

31 D.F. McKenzie, *Bibliography and the Sociology of Texts* (Cambridge: Cambridge University Press, 1999), 45.

32 Heather Wolfe, Principal Investigator, *Early Modern Manuscripts Online*, Folger Shakespeare Library, emmo.folger.edu [accessed 20 March 2019] See also Wolfe, curator, *Shakespeare Documented* (Folger Shakespeare Library), shakespearedocumented.org [accessed 20 March 2019], which documents selected Shakespearean dramatic extracts.

33 Robert Morissey and Min Chen, Primary Investigators, *Commonplace Cultures: Digging Into 18th-Century Literary Culture* (University of Chicago and University of Oxford), commonplacecultures.org/ [accessed 20 March 2019].

34 Estill and Montedoro, eds., *DEx: A Database of Dramatic Extracts*, Iter: Gateway to the Middle Ages and Renaissance, dex.itercommunity.org (in beta) [accessed 20 March 2019].

35 *DEx* links to library catalogue entries and facsimiles when available online, while also pointing to *CELM*, the Folger's *First Line Index*, and other relevant digital resources.

10

Typography *After* Performance

Claire M. L. Bourne

Are printed playbooks 'theatrical documents'? They were, as far as we know, not typically used to facilitate performance in the commercial theatre before 1642, but determining the extent to which they preserve traces of theatrical practice, and even specific performances, has been the aim of early modern drama scholarship from the New Bibliographers to current Performance as Research (or, Research in Action) practitioners.[1] W. W. Greg, A. W. Pollard, John Dover Wilson and others spent their careers trying to establish just how much 'theatrical' residue had stuck to playtexts as they were transmitted – in varied, circuitous ways – among playwrights and theatre personnel and, ultimately, into the hands of publishers, printers, and (finally) readers. For the New Bibliographers, reconstructing elusive (illusive, really) authorial manuscripts involved not only lifting 'the veil of print' – eradicating the vagaries of typesetting – but also stripping the text of playhouse interventions. Printed playbooks were *too* theatrical. More recently, reconstructions of early modern theatres, such as the Globe and the Blackfriars, have made it easier for researchers to experiment with simulating performance conditions and what that can teach us about how plays by Shakespeare and his contemporaries once inhabited those spaces. These experiments have entailed the reverse engineering of actors' parts, backstage plots, and other 'documents of performance' from published playbooks and, as such, have tested the potentials and limits of printed plays as scripts. In these cases, printed playbooks are often not theatrical *enough*.

Over the last two decades, though, book historians have insisted that printed playbooks, while they contain texts initially written for performance, were (and are) *books* designed to circulate in new, non-theatrical (although sometimes related) contexts from the embodied iterations of plays that readers might have seen on London stages. Viewed as independent, viable entities in their own right, playbooks are not 'theatrical documents' at all but rather objects made for the book trade.[2] They are neither 'contaminated' by the theatre nor created to function as records of past or scores for future performance. Instead, they are books of imaginative writing published to be bought, bound, and read alongside other print genres: from poetry to polemic, sermon to ballad, travelogue to newsbook, and so forth.

But how can a textual object designed to be enjoyed alongside other textual objects in the 'chamber-room at your lodging' be simultaneously 'theatrical'?[3] One answer inheres in the term 'document', a word that derives from the Latin *docēre* (to teach) and which was used in the sixteenth and seventeenth centuries exclusively to mean a lesson or instruction.[4] For all the inconsistencies and perceived messiness of moveable-type printing, printed plays were – and are – 'theatrical documents' insofar as they teach readers how to navigate and encounter the texts in front of them as *plays*. By the 1590s, the particular design characteristics of playbook *mise-en-page* evoked many of the extra-lexical, meaning-making effects of theatricality, most of which we assume to have been lost or erased or ignored in the process of repackaging playtexts made for one media environment (the theatre) to suit a different medium: the printed book. Typographic arrangements that accounted for the visual, sonic, and emotional 'energetics' of performance (the term is borrowed from Marta Straznicky) were vital to the legibility of printed matter specifically as *play-matter*.[5] These arrangements activated generic recognition, making it possible for readers (before reading a word) to know that what they were looking at was a play.[6]

The term 'document' did not come to refer to 'something written or inscribed' and, more specifically, something that could serve as material evidence for an external event or phenomenon until the early eighteenth century. Nevertheless, it has been widely adopted in modern scholarship – from Greg's *Dramatic Documents from the Elizabethan Playhouses* (1931) to Tiffany Stern's *Documents of Performance in Early Modern England* (2009) to the present volume – to denote any one of the variety of texts, including actors' parts, backstage plots, 'free-floating' songs and letters, and what Greg called 'prompt books' that enabled performance in the early modern theatre. Printed playbooks are certainly 'documents' in this anachronistic sense in that they are both physical texts ('something written or inscribed') *and* have been used as evidence – of authorial intention, of performance, of printing house practices. But what, exactly, do printed playbooks 'document'?[7]

To suggest that printed playbooks 'document' something external *at all* is to assert that they post-date (and are intrinsically linked to) previous events or phenomena. Yet they do not thoroughly describe performance, nor do they reproduce performance in a new medium. They do, however, 'document' a shifting set of distributed agencies – from company managers to playwrights to compositors. Their interventions are (together) evident on the printed page, but their individual contributions often cannot be isolated from the impacts of other hands, minds, bodies, machines, spaces, etc., that touched the text as it was – or the *texts* as they *were* – ultimately transmitted to readers. The typographic arrangements in most printed playbooks thus come *after* performance chronologically.[8]

Indeed, Francis Beaumont called the book a play's 'second publication'.[9] It is tempting therefore to treat playbooks as backwards-looking or as 'souvenirs'. Title-page marketing claims – 'as it was acted' – moreover encourage this kind of reading. And we often take these claims at face value and use them to dismiss printed plays as emaciated or inferior surrogates, just as some early modern playwrights did.[10] The book always already fails to capture the play 'as it was acted'.[11]

Yet playbooks were initially designed not as proleptic textual archives of performance but as commercial objects for contemporary readers. Scholarship in the history of reading over the last two decades has pushed back against the performance-oriented criticism of the 1980s and 1990s, which insisted that performance was the dominant 'end' of playwriting. It might have been the first 'end', but early modern playbooks are now understood to have been viable and popular entertainments in their own right. D. F. McKenzie in the early 1980s suggested that playbook typography could 'bridge a gap' between play-going and play-reading[12]; in his wake, others have started taking seriously the typography – broadly conceived as the disposition of printed matter on the page – of the earliest commercial-theatre playbooks.[13] Typographic reading as a method of inquiry comes *after* years of looking through the pages of playbooks to access something about performance. Only by understanding how early playbooks were designed to be read on their own terms and in their own moment can we start to understand how to read them as 'documents' of prior theatrical phenomena.

The typography of early modern playbooks, therefore, comes *after* performance both chronologically and methodologically (that is, as a valid object of study). But typography also comes *after* performance insofar as it correlates with performance and its effects. Instead of recording what happened on stage, playbooks document – to greater and lesser degrees – how a completely different medium (moveable-type printing) was mobilized to accord with theatrical effects. This rest of this chapter uses the earliest extant edition of

Love's Labour's Lost (1598) as a case study in typography that creatively accounts for those effects. Despite its title-page claim to present the play 'As it vvas presented before her Highnes this last Christmas', Q1 *Love's Labour's Lost* does not record an actual performance, nor prescribe future performances.[14] Indeed, scholars and editors sometimes call it 'unactable' because it is full of textual infelicities: variable speech prefixes for the same characters, orthographic errors, possible 'ghost' characters, and an unattributed final line, among others.[15] However, 'unactable' does not mean unreadable. In fact, the quarto contains an unusually varied range of typographic strategies that help 'vitalize' the play's non-verbal theatricality for readers. For a play whose plot turns on the (un)successful reading and performance of textual matter, it makes sense that Q1 positions readerly activity in the interstice between the idea of the play as a book and the idea of the play in performance. Q1 teaches readers how to see and hear the play's more complex theatrical moments and, in doing so, provides one of the best examples of an early modern playbook functioning as a 'theatrical document' for readers.

*

Q1 *Love's Labour's Lost*'s *mise-en-page* is unusually attentive to moments of theatricality where the effect of an exchange *for audiences* would have been staked on non-lexical business. These moments include instances of simultaneous speech and action; changes in tone or addressee (especially quick transitions from public to guarded speech); and longer episodes that switch between different layers of performance, such as the reading aloud of sonnets and letters; the Muscovite masque; and the Nine Worthies pageant. Published in 1598, when English playbook page design was still highly experimental, Q1 demonstrates dramatic typography's ability to display (that is, re-present) theatricality before even Ben Jonson began to micro-manage the typographic minutiae of his earliest quartos.[16]

The edition of *Love's Labour's Lost* now referred to as Q1 was quite possibly the second printed edition of the play. Its title page advertises a 'Newly corrected and augmented' text, and its printer William White was hired almost exclusively for reprints. The nature of the 'exit manuscript' (John Jowett's catch-all term for the variety of texts that 'migrate[...] from the theatre to the printing house') used as copy-text for Q0 (if it existed) or Q1 (if there was no Q0) has been extensively debated.[17] Whether set primarily from a working, possibly collaborative, draft of the play or a scribal transcript or an earlier printed edition set from one of these two kinds of manuscripts, Q1 is the material result of several agencies, and does not express the singular intention of playwright, scribe, publisher, printer, or compositor.[18] Even if the *mise-en-page* of the exit manuscript behind Q0 or Q1 cued the typographic arrangements now evident on the pages of Q1, those arrangements would survive not as the unthinking residue of textual transmission, but as choices: decisions to reproduce copy-text. And whether these arrangements were set out in a copy-text or originated in the printing house, their effects would have been the same for readers.

Love's Labour's Lost is undoubtedly a 'bookish' play. Its plot is animated by the circulation and 'miscarrying' of letters, as well as by the performance of lyric poetry not only from memory but also from papers brought on stage. The art of courtship is displayed by acts of inscription and reading. The King of Navarre's fellowship with his gentlemen companions is defined by their sworn commitment to book learning: they are called both 'bookmen' and 'book-mates'.[19] And Holferness's pedantry derives from his use (and misuse) of schoolbooks and dictionaries. In this play, books create the conditions for exploring the limits of self and identity.[20] At several moments, the play also anticipates knowledge of publishing conventions. Most notably, the comically smitten Don Armado's gleeful declaration that he will write sonnets to fill 'whole volumes in folio' registers his excess to anyone who understood that a folio was a big book; to the most literate auditors and readers, it also characterizes him as an incompetent lover, unaware that sonnets (and lyric poems, more broadly) were typically published in the smaller, more portable formats.

The overall conceit of *Love's Labour's Lost* – and Q1 is advertised as 'conceited' (witty *and* well-made) on its title page – concerns failed or interrupted performances within the play's fictional world: the selective reading aloud of letters; the guarded recitation of love poems while others (unseen) overhear; the pre-empting of inset performances. It is at these specific moments of performance that the play's dependence on theatricality – non-lexical business – to generate humour and tension intersects with its bookishness most explicitly *and* strains the capacity of print. But it is also at these moments that Q1 offers inspired typographic arrangements, which were completely novel to English playbook *mise-en-page* in 1598. Q1 is therefore at its most theatrical when it is at its most bookish.

The typographic treatment – and even presence – in printed plays of 'free-floating' texts (songs, letters, poems, proclamations) varies widely in play quartos of the 1590s. As Tiffany Stern has shown, these texts, many of which appeared or were represented in some physical form on stage (as was evidently the case in *Love's Labour's Lost* see Figure 10.1), often circulated apart from the 'allowed' book in the theatre. As a result, they did not always make it to the printing house with (or in) whatever kind of manuscript the publisher acquired. For instance, the lyrics of the song that Don Armado asks his page Moth to 'warble' are not present in Q1, which only supplies what seems to be its title: 'Concolinel'.[21] But elsewhere, letters and poems read aloud are carefully disposed on the page, none more so than the letter from the 'magnifisent [sic] *Armado*' that Dull, the constable, and Costard (also called '*Clowne*' in Q1) deliver to Ferdinand, the king, towards the beginning of the play.

(See Fig 10.1.) Before Ferdinand reads the letter, which reveals that Costard was caught consorting with the dairymaid Jaquenetta, Costard admits 'The matter is to me' (meaning, the

Ferd. Will you heare this Letter wth attention?
Bero. As we would heare an Oracle.
Clow. Such is the simplicitie of man to harken after the flesh.
Ferd. GReat Deputie the welkis Vizgerent, and sole dominatur of
       Nauar, my soules earthes God, and bodies fostring patrone:
Cost. Not a worde of *Costart* yet.
Ferd. So it is

Cost.

called Loues Labor's lo

Cost. It may be so: but if he say it is so, ne is in telling true:
but so.

Ferd. Peace.

Clow. Be to me, and euerie man that dares not fight.

Ferd. No wordes.

Clow. Of other mens secrets I beseech you.

Ferd. So it is besedged with sable coloured melancholie, I did
commende the blacke oppressing humour to the most holsome phisicke
of thy health-geuing ayre: And as I am a Gentleman, betooke my
selfe to walke: the time When? about the sixt houre, When Beastes
most graze, Birdes best peck, and Men sit downe to that nourishment
which is called Supper: So much for the time When. Now for the
groun.d Which? which I meane I walkt vpon, it is ycliped *Thy Park.*
Then for the place Where? where I meane, I did incounter that obseene & most propostrous euent that draweth fro my snowhite pen the
ebon coloured Incke, which here thou viewest, beholdest, suruayest, or
seest. But to the place Where? It standeth North North-east & by
East from the West corner of thy curious knotted garden; There
did I see that low spirited Swaine, that base Mnow of thy myrth,
(*Clowne.* Mee?) that vnletteed smal knowing soule, (*Clow.* Mee?)
that shallow vassall (*Clown.* Still mee.) Which as I remember,
hight *Costard,* (*Clow.* O mee) sorted and consorted contrary to
thy established procleymed Edict and continent Cannon: Which
with, ò with, but with this I passion to say wherewith:

Clo. With a Wench.

Ferd. With a childe of our Grandmother *Eue, a female;* or for thy
more sweete vnderstanding a Woman: him, I (as my euer esteemed
duetie prickes me on) haue sent to thee, to receiue the meede of pu-
nishment by thy sweete Graces Officer Anthonie Dull, *a man of
good reput, carriage bearing, and estimation.*

Anth. Me ant shall please you? I am *Anthony Dull.*

Ferd. For Iaquenetta (*so is the weaker vessell called*) which I
apprehende I with the foresayd Swaine, I keepe her as a vessell of
thy Lawes furie, and shall at the least of thy sweete notice, bring
her to tryall. Thine in all complements of deuoted and hartburning
heate of duetie.

                                              Don Adriano de Armado.

B.   *Ber.*

FIGURE 10.1 *A Pleasant Conceited Comedie Called, Loues labors lost* (London: Cuthbert Burby, 1598), A4v–B1r. By permission of the Folger Shakespeare Library.

letter concerns his behaviour), while Berowne anticipates the comic effect of the letter's 'stile' (it 'shall giue vs cause to clime in the merrines[s]').[22] Having already mentioned Don Armado's penchant for 'fire-new words', Berowne is eager to hear *what* Armado has written. But just as critical as the letter's words is the 'stile' in which Armado wrote it – and, presumably, the 'stile' in which it will be performed by Ferdinand. The shift in tonal register from Ferdinand speaking in his own voice to his ventriloquising of Armado's voice is marked by a change in typeface.[23] The beginning of the letter – the superscription – is articulated with a dropped initial, and the inscribed words are in italics, in contrast to the roman of the dialogue. The different typefaces made it easier for readers to know when to 'hear' the king's voice and when to 'hear' him voicing Don Armado.

But this episode of reading aloud also has an onstage audience whose interactions with the king's performance are rendered typographically, making lengthy descriptions of the encoded action unnecessary. In the course of Ferdinand's reading of the letter, Costard has nine lines in total. In three cases, he interrupts the king – the breaking off of the king's reading is signalled in two instances by colons and in one instance by a lack of punctuation.[24] In two other cases, the king tries to silence Costard so that he can continue to read. Even though each of these directives is followed by a full stop, Costard takes each one as the start of a longer syntactical unit: 'Peace.' / 'Be to me, and euerie man that dares not fight.' and 'No wordes.' / 'Of other mens secrets I beseech you.' The periods after the king's demands for silence signal that, at these moments, Costard is not interrupting.

Costard's other four lines are set inside parentheses and embedded in the text of the letter, an arrangement not used before, to my knowledge, in a printed commercial theatre playbook.[25] As Ferdinand reads Armado's account of witnessing the '*obseene & most propostrous euent*' that inspired him to write (sexual cavorting on the king's property), Costard slowly recognizes that the person Armado describes in the letter is he himself. Costard's parenthetical utterances, where both speech prefix (in italic type) and words uttered (in roman type) are set between round brackets, suggest a quite different temporal, tonal, and even spatial dynamic between the king's performance and Costard's verbally annotated audition. Instead of being sequential like the prior series of interruptions, the king's act of reading aloud and Costard's utterances are simultaneous.

Parenthesis is both a rhetorical figure and a typographic arrangement.[26] In speech, as on the page (thanks to the two 'half moon' glyphs that circumscribed parenthetical content), parenthesis provided the means by which to 'peece or graffe' together what George Puttenham called 'larger information' in the middle of an otherwise grammatically complete sentence.[27] That 'parcell' could be removed 'without any detriment to the rest' but was nevertheless considered important to the matter being presented.[28] Parenthesis simultaneously subordinated *and* drew attention to the words inside the brackets. And those words had the power not only to supplement the sentence but also to offer vital context (which allowed writers and speakers to clarify their attitude to the main issue at hand) for the extraparenthetical content. In particular, the use of typographic parentheses conveyed tone in early modern print. As Richard Mulcaster explained, parentheses 'warneth vs, that the words inclosed by them, ar to be pronounced with a lower & quikker voice, then the words either before or after them'.[29] Typographic parentheses invite readers to *hear* the words inside them differently.

Words contained inside typographical parentheses, according to Mulcaster, are neither 'impertinent' (i.e., irrelevant) to nor 'fullie concident [sic]' with the rest of the sentence: they indicate that the 'branch' of speech placed inside them is connected to the matter at large, while also distinguishing it in time, space, and quality. The parentheses around the text of Costard's reactions to the king's voicing of Armado's letter are designed to make Costard's reactions read as both unnecessary to but also not 'fullie concident' with the content of the letter. In other words, the letter itself is complete without them, but the dramatic situation is not. The *typographic* parentheses indicate that Costard's *verbal* parentheses do not interrupt Ferdinand but show him reacting verbally *at the same time as* the king reads the bulk of the letter. Though directly related to the content of the letter, they leave open the possibility that Ferdinand, who is Costard's primary onstage auditor, does not hear these tiny outbursts as his italicized reading proceeds.[30] The king reads the catalogue of derogatory epithets Armado uses to describe Costard ('*low spirited Swaine*', '*base Minow of . . . myrth*', '*vnlettered smal knowing soule*', and '*shallow vassall*'), and after each one, Costard goes from vocalizing 'Mee?' to 'Mee?' to 'Still mee.' to 'O mee.' If Q1's question marks are meant to be read *as question marks*, then Costard might initially doubt that he is the one being arraigned in the letter, or feign innocence. But, if they are read as exclamation marks (a distinct possibility since question marks were often used in early print to indicate both '?' and '!'), then readers would get the sense that he has been eagerly waiting to recognize himself in the letter: *There I am!* The ambiguity of this arrangement means that it does not record or provide a score for performance – but it *does* convey the complex non-lexical business of this episode. The arrangement of Costard's reactions inside parentheses and embedded in the longer letter not only accounts for the stage's capacity to show two things happening at once; it also demonstrates that typography has the capacity to offer multiple interpretive possibilities at once.[31]

These typographic parentheses probably cued readers to read for action as well as tone since, when the figure of parenthesis is explicitly evoked in dialogue of plays from the period, it is often used to describe (usually comic) action that dilates or breaks into speech. In Lodge's *Wounds of Civil War* (1594), for instance, the clown declares that he 'must make a parenthesis of this pint pot, for words make men dry'.[32] Here, the act of drinking from 'this pint pot' creates a parenthesis in the clown's speech. In *The Fair Maid of the Exchange* (1607), Cripple describes Bowdler as a 'due fond humorist, a Parenthesis of iests': Bowdler's jests are both physical and verbal.[33] Parenthesis can play *and* read as visible, antic digression. By presenting Costard's utterances embedded in the letter rather than set on their own lines, Q1 bifurcates the episode into two focal points. It is as much about Costard's comic self-incrimination as it is about Don Armado's hapless officiousness. The parentheses in Q1 *Love's Labour's Lost* supply both 'accent' (tone) and 'action' to produce an efficient textual arrangement that assumes readers' familiarity with typographical parentheses as signs of both subordination and significance.

*

In some of the play's other episodes of onstage reading, Q1 again signals the distinction between dialogue and text read aloud from a sheet of paper or performed in a different vocal register. Both Holferness's bawdy 'extemporal Epytaph on the death of the Deare' and the sonnet Longaville reads aloud as Ferdinand observes him unseen are inaugurated by glyphs that traditionally (that is, in printed plays and other genres) open new units of sense. Holferness's verse is introduced by a fleuron (❧), a symbol used in medieval manuscripts as well as early print to distinguish commentary from passages of main text, see Figure 10.2.[34] Holferness's poem indeed is a comment on the play's preoccupation with venery, both the hunting of animals and the pursuit of sex.

Then, in the scene that follows, Ferdinand (here, '*King*'), Longaville, and Dumaine – each believing himself to be alone – recite love lyrics composed for the ladies they are secretly pursuing. Modern editions typically specify that each man *reads* his poem, but Q1 specifies that only Longaville and Dumaine read theirs. There is no indication that the king speaks his sonnet from a paper. Instead, he recites it. And indeed the lines of the sonnet are set like normal dialogue – left-justified in roman type with no special typographic dispensation, see Figure 10.3. By contrast, the king states that Longaville enters 'reading' and a stage direction details that Longaville '*reades the Sonnett*'. Furthermore, a pilcrow (¶) is situated at the start of Longaville's poem giving it a visual separation from his other *called Loues Labor's loſt.*

Holo. Sir *Nathaniel,* will you heare an **extemporall Epy-**
taph on the death of the Deare, and to humour the igno-
rault cald the Deare: the Princeſſe kild a Pricket.

Nath. Perge, good M. *Holofernes perge,* ſo it ſhall pleaſe
you to abrogate ſquirilitie.

Holo. I wil ſomthing affect the letter, for it argues facilitie.

❧ The prayfull Princeſſe pearſt and prickt
   a prettie pleaſing Pricket,
Some ſay a Sore, but not a ſore,
   till now made ſore with ſhooting.
The Dogges did yell, put ell to Sore,
   then Sorell iumps from thicket:
Or Pricket-ſore, or els Sorell,
   the people fall a hooting.
If Sore be ſore, then el to Sore,
   makes fiftie ſores o ſorell:
Of one ſore I an hundred make
   by adding but one more l.

Nath. A rare talent.

Dull. It a talent be a claw, looke how he clawes him
with a talent.

FIGURE 10.2 *A Pleasant Conceited Comedie Called, Loues labors lost* (London: Cuthbert Burby, 1598), E1r. By permission of the Folger Shakespeare Library.

dialogue, see Figure 10.4. Inspired by the long-standing practice of medieval scribal rubrication (where red ¶ symbols were used to divide manuscripts into discrete parts), pilcrows, which were known earlier as *capitula*, or heads, were deployed in a variety of sixteenth-century printed texts to mark new units of text. They were used frequently in sixteenth-century printed plays to articulate units of dialogue and in books of lyric poetry to begin new poems.[35] The pilcrow at the start of Longaville's poem, like the fleuron at the beginning of Holferness's, signals that the text of the poem is qualitatively distinct from the

> *He ſtandes aſide.*   *The King entreth.*
> *King.* Ay mee!
> *Be.* Shot by heauen, proceed ſweet *Cupid*, thou haſt thumpt
> him with thy Birdbolt vnder the left papp: in fayth ſecrets.
> *King.* So ſweete a kiſſe the golden Sunne giues not,
> To thoſe freſh morning dropps vpon the Roſe,
> As thy eye beames, when their freſh rayſe haue ſmot.
> The night of dew that on my cheekes downe flowes,
> Nor ſhines the ſiluer Moone one halfe ſo bright,
> Through the tranſparent boſome of the deepe,
> As doth thy face through teares of mine giue light:
> Thou ſhinſt in euerie teare that I do weepe,
> No drop but as a Coach doth carrie thee:
> So rideſt thou triumphing in my wo.
> Do but beholde the teares that ſwell in me,
> And they thy glorie through my griefe will ſhow:
>   But
>
> *called Loues Labor's loſt.*
> But do not loue thy ſelfe, then thou will keepe
> My teares for glaſſes, and ſtill make me weepe.
> O Queene of queenes, how farre dooſt thou excell,
> No thought can thinke, nor tongue of mortall tell.
> How ſhall ſhe know my griefes? Ile drop the paper.
> Sweete leaues ſhade follie. Who is he comes heere?
>   *Enter Longauill.*   *The King ſteps aſide.*

FIGURE 10.3 *A Pleasant Conceited Comedie Called, Loues labors lost* (London: Cuthbert Burby, 1598), E2v–E3r. By permission of the Folger Shakespeare Library.

surrounding dialogue. In this way, the most abstract of typographic symbols teach readers to *hear* the poems in different vocal registers and to *see* their recitation as capsule performances inside a larger theatrical event.[36]

Elsewhere, too, typographic strategies for differentiating kinds of theatrical speech make it easier for readers to navigate

> *Long.* I feare thefe ftubborne lines lacke power to moue,
> O fweete *Maria*, Empreffe of my Loue,
> Thefe numbers will I teare, and write in profe.
>   *Ber.* O Rimes are gardes on wanton *Cupids* hofe,
> Disfigure not his Shop.
>   *Long.* This fame fhall go.   *He reades the Sonnet.*
> ¶ Did not the heauenly Rethorique of thine eye,
>   Gainft whom the world cannot holde argument,
>   Perfwade my hart to this falfe periurie?
> Vowes for thee broke deferue not punifhment.
> A Woman I forfwore, but I will proue,
> Thou being a Goddeffe, I forfwore not thee.
> My Vow was earthly, thou a heauenly Loue.
> Thy grace being gainde, cures all difgrace in mee.
> Vowes are but breath, and breath a vapoure is.
> Then thou faire Sunne, which on my earth dooft fhine,
> Exhalft this vapour-vow in thee it is:
> If broken then, it is no fault of mine:
> If by mee broke, What foole is not fo wife,
> To loofe an oth, to winn a Parradife?
>   *Bero.* This is the lyuer veine, which makes flefh a deitie.
>   E 3   A greene

FIGURE 10.4 *A Pleasant Conceited Comedie Called, Loues labors lost* (London: Cuthbert Burby, 1598), E3r. By permission of the Folger Shakespeare Library.

the play's complex business in which onstage audiences interact with onstage performers. For example, Moth's struggle to deliver his learned speech at the beginning of the so-called Muscovite masque is clearly illustrated by the use of italics to indicate his words, where roman type is used for Berowne and Boyet's interjections, see Figure 10.5.

At the sound of a trumpet, Moth enters '*with a speach*', says the stage direction, which suggests he (the character) might have had the option to read the speech from a paper though he attempts to perform it from memory. No sooner has he spoken his first line ('*All haile, the richest Beauties on the earth*'), but Berowne asserts that the women's beauty is 'no richer then rich Taffata', i.e. not visible because they are wearing taffeta masks.

> *Boy.* The Trompet foundes, be maſkt, the maſkers come.
>
> *Enter Black-moores with muſicke, the Boy with a*
> *ſpeach, and the reſt of the Lordes diſguyſed.*
> *Page.* All haile, the richeſt Beauties on the earth.
> *Berow.* Beauties no richer then rich Taffata.
> *Page.* A holy parcell of the fayreſt dames that euer turnd their
> backes to mortall viewes.
>   The Ladyes turne their backes to him.
> *Berow,* Their eyes villaine, their eyes.
> *Pag.* That euen turnde their eyes to mortall viewes.
> *Out*
> *Boy.* True, out in deede.
> *Pag.* Out of your fauours heauenly ſpirites vouchſafe
> Not to beholde.
> *Berow.* Once to beholde, rogue.
> *Page.* Once to beholde with your Sunne beamed eyes,
> With your Sunne beamed eyes.
> *Boyet.* They will not anſwere to that Epythat,
> You were beſt call it Daughter beamed eyes.
> *Pag.* They do not marke me, and that bringes me out.
> *Ber.* Is this your perfectnes? begon you rogue.
>   *Roſa.*

FIGURE 10.5 *A Pleasant Conceited Comedie Called, Loues labors lost* (London: Cuthbert Burby, 1598), G3v–G4r. By Permission of the Folger Shakespeare Library.

Berowne's intervention distracts Moth, who makes a mistake in his next line calling the women '*the fayrest dames that euer turnd their backes*' – rather than 'eyes' – '*to mortall viewes*', After this line in Q1 is a stage direction set in roman type (the only one in the whole quarto) to distinguish it visually from Moth's italics: 'The Ladyes turne their backes to him.' Berowne corrects Moth ('Their eyes villaine, their eyes'), and Moth then corrects himself: '*That euen* [sic] *turnde their eyes to mortall viewes.*' He then begins the next line with the word '*Out*' but now Boyet interrupts him to make a joke: 'True, out in deede.'

(The lack of a period after the single word set on its own line suggests the interruption.) What Boyet means is that Moth has been put 'out of his part' by the actions (and words) of his audience. Feeling their 'contempt', Moth's mistakes continue until he forgets his lines completely:

> *Pag. Out of your fauours, heauenly spirites vouchsafe*
> *Not to beholde.*
> *Berow.* Once to beholde, rogue.
> *Page. Once to beholde with your Sunne beamed eyes,*
> *With your Sunne beamed eyes.*

As Moth (here, '*Page*') repeats several words to jog his memory or cue Boyet to cue him, Boyet makes fun of the repetition, telling Moth that the ladies will not respond ('answere') to the 'Epythat' (epithet) '*Sunne beamed eyes*' (and presumably turn back around) even if he repeats it: 'You were best call it Daughter beamed eyes.' Moth's frustration comes to a head; he leaves his part completely. Here, his lines turn from italics to roman type: 'They do not marke me, and that brings me out.' The 'bringing out' that results from the onstage audience's mockery of Moth's performance is made clear by this shift in typeface; the lack of subsequent italics indicates that the masque itself is over.

The much longer and frequently interrupted performance of the Nine Worthies pageant towards the end of the play uses the same system of typographic differentiation to indicate where Costard, Nathaniel, Holferness, and Moth are speaking their parts and when they are directly engaging with the barbs and reactions of their onstage audience. In this way, italics are used fairly consistently throughout the playbook both to teach readers what dialogue is (i.e., the lines set in roman type) and to mark speech that is read or performed by characters within the fictional world of the play. Actual actors perform in roman type. Fictive actors – characters performing within the fiction – perform in italics.

*

Love's Labour's Lost is a play that dramatizes women's capacity to 'turn tutor' to men (that is, to instruct them) in the ways of love *and* the capacity of documents to communicate first- and second-hand truths (that is, to teach) about suffering for love on behalf of male authors.[37] The play has been described (and sometimes dismissed) as a loose patchwork of episodes that lacks a plot. But as Stern has shown, it was the nature of early modern plays to be patched in the first place, and in *Love's Labour's Lost*, this patchiness is, in a way, the point. Free-floating poems, letters, and dramatic set-pieces are stitched into the fabric of the play, where they serve as plot devices. Information only circulates through texts and the points of the plot are only linked through the failed, miscarried, and interrupted performances of those texts. The typography of Q1 manages to articulate both the presence of these texts and some vital effects of their performance: typeface differentiation, the choice placement of glyphs, and the parenthetical embedding of one character's words inside another's all document the tone and action of episodes where bodies make meaning. In doing so, typography renders legible (and audible) key aspects of the play's multi-vocal and multi-perspectival – and decidedly theatrical – meditation on the limited potential of courtship rituals and, in turn, mitigates against the failure of transmitting a text that is also a play to readers. Q1 therefore serves as a test case for printed playbooks as theatrical documents. Instead of being designed to facilitate performance, it was designed to facilitate reading *after* – in accordance with the meaning-making effects of – the play's theatrical incarnations.

Notes

1 On the possibility that printed playbooks were used to mount performances before 1642 despite the lack of extant evidence for such a practice, see Leslie Thomson, 'A Quarto "Marked for Performance": Evidence of What?', *Medieval and Renaissance*

Drama in England 8 (1996): 176–210. Some pre-1642 printed folios and quartos were certainly used as prompt books for professional revivals after 1660. See G. Blakemore Evans, *Shakespearean Prompt-Books of the Seventeenth Century*, 8 vols (Charlottesville: Bibliographical Society of the University of Virginia, 1960); and Edward A. Langhans, *Restoration Promptbooks* (Carbondale: Southern Illinois University Press, 1981).

2. See Zachary Lesser, *Renaissance Drama and the Politics of Publication* (Cambridge: Cambridge University Press, 2004); Jeffrey Todd Knight, *Bound to Read: Compilers, Collections, and the Making of Renaissance Literature* (Philadelphia: University of Pennsylvania Press, 2013); Aaron T. Pratt, 'Stab-Stitching and the Status of Early English Playbooks as Literature', *The Library*, 7th series, 16.3 (2015): 304–328; and Adam G. Hooks, *Selling Shakespeare: Biography, Bibliography, and the Book Trade* (Cambridge: Cambridge University Press, 2016).

3. Thomas Middleton and Thomas Dekker, *The Roaring Girle* (London: Thomas Archer, 1611), sig. A3r.

4. Lisa Gitelman, *Paper Knowledge: Toward a Media History of Documents* (Durham: Duke University Press, 2014), introduction.

5. Marta Straznicky, 'Plays, Books, and the Public Sphere', in *The Book of the Play: Playwrights, Stationers, and Readers in Early Modern England*, ed. Straznicky (Amherst: University of Massachusetts Press, 2006), 19.

6. On generic recognition see Knight, 'Economies of Scale: Shakespeare and Book History', *Literature Compass* 14.6 (2007).

7. For a particularly rich analysis of what printed playbooks do not document, see Richard Preiss's chapter 'Undocumented: Improvisation, Rehearsal, and the Clown' in this volume.

8. On this model of chronology, see, for example, Roslyn L. Knutson, *The Repertory of Shakespeare's Company, 1594–1613* (Fayetteville: University of Arkansas Press, 1991), 10–11. Masques, which were sometimes printed ahead of the performance event, are one obvious exception, as are William

Davenant's interregnum entertainments, which were printed with advertisements for performance.

9 Francis Beaumont, 'To my friend Maister *Iohn Fletcher*', in *The Faithfvll Shepheardesse* (London: Richard Bonian and Henry Walley, [1610?]), sig. ¶4v.

10 For evidence and discussions of this phenomenon, see Stephen Orgel, 'The Poetics of Spectacle', in *The Authentic Shakespeare and Other Problems of the Early Modern Stage* (New York: Routledge, 2002), 49; Laurie Maguire, *Shakespearean Suspect Texts* (Cambridge: Cambridge University Press, 1996), 56; and Jeffrey Masten, *Textual Intercourse: Collaboration, Authorship, and Sexualities in Renaissance Drama* (Cambridge: Cambridge University Press, 1997), 115.

11 This does not mean that printed playbooks have nothing to offer about early modern performance practices. Theatre historians have shown that printed playbooks preserve the contours of crucial localized moments and broader theatrical protocols. But treating playbooks as failures for proffering 'unactable' texts or texts that interfere with the scholarly aim of reconstructing performance ignores the status of printed plays as texts designed for reading.

12 D. F. McKenzie, 'Typography and Meaning: The Case of William Congreve', in *Buch und Buchhandel in Europa im achtzehnten Jahrhundert*, ed. G. Barber and B. Fabian, *Wolfenbüttler Schriften zur Geschichte de Buchsewens* 4 (1981): 83.

13 They include Linda McJannet, 'Elizabethan Speech Prefixes: Page Design, Typography, and Mimesis', in *Reading and Writing in Shakespeare*, ed. David M. Bergeron (Cranbury: Associated University Presses, 1996), 45–63; Zachary Lesser, 'Typographic Nostalgia Play-Reading, Popularity, and the Meanings of Black Letter', in *The Book of the Play*, 99–126; Holger Schott Syme, 'The Look of Speech', *Textual Cultures* 2.2 (2007), 34–60 and 'Jonson, Marston, and the Theatrical Page', *English Literary Renaissance* 38.1 (2008): 142–171; Claire M. L. Bourne 'Dramatic Pilcrows', *Papers of the Bibliographical Society of America* 108.4 (2014): 413–452; and Laurie Maguire, 'Typographical Embodiment: The Case of Etcetera', in *The Oxford Handbook of Shakespeare and Embodiment: Gender, Sexuality, and Race*, ed. Valerie Traub (Oxford: Oxford University Press, 2016), 527–548.

14 *A Pleasant Conceited Comedie Called, Loues labors lost* (London: Cuthbert Burby, 1598), [t.p.].

15 Georg Brandes, *William Shakespeare: A Critical Study*, vol. 1 (New York: The Macmillan Company, 1898), 48; and G. R. Hibbard, ed., *Love's Labour's Lost* (Oxford: The Clarendon Press, 1990), 65. The 1623 Folio text redistributes speech prefixes and assigns the play's final line, but also replicates some of Q1's arrangements.

16 On the shifting conventions of playbook typography in the sixteenth century, see T. H. Howard-Hill, 'The Evolution of the Form of Plays in English During the Renaissance', *Renaissance Quarterly* 43.1 (1990): 112–155; Bourne, 'Dramatic Pilcrows'; and Tamara Atkin, "Playbooks and Printed Drama: A Reassessment of the Date and Layout of the Manuscript of the Croxton "Play of the Sacrament"', *Review of English Studies* 60.244 (2009), 194–205.

17 John Jowett, 'Exit Manuscripts: The Archive of Theatre and the Archive of Print', *Shakespeare Survey* 70 (2017), 119.

18 For an overview of textual transmission theories, see Henry Woudhuysen, ed., *Love's Labour's Lost*, The Arden Shakespeare (London: Bloomsbury Publishing, 1998), Appendix 1.

19 *Loues labors lost* (1598), sigs. C3r and D3v.

20 Charlotte Scott, *Shakespeare and the Idea of the Book* (Oxford: Oxford University Press, 2007), 57; and Carla Mazzio, 'The Melancholy of Print: *Love's Labor's Lost*', in *Historicism, Psychoanalysis, and Early Modern Culture*, ed. Mazzio and Douglas Trevor (New York & Abingdon, Oxfordshire: Routledge, 2000), 189–190.

21 *Loues labors lost* (1598), sig. C3v. See Tiffany Stern, *Documents of Performance in Early Modern England* (Cambridge: Cambridge University Press, 2009), 122.

22 *Loues labors lost* (1598), sig. A4v.

23 On the typographic articulation of letters in plays, see Claire M. L. Bourne, 'Dramatic Typography and the Restoration Quartos of *Hamlet*', in *Canonising Shakespeare: Stationers and the Book Trade, 1640–1740*, ed. Emma Depledge and Peter Kirwan (Cambridge: Cambridge University Press, 2017); and Seth Lerer, 'Hamlet's Poem to Ophelia and the Theater of the Letter', *English Literary History* 81.3 (2014): 841–863.

24 See Woudhuysen, '"Dead, for my life": Stopping, Starting and Interrupting in Love's Labour's Lost', *Actes des congrès de la Société; française Shakespeare* 32 (2015): 2–3. On the use of colons, as well as a lack of punctuation, to mark interruption, see Percy Simpson, *Shakespearian Punctuation* (Oxford: The Clarendon Press, 1911), 71–74 and 98–99.

25 This observation is based on an original survey of typographic arrangements in playbooks printed in England from the sixteenth to eighteenth centuries.

26 John Lennard, *But I Digress: The Exploitation of Parentheses in English Printed Verse* (Oxford: Oxford University Press, 1991), 37; Jonathan Lamb, 'Parentheses and Privacy in Philip Sidney's Arcadia', *Studies in Philology* 107.3 (2010); and Jenny C. Mann, 'Sidney's "Insertour": *Arcadia*, Parenthesis, and the Formation of English Eloquence', *English Literary Renaissance* 39.3 (2009): 460–498.

27 George Puttenham, *The arte of English poesie* (London: Richard Field, 1589), sig. T4v.

28 Puttenham, *English poesie*, sig. V1r.

29 Richard Mulcaster, *The First Part of the Elementarie* (London: Thomas Vautroullier, 1582), sig. T3r.

30 Q1 *Love's Labour's Lost* features an extraordinary (for a playbook printed in the 1590s) number of parentheses, many of which could signal guarded speech or shifts in tonal register. Later, the King's Men scribe Ralph Crane would use parentheses more abundantly – and to similar effect – in his dramatic manuscripts. See Amy Bowles, 'Dressing The Text: Ralph Crane's Scribal Publication of Drama', *Review of English Studies* 67.280 (2016): 418–423.

31 Syme describes Jonson's varied strategies for articulating in print theatrical simultaneity in 'Unediting the Margin'.

32 Thomas Lodge, *The Wovnds of Ciuill War* (London: John Danter, 1594), sig. G3r.

33 *The Fayre Mayde of the Exchange* (London: Henry Rocket, 1607), sig. I2r.

34 Malcolm B. Parkes, *Pause and Effect: An Introduction to the History of Punctuation in the West* (Berkeley and Los Angeles: University of California Press, 1993), 181.

35 Bourne, 'Dramatic Pilcrows'.

36 On the next page, there is no glyph to introduce Dumaine's poem, but each line is indented to differentiate it visually, and a stage direction notes that Dumaine '*reades*'.

37 Kathryn Moncrief, '"Teach Us, Sweet Madam": Masculinity, Femininity, and Gendered Instruction in Love's Labor's Lost', in *Performing Pedagogy in Early Modern England: Gender, Instruction and Performance*, ed. Kathryn Moncrief and Kathryn Read McPherson (Aldershot: Ashgate, 2011), 214; and Mazzio, 'Melancholy of Print'.

11

Shakespeare the Balladmonger?

*Tiffany Stern**

This chapter is on the strange and complicated connections between ballads and the plays of Shakespeare. It considers, on the one hand, Shakespeare's explicit use of ballads both in performance and as printed texts in his plays; on the other the 'play ballads' for which he may or may not have been responsible, that tell the stories of bits of, and sometimes the entirety of, his plays. Asking whether Shakespeare promoted links between ballads and plays, or simply used them when they were there, it raises questions about the form and nature of theatrical marketing. How and why did plays batten on ballads? Did Shakespeare, or his theatre, ever market ballads to market plays?

Shakespeare, ballads and print

As is well-known, Shakespeare had a deep interest in producing what have come to be called 'art songs': coterie ditties – like '*Full fathom five*' (*The Tempest*, 1.2.397) – that he wrote as 'gifts' for the audience of specific plays and that seem to have been intended, at least from 1603, when his company became The King's Men, to be set to music by specific, often royal, composers.[1] But throughout his writing career, Shakespeare also made repeated use of songs with a different range and register: ballads.

Ballads are hard to define as texts. They are narrative songs, sometimes said to be identifiable by their 'ballad meter' – alternating tetrameter and trimeter iambic lines in an a.b.c.b. rhyme scheme – though many ballads of the early modern period do not actually take that metrical form. They are also said to be characterized by their well-known popular tunes, which often include a repeating chorus in which listeners can join, muddying the distinction between performer and audience. Yet ballads of the time regularly introduce new tunes as well as being set to old ones, and not all of them have a chorus or 'burden'.[2] The most consistent main 'ballad' indicator at the period was, perversely, not its form at all, but its dissemination. Unlike an 'art' song, which was play-specific, and was a gift for a specific audience (though not a gift that could be taken home), a ballad – in a play, about a play, or about anything else – was sung and sold from a published text. Ballads therefore were widely and easily available, had a clear, visual, print form, as well as an aural one, and could be acquired, carried home, owned, and (re)performed by anyone prepared to pay for the privilege.

'Broadside' or 'broadsheet' ballads, as they are called, consisted of folio-sized pages: they were large enough to be held up for communal performance and, as they were printed on one side only, they could also be pinned onto walls as singable texts that doubled as decoration. Their typical content was: a title; the name of the tune (using the formula 'to the tune of': no musical notation was supplied); one or a row of woodcuts; and, typically in black letter, the lyrics. Providing, then, sound, poetry and image on one single paper, ballads were multimedia print texts; but as they also brought singing about, they were oral, performance texts too. They were the most prominent bulk-selling texts on the market, and, at a penny or less, were also the most commercially viable.

Shakespeare's own interest in ballads may have stemmed from sales. Ballads covered the same range of topics that plays did – history, religion, contemporary politics, domestic drama; and took the same variety of approaches – tragical, comical, historical, pastoral (satirical, romantic, etc.). Like plays, they were often, but not always, anonymous; reliant on poetry; and did not have to be good to be popular. They even used the same lures – 'excellent', 'lamentable', 'true' – that were to be found on printed plays (plays may, indeed, have acquired their vocabulary from ballads). Moreover, ballads, like plays, gathered an audience to make money and relied upon performance for sales, as ballad-singer/sellers marketed their wares by singing them. What differentiated ballads from plays, however, was that their performances were designed to lead to print sales, while their print sales were designed to lead to further performances, as the purchaser of a ballad usually sang the text. Ballads may have seemed, then, a model for what plays could be: they sold excellently both as performance and print, without letting the one ever fully give way to the other.

The reach and coverage that print ballads offered, which extended well beyond London, seems to have fascinated Shakespeare. When Mopsa in *Winter's Tale* learns that Autolycus is selling ballads – nowhere near the town that will have generated them – she instantly declares both her familiarity with the form and her 'love' for it, specifically for 'a ballad in print' because 'then we are sure they are true' (*Winter's Tale*, 4.4.260–1). That observation, which on one level highlights her naivety, also witnesses the authority, and linked pleasure, the print form itself had for the buyer, 'love' not being a word Shakespeare used casually. As Mopsa's next request is that the Clown 'buy' her a ballad – and as she then sings one – so she, and behind her, Shakespeare, indicates how the fact of print ballads generated performances and sales far away from the site of origin.

A sizeable part of the rest of the scene is given over to the sale of one particular ballad. The thief-pedlar-balladmonger Autolycus presents *Get you Hence for I must Go*, and, as a routine part of his sales pitch, sings it; Mopsa and Dorcas join in. In terms of the fiction of *Winter's Tale*, the song's narrative, about two women who lay claim to one man, highlights the themes of fidelity, love and faith that are the focus of the rest of the play. But Autolycus, as he sings and sells in the fiction, also teaches the ballad's tune to the play's real audience, just as a genuine balladmonger would do (when a ballad was set to a new rather than old tune, it had to be learned from the singer). Here, the play may be teasingly parading a King's Men's inaccessible 'art song' as though it is a ballad – *Get you Hence* was, it seems, written by Shakespeare to music by Robert Johnson.[3] Alternatively, 'Autolycus', who on stage sings from a printed ballad text, is marketing the theatre's actual ballad, fictionally to Mopsa and Dorcas, and factually to us. We have paid for Shakespeare's play and for Autolycus' ballad, so we are already an extension of the naïve Mopsa and Dorcas. But are we even closer to them than we might care to think – taught a ballad that we are then, at the playhouse, given the opportunity to buy? If so, then 'ballads' can 'play' themselves (or, if not so, other ballads can enact them) in the complex way that books are shown to do in Wall-Randell's chapter in this volume.

To know whether Shakespeare was, in *Winter's Tale*, marketing an actual ballad sheet would require knowing whether *Get You Hence* really existed as a broadside. But here we come up against the problem that dogs all researchers of ballads. Ballads were ephemeral, and of the 4,000 ballads probably published before 1600 only about 260 survive.[4] Most ballads, that is to say, are lost. And, though some lost ballads can be learned about from the Stationers' Registers, remarkably few, proportionately, are to be found there: as it seems, many publishers simply did not register their ballads (or registered them without paying the additional charge for entrance). That means that this chapter is dependent on the few records in the Stationers' Registers, for which, often, no broadside survives, and the broadsides that are extant, for which, often, there is no trace in the Stationers' Registers. As a result, dating ballads is difficult: even if one can date a specific iteration of a ballad, whether it is a first edition or a reissue is often impossible to know, making it hard to assess whether plays adopt old ballads or introduce them for the first time. What has revolutionized ballad research, however, and made this chapter possible, is the brilliant *English Broadside Ballad Archive* (EBBA) website, which, over the years, has made surviving ballads gathered from different places publicly available online.[5] EBBA does not, alas, include *Get You Hence* and nor do the Stationers' Registers – but that does not mean that the song never existed as a broadside, or, of course, that it did. To trace Shakespeare's relationship to ballad sales, then, requires a closer analysis, both of the use he definitely made of them in performance, and of the use he may have made of them in print.

Ballads and performance

Many of Shakespeare's characters, including Falstaff, Sir Toby Belch, Mercutio, Edgar, Iago and Moth sing snatches and quotations from ballads as an aspect of their characterization.[6] That makes dramaturgical sense, both because the audience are likely to have associations with the lyrics, and because they are likely to have associations with the tune: tune, indeed, lodges in an audience's minds more powerfully than words, and using it is an easy way to change or shape mood.

Several Shakespeare plays, however, rely not on brief, haunting or delightful references to snatches of words and tune, but on sustained ballad performances.

In *Merry Wives*, the Welsh parson Sir Hugh Evans, thinking that he is going to have to fight a duel, tries to cheer himself up by singing lines from a ballad: 'pless my soul, how full of cholers I am, and trempling of mind ... How melancholies I am! ... To shallow rivers, to whose falls / Melodious birds sings madrigals –' (*Merry Wives,* 3.1.11–17). Evans eventually sings bits of two stanzas from what is called in broadsheet form *A most excellent Ditty of the Lovers promises to his beloved*.[7] What is seldom addressed, however, is that this passage of *Merry Wives* marks the earliest known outing *as a ballad* of what is often thought of as a pastoral poem, 'Live with me and be my love' (first published in *The Passionate Pilgrim* [1599] as a Shakespeare text, though it is attributed to Christopher Marlowe now).[8] In fictional terms, Evans's song brings out the play's theme of misplaced eroticism, while its reference to 'shallow rivers' jokily prepares the way for Justice Shallow, who then enters. In factual terms, however, *Merry Wives* features a ballad so new that, though sung in the play's first publication (1602), it was not to enter the Stationers' Register as a ballad until the next year (11 June 1603: showing that even entrance in the Stationers' Register is not always useful for dating). Perhaps 'Live with me' was always a ballad – it is, after all, listed as a 'song' in *Passionate Pilgrim* – Marlowe (or Shakespeare) emerging as a sometime balladwriter; perhaps the lyric circulated in two forms, song and poem. Either way, as the surviving broadside ballad text (a reissue from *c.* 1619–29) shows that the song had a specific tune written for it – 'to a sweet new tune called, *Live with me and be my Love*'[9] – the play may well have taught the tune to its audience as, it has been suggested, Autolycus did; an obvious way of promoting a broadsheet, of course, or of heralding one in advance of publication.

Another play that relies deeply upon the performance of a ballad – and, in this instance, one seemingly already in print – to make its point is *Othello*. In the Folio version of *Othello* there is a moment in which Desdemona recalls her mother's maid's unhappiness in love and how it found expression in an 'old' song; Desdemona sings the same song, which is later to be echoed by her own maid, Emilia.[10] The song, then, is a 'female lament', conveying women's shared sorrow over time and class:

DESDEMONA
> My mother had a maid called Barbary,
> She was in love, and he she loved proved mad
> And did forsake her. She had a song of 'willow',
> An old thing 'twas, but it expressed her fortune
> And she died singing it. . . .
>
> *[Sings.]*
> The poor soul sat sighing by a sycamore tree,
> Sing all a green willow:
> Her hand on her bosom, her head on her knee,
> Sing willow, willow, willow.
>
> (4.3.24–42)

The ballad that Desdemona sings survives in various manuscript witnesses as well as a printed broadsheet of the time, where it is called *A Lovers complaint being forsaken of his Love* and advertised as sung 'To a pleasant new tune' – another tune, then, that may need to be learned from a ballad-singer/seller or onstage.[11] The print text is both similar to and strikingly different from Desdemona's song, however. Though the words are almost the same in play and ballad, the subject of the ballad song is not a woman let down by a man, but a man let down by a woman:

> A poore soule sat sighing under a Sycamore tree
> *O willow, willow, willow,*
> With his hand on his bosome, his head on his knee,
> *O willow, willow, willow.*

For an audience who know the ballad, the changed sex of the hero allows Desdemona's song of female lamentation to gather up men's too: in 'The Willow Song', Desdemona's and Othello's unhappy fates are, to the initiated, conjoined. But to what extent did Shakespeare expect his audience to know the original ballad? Seemingly pretty well, for his text expects recognition of the ballad's words up to the seventh stanza, which Desdemona starts to sing and then makes a point of saying she has misremembered: '*Let nobody blame him, his scorn I approve* – / Nay, that's not next' (4.3.51–2, my italics). In so doing, she shows how 'conscious of the presence of a fixed (that is, printed) text' she is, as Porter points out.[12] But she also seems to ask those in the know to summon up the correct line, 'Let no body blame me, her scornes I do prove / She was borne to be faire, and I die for her love', a line that eerily foreshadows the play's end. Once again, this seems to be a Shakespeare who anticipates an audience with, or with close access to, a broadside.

Another play seemingly reliant on broadside knowledge is *Hamlet*. In all three surviving texts of *Hamlet*, variant in so many ways, Hamlet recites, or perhaps sings, sections of *Jephthah Judge of Israel*: 'One fair daughter and no more, / The which he loved passing well', 'as by lot, / God wot', 'It came to pass, / As most like it was' (*Hamlet*, 2.2.343–56). He too seems to expect detailed knowledge of the ballad's whole first verse:

> I Read that many yeares agoe,
>   when *Jepha* Judge of *Israel*,
> Had one faire daughter and no moe,
>   whom he beloved passing well:
> And as by lot God wot,
> It came to passe most like it was,
> Great Warres there should be,
>   and who should be the chiefe but he, but he.[13]

The many prompts that Hamlet gives seem designed to position Polonius as Jephtha, bad judge, and misguided chief in a war – the 'war', in *Hamlet* terms, being the brewing conflict between Claudius and Fortinbras, or the local battle between Claudius and Hamlet. And, as Jephtha, in ballad (and bible, of course) promised to pay for his victory by sacrificing the first living thing he comes across – only for it to be his virgin daughter – so Polonius, the parallel suggests, will end up sacrificing Ophelia. This seemingly marked and insistent use of intertextuality to enrich subtext, however, only works if the audience have comprehensive knowledge of – and perhaps easy access to – the ballad text itself.

Hamlet is, of course, a ballad-focused play. In it, mad Ophelia also performs well-known ballads, singing popular songs that reflect on the death of her father ('They bore him bare-faced on the bier') and the frustrations of her relationship with Hamlet ('I a maid at your window / To be your valentine') (4.5.48–161). The shattered heroine also asks the characters onstage to join her in singing the chorus, 'You must sing "a-down a-down", and you … "a-down-a"' (4.5.165–6), prompting the play's audience, too, to 'join in' the choruses, at least in their heads. She too advertises or extols particular ballads: her ballad references enhance our understanding of the text and, by sharing familiar tunes with us, she deepens our relationship with her while showing how permeable the distinction is between what is fictional and what is real.

Some plays seem particularly focused on selling ballads. In *The Tempest*, the drunken Stephano attempts to sing a song, 'Flout 'em and scout 'em', but gets the tune wrong; he is 'corrected' by the invisible Ariel, who, according to the stage direction, '*plays the tune on a tabor and pipe*', typical instruments for accompanying a ballad (3.2.121–4). As Ariel cannot be seen, however, the onstage characters are not able to determine the source of the music:

STEPHANO
  What is this same?
TRINCULO
  This is the tune of our catch, played by the picture of
  Nobody.

(3.2.125–6)

This reference, not just to 'nobody' – Ariel's invisibility – but to 'the picture of Nobody', is to a specific, purchasable, image. On 8 January 1606, the publisher John Trundle entered 'The picture of No bodye' in the Stationers' Register; three months later, on March 12 1605/6, he marketed the anonymous play

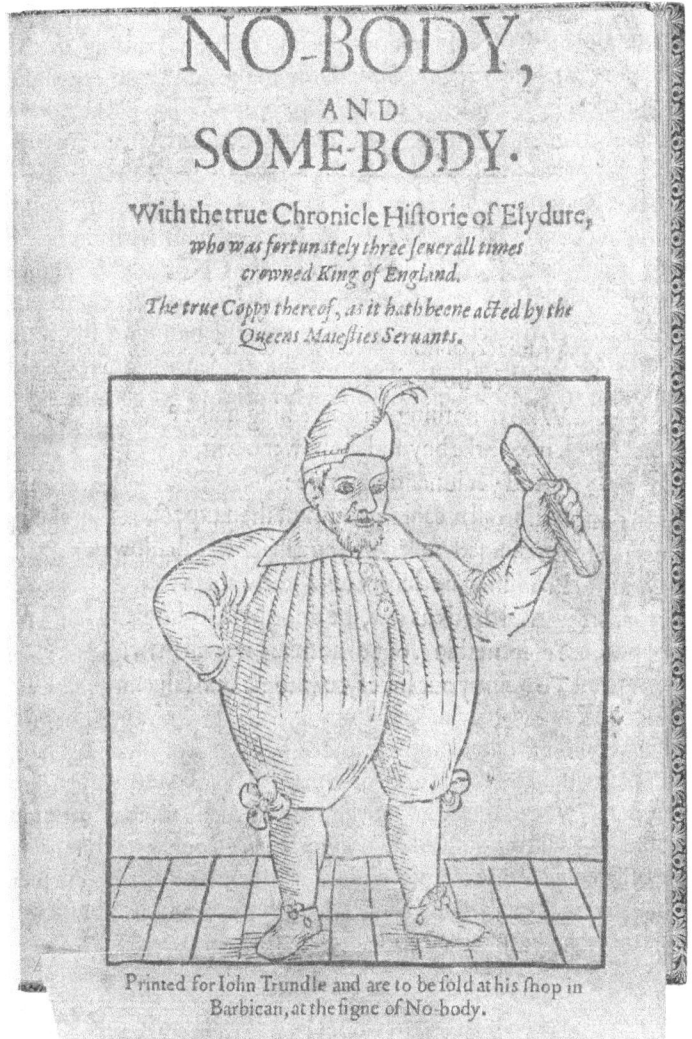

FIGURE 11.1 Anon, *No-body, and some-body* (1606), title page. By permission of the Folger Shakespeare Library.

that had made it famous, *Nobody and Somebody* with, on its title-page, the 'Nobody' picture; he also took to trading, as the title-page of *Nobody and Somebody* makes clear, at 'the signe of No-body'.[14] The pull of the *Nobody* picture is that, in a language-dependent joke, 'Nobody' has 'no body': just breeches from his neck downwards.

As the ballad *Nobody his Counsaile to chuse a wife*, featuring 'Nobody' and his ideal wife (a woman with no body, only a skirt) suggests, Trundle extended his 'Nobody' franchise into ballads.[15] *The Tempest*'s reference, then, to 'the picture of Nobody', seems to tell the audience that the ballad of the song is printed by Trundle. If so, then Shakespeare's only staged reference to a publisher, and one who printed playbooks, is in his ballad-making capacity – indeed, Shakespeare seems here to be promoting Trundle's ballad sales.

Whether 'Nobody' is a direct reference, or a hint, or a suggestion, Shakespeare was obviously intrigued by all print aspects of the ballad form. So, too, was Ben Jonson, whose *Caveat for Cut-purses*, the ballad for *Bartholomew Fair*, does survive as a broadside; woodcut images for other Jonson ballads, originally for masques but seemingly also sold as regular broadsides, are also extant.[16] In none of these instances is it clear who 'releases' the ballad as a broadsheet – author, company, no-one (a stage ballad could be 'taken' and expanded by ballad-printers instead). But given that Shakespeare often used ballads, and sometimes apparently wrote them, and given that all such ballads if printed would double as souvenirs and advertisements – while also making money in their own right – it is worth exploring further whether the theatre-ballad link might have been an intentional aspect of playhouse marketing.

Shakespeare play ballads

One reason why Shakespeare was partial to ballads will have been that he, and his company, participated in ballad culture. It was usual for plays of the period to close on a 'jig': a playlet in dance form ('jig' signifies a dance in a circle), typically set to one or several ballad tunes – indeed, as 'ballad' comes from 'ballare', to dance, the jig was the ultimate ballad. As a result, most plays in most theatres, until 1612 (when Middlesex magistrates attempted to suppress jigs, not necessarily successfully) ended with ballads, and most playgoers' final theatrical experience was a tune.

Because of jigs, Shakespeare's company, like all companies, needed ballad writers. Surviving music to 'Kemps Jegg' – i.e. music by William Kemp, the company's clown up to 1600 – together with Stationers' Register entrances for other Kemp jigs and ballads, suggests that clowns, who danced the jigs, sometimes 'wrote' them (see Preiss, in this volume).[17] Kemp's replacement, the 'wise fool' Robert Armin, meanwhile, is often linked with the ballad-writers Thomas Deloney, Philip Stubbs and William Elderton, and may even have been a professional ballad writer before becoming an actor.[18] Shakespeare, too, seems to have written jigs; one, 'When that I was and a little tiny boy', is latched to the end of *Twelfth Night* (5.1.382). 'When that I was' provides a narrative of the life of its clown-singer that supplies his own ironic take on marriage ('when I came, alas, to wive', 390). Raising questions about the happy ending of the play we have just watched, 'When that I was' seems the culmination of all the songs by Feste in the play, which, collectively, may tell the story of a man brought down by love, and ruined by marriage – thus offering a counter-narrative to the play.[19] This 'Shakespeare' or 'company' jig (it need not be by Shakespeare himself) shows plays and ballads to be performed in the same places for the same audience – and perhaps written by the same people too.

The fact that the company contained ballad writers may (but may not) explain the existence of another kind of ballad: one that told the story of the play. There is, for instance, an entrance on the Stationers' Register on 6 August 1596 for 'A newe ballad of Romeo and Juliett'. Though that ballad is lost, it was presumably inspired by Shakespeare's the bullard of *Romeo and Juliet*, in performance at the time, but not published as a playbook until the following year. By design or circumstance, the ballad of *Romeo and Juliett* will have advertised the play in performance, and potentially constituted one of its mementos. Ballads might equally advertise books. There is a double entrance on the Stationers' Register of 6 February 1594 for John Danter who records not just 'a booke intituled a Noble Roman Historye of TYTUS ANDRONICUS' – Shakespeare's play – but 'the ballad thereof'. He intends to publish both together, apparently expecting playbook and ballad to co-advertise one another. That gives evidence, then, of ballads printed apparently to advertise (or batten on) performance; and ballads printed to advertise (or batten on) a printed text. The issue is more complicated yet, however. The *Titus* ballad survives and in more than one

FIGURE 11.2 *Anon, A Ballad of the Lamentable and Tragical History of Titus Andronicus* (c. 1660), Huth 50 (69). By permission of the British Library.

version; some broadsheets for it contain a ballad-specific picture supplying highlights from the play/ballad – Lavinia writing her name in the sand; Aaron buried and lamenting; Lavinia and Titus cutting the throats of Chiron and Demetrius; Tamora and Saturninus getting ready to eat 'son' pie (the story is told out of sequence).

In its top right-hand corner is a depiction of a city which has, as its focal point, a large round theatre with its flag raised for performance. This picture seems, then, to refer not so much to Rome, the fictional city in which *Titus Andronicus* is located, as the factual city in which *Titus* can be seen as a play, London. That suggests that Danter, who may have published the ballad to help sell a playbook, or as an alternative text to a playbook, also ensured (or his successor ensured) it equally sold, reflected upon, or could be a memento of, performance. As Danter published, by my count, at least nine other 'play ballads' in the 1590s, for a range of authors and companies – the Stationers' Registers contain entrances from him for the ballads of 'the storye of tamburlane the greate', 'the murtherous life and terrible death of the riche jew of malta', 'a knacke howe to knowe an honest man from a knave', amongst others – he may have exploited theatre performances as an 'advertiser', or he may even have been paid by companies to produce texts that promoted, provided plot-summaries for, or were souvenirs of their productions.

The issue is only made more complicated by looking at other surviving 'Shakespeare' play ballads. There is the *Lamentable Song of the Death of King Leare*, gathered into Richard Johnson's *Golden garland of princely pleasures and delicate delights* (1620, but seemingly from an earlier broadsheet). But there are also ballads with a hazier connection to his dramas which, because hard to date, may be sources, reflections, fan-fiction-style extensions, or simply different versions of stories that Shakespeare told. *The Frolicksome Duke* tells the 'frame' story of *The Taming of the Shrew*: '*The Tinker's good Fortune. Who being found Dead Drunk, was conveyed to the Duke's Palace, . . . the next day being honour'd as the real Duke till they made him as Drunk as before, and then left him where they first found him*'.[20] But how does it relate to Shakespeare's play, and how to the play that may be source or reflection of it, *Taming of a Shrew*? The ballad '*shewing the crueltie of Gernutus a Iew, who lending to a Marchant a hundred Crownes, would haue a pound of his Flesh, because he could not pay him at the day appointed*' must relate to *The Merchant of Venice* – but, again, how, exactly? And then there is *Pyramus and Thisbe: or Love's Master-Piece*. Does that borrow from *A Midsummer Night's Dream*, give to it, or simply, as the play does, retell in somewhat jokey form a well-known story from Ovid's *Metamorphoses*. Given the number of 'play ballads' that survive for a range of texts, by Shakespeare and others, Bruce Smith concludes that some ballads were designed to perpetuate stage performance 'in another medium' as 'commercially produced residuals', the predecessors to today's marketing campaigns.[21] It is certainly the case that the topics picked by Shakespeare for his plays often had or forged ballad-relationships, seeming in some instances to be inspired by them, and in others to inspire them (there are several Robin Goodfellow and Poor Tom ballads that have the same 'tone' of the Shakespearean characters) – a fact that is hardly surprising given how ballad-conscious Shakespeare was throughout his writing career.

Ballads in the playhouse

That brings us to the heart of this chapter, and also its most speculative aspect: the relationship that Shakespeare and/or the Chamberlain's/King's Men and/or all theatres had commercially with the ballad trade. Were ballads, for instance, specifically sold in the playhouse?

As ballad-singer/sellers could set up anywhere they wanted – they did not need 'shops' – and were found wherever crowds gathered, they are likely to have stationed themselves around theatres. And, indeed, Robert Greene in 1592 writes of ballad-singer/sellers and their 'unsufferable loytring qualitie, in singing of Ballets and songs at the doors of such houses where plaies are used';[22] while years later, William Cartwright, follower of Ben Jonson and so-called 'son of Ben', in his university play *The Ordinary* has Catchmay and Sir Christopher trade insults:

SIR CHRISTOPHER
Thou'lt be . . . a Balladmonger.
CATCHMAY
I shall live to see thee
Stand in a Play-house doore . . . and cry small Books.[23]

The playhouse door of entrance is, of course, an obvious place for salespeople of all kinds, but particularly ballad-singer/sellers, to congregate: it is where queues form, both before and after plays, made up of people who have chosen to spend their money on entertainment and hence are natural ballad purchasers. But if, as these quotations may suggest, ballad-singer/sellers touted their wares around theatre doors as a matter of course, then an audience's experience of visiting a theatre was potentially bracketed at the start *and* end by ballads. The liminal nature of the space of sale, however, raises questions of its own. Did ballad-seller/singers only sometimes choose to station themselves around playhouses, or could they be relied on to be there, a daily part of the daily play? When there, did they have the theatre's tacit blessing or active encouragement? Or did they pay for – or alternatively were they paid for – access to the theatre's audience?

It is worth thinking about the role of ballads in the context of broader playhouse finances. The playhouse was a space in which not only plays, but linked entertainments – food, drink, books – were marketed.[24] At least some of these were sub-contracted as concessions: Henslowe in 1587 'will not permit . . . any person . . . other than . . . John Cholmley . . . to utter, sell or put to sale in or about the . . . playhouse . . . any bread or drink';[25] while at Whitefriars 1607/8 'if any . . . profit can or may be made in the said [play]house either by wine, beer, ale, tobacco, wood, coals, or any such commodity, ... Martyn Slater ... shall have the benefit thereof'.[26] And, looking forward in time, by the eighteenth century, theatres were offering concessions to the 'fruit women' who sold not only fruit and 'nonpareils' (candied sweetmeats), but also playbills and play songs.[27] Might sales of ballads always have been a purchasable concession? Alternatively (or, as well) might the theatre – which had, of necessity, a link to the print trade (the playbills that advertised performances were printed texts, and James Roberts, playbill-printer *c*. 1594–1606, was also a well-known ballad-printer) – have put money into the production of ballads, just as, by the eighteenth century, the theatre arranged for the publication of some of its songs?[28] On one level, it all depends on how 'knowing' the theatre was about marketing practices, like 'residuals', in the early modern period; on another, it depends on how 'knowing' Shakespeare himself was.

Shakespeare certainly seems to make regular, seemingly pointed attempts, to market ballads as shown by this chapter. Other examples seemingly of his pushing ballads include *Antony and Cleopatra*, in which Cleopatra, now Caesar's captive, has two concerns. One is that 'The quick comedians / Extemporally will stage us ... [and] I shall see / Some squeaking Cleopatra boy my greatness', a fear that is metatheatrically underlined by the fact that that is indeed happening; another that 'scald rhymers [will] / Ballad us out o' tune' (5.2.214–6). Metatheatrically – metaballadically – the second worry only makes sense if such a ballad is available, ideally where the very squeaking Cleopatra is performing. Likewise, in *A Midsummer Night's Dream*, Bottom 'awaking' from his extraordinary encounter with Titania, determines to 'get Peter Quince to write a ballad of this dream. It shall be called "Bottom's Dream and I will sing it in the latter end of a play"' (*MND*, 4.1.212–15). This too seems to herald a ballad, perhaps to be sung as a jig, maybe in the form of a burgomask, at the end of *Midsummer Night's Dream* – but, again, the promotion seems pointed: might it too have been purchasable as a souvenir?

When Falstaff, in *2 Henry IV*, says that if his bravery is not 'booked' (he wants it recognized textually), he will have his capture of Sir John Coleville printed in 'a particular ballad ... with mine own picture on the top on't, Colleville kissing my foot' (*2 Henry IV*, 4.2.47–8), he jests, but does he also build an interest in acquiring his outrageous song? After all, *The Winter's Tale*'s acknowledgement that its actual story is too complicated for a 'play ballad' – 'such a deal of wonder is broken out within this hour that ballad-makers cannot be able to express it' (5.2.23–5) – could potentially be seen as an explanation for the absence of a play ballad, and the existence of *Get You Hence* as the play's (only) memento.

These examples *may* show Shakespeare, individual in so many other ways, having a private, individual relationship with ballad publishers and/or singers, that involved channelling work to them – which he had sometimes also written – himself. Alternatively, as he was financially invested in the success of his company – he became one of its 'sharers' in 1594, and a 'housekeeper' in its buildings from 1599 – it may show him exploiting and teaching the use of ballads as pre-play publicity, plot summaries, or/and as post-play souvenirs.

Given that ballads linked to plays could serve as direct marketing, advertising, personal selling, sales promotion, and publicity – said to be five quintessential elements of sales promotion – they certainly provided in their natures all the elements of a powerful marketing campaign. And, in view of the fact that a host of plays of the period employ ballads – Ross Duffin, writing just on English Renaissance comedies up to 1625, identifies over 600 such ditties – and many plays of the period also have 'play ballads' written about them (my researches have so far revealed over 60 play ballads), could it be that that ballads were a potential extension of the 'playbill' and that all companies used them on occasion?[29]

Whatever is the case, as the word 'balladmonger' ('monger' meant 'trader') in the period sometimes indicated a balladseller and sometimes ballad-writer, Shakespeare emerges as at least one form of balladmonger, and perhaps both. That raises questions about how to interpret ballads 1) in plays and 2) about plays. As the only published bits of play generally available at the time of performance are ballads – in and about plays – are they a part of theatrical marketing or cross-marketing? Or are they sometimes, or always, neglected textual extensions of plays themselves? Perhaps, they are intermediate: part of the play if to hand and not if not, in a confusion of permanence and impermanence, print and performance, peritext and epitext, that mirrors the complex life of early modern plays, and Shakespeare's ambiguous role in their popularity and survival. Whatever is the case, Shakespeare seems to have used ballad performances to make points that extended beyond interpretation into the confusing world of shared experience that joined fictional characters and audience. He reverenced, referenced – and on occasion expected access to – broadside ballads. This chapter has suggested reasons as to why that may be.

Notes

* This chapter is dedicated to the memory of brilliant, passionate, kind, thoughtful, driven, wonderful Stephanie Dumke (1981–2018).

1 Discussed in William Shakespeare, *The Tempest*, ed. Alden T. Vaughan and Virginia Mason Vaughan (London: Bloomsbury Arden Shakespeare, 2011), 18–19, where the musical setting is also reproduced. All subsequent Shakespeare references are to Arden 3 editions. That the company regularly used the royal composer is suggested by Tiffany Stern in *Documents of Performance in Early Modern England* (Oxford: Oxford University Press, 2009), 149.

2 Different definitions of ballad in the period are discussed in David Lindley, *Shakespeare and Music* (London: Thomson Learning, 2006), 70–76.

3 A manuscript of theatre songs *c.* 1630 survives, many of which are by Robert Johnson. It is discussed in 'Music and Song' in

The Winter's Tale, ed. John Pitcher (London: Bloomsbury Arden Shakespeare, 2010), 389.

4   Bruce R. Smith, *The Acoustic World of Early Modern England: Attending to the O-Factor* (Chicago: University of Chicago Press, 1999), 170.

5   *The English Broadside Ballad Archive* (EBBA), ed. Patricia Fumerton (http://ebba.english.ucsb.edu; accessed 19 July 2018). All broadsides quoted in this chapter are from this website (but with i/j and u/v regularized for ease of reading).

6   For a full list of ballads referred to in Shakespeare's plays, see Helen Sewell, 'Shakespeare and the Ballad: A Classification of the Ballads Used by Shakespeare and Instances of Their Occurrence', *Midwest Folklore*, 12 (1962), 217–234.
    For their musical settings, certain and conjectural, see Ross Duffin, *Shakespeare's Songbook* (London: W. W. Norton, 2004).

7   British Library, Roxburgh, EBBA 30141 (1619–1629?).

8   The book is attributed in its entirety to Shakespeare, though many of its poems – which seem to have been collected together by the publisher William Jaggard – are apparently by other people. When 'Live with Me' is reprinted in a year later in John Bodenham's *England's Helicon* (1600), it is longer; has a new first word 'come'; a new title, 'The passionate Sheepheard to his loue'; and a new attribution, 'Chr. Marlow'. It is that version, and that authorship, that is generally accepted now – though Shakespeare's use might give us pause.

9   A musical setting for the song survives in William Corkine's *Second Book of Aires* (1612).

10 The ballad is prepared for, but not sung in the Quarto, probably because of vocal issues in the playhouse. See *Othello*, ed. E. A. J. Honigmann (London: Bloomsbury Arden Shakespeare, rev edn with new introduction by Ayanna Thompson, 2016), appendix one, 349–356.

11 Magdalene College, Pepys, EEBA 20167 (1615?).

12 Gerald Porter, 'Telling the Tale Twice Over: Shakespeare and the Ballad', in *Ballads into Books: The Legacies of Francis James Child,* ed. Tom Cheesman and Sigrid Rieuwerts (Bern: Peter Lang, 1997), 171.

13 *[A proper new ballad, intituled], When Jepha Judge of Israel*; Manchester Central Library, EBBA 36107 *c.* 1620.

14 All references to the Stationers' Register are quoted from Edward Arber, *A Transcript of the Registers of the Company of Stationers of London,* 5 vols (London: 1875–1884).

15 Magdalene College, Pepys, EBBA 20177. Printed in *c.* 1622, this is apparently a later iteration of a Trundle text.

16 British Library, Roxburgh, EBBA 30274 *c.* 1647; pictorial traces from Jonson broadside ballads from masques are discussed in John P. Cutts, 'Seventeenth-Century Illustrations of Three Masques by Jonson' *Comparative Drama,* 6 (1972), 125–134.

17 For more on this subject, see Roger Clegg and Lucie Skeaping, *Singing Simpkin and Other Bawdy Jigs* (Exeter: University of Exeter, 2015), 21–23.

18 Thomas Nashe, *Strange Newes* (1592), D4v.

19 Tiffany Stern, 'Inverted Commas around the "Fun"': Music in *Twelfth Night*', *Twelfth Night: A Critical Guide*, ed. Alison Findley and Liz Oakley-Brown (London: Methuen, 2013), 166–188, 175.

20 Magdalene College, Pepys, EBBA 21895 (*c.* 1664–1703).

21 Bruce R. Smith, 'Shakespeare's Residuals,' in *Shakespeare and Elizabethan Popular Culture,* ed. Stuart Gillespie and Neil Rhodes (London: Arden Shakespeare, 2006), 194–195.

22 Robert Greene, *The third and last part of conny-catching* (1592), B1v.

23 William Cartwright, *The ordinary* (1651), 51–52.

24 See Tiffany Stern, '"Fill thy Purse with Money": Shareholders, Shakespeare and Theatrical Finance', *Shakespeare Jahrbuch,* 150 (2014), 65–78.

25 Dulwich, Mun.16, *English Professional Theatre, 1530–1660,* ed. Glynne Wickham, Herbert Berry and William Ingram (Cambridge: Cambridge University Press, 2000), 425.

26 PRO, C2 Jas.I/A6/21, transcribed in *English Professional Theatre, 1530–1660,* 270.

27 Valerie Fairbrass, '"Books of the Songs to Be Had at the Theatre": Some Notes on Fruit Women and Their

Contribution to Theatre Finances', *Theatre Notebook*, 66 (2012), 66–84.

28 See Tiffany Stern, 'Playbills and Title-Pages', in *Documents of Performance in Early Modern England* (Oxford: Oxford University Press, 2009), 36–62; and Fairbrass, *passim*.

29 Ross W. Duffin, *Some Other Note* (Oxford: Oxford University Press, 2018).

PART FOUR

Lost Documents

12

Lost Documents, Absent Documents, Forged Documents

Roslyn L. Knutson and David McInnis

To speak of a 'lost play' and an 'extant play' is ostensibly to posit a simple dichotomy in ontological status, but the reality is more complex and involves a continuum of 'lostness'. This is in part because, as Tiffany Stern has noted, 'a play was pieced together out of a collection of odds and ends; it was not a single whole entity' but something 'patchy' – any one of these odds and ends could easily become separated from its group and subsequently lost altogether.[1] In addition to the documents that constitute a play, there are also the documents a play generates through the processes of composition, performance, and publication (as previous chapters in this volume have demonstrated). Scholars who attend to this vast assemblage of documentation find that their sense of how much is lost and how little survives changes radically. For example, *Titus Andronicus* – now widely believed to have been co-authored by William Shakespeare and George Peele – appears to be an early modern play near the 'extant' end of a lost-to-extant spectrum due to its many surviving records. *Titus* was registered for publication by John Danter at Stationers' Hall on 6 February 1594, and printed by him later that year (Q1, STC 22328). It was published twice more in quarto (1600) and octavo (1611), and twice with other plays in folio (1623, 1632) prior to 1642, appearing in the Stationers' Register three more times (1602, 1626, 1630). This paper trail provides substantial information on its company affiliations. The title page of the 1594 Quarto advertises that three companies had performed the play: the Earl of Derby's Men (formerly Lord Strange's Men), the Earl of Pembroke's Men, and the Earl of Sussex's Men; the title page of the 1600 Quarto adds a fourth, the Lord Chamberlain's Men (later the King's Men, who are advertised on the 1611 title page).

The stage history of the play in London is also well documented in the book of accounts, or 'diary', kept by Philip Henslowe between 1592 and 1603. Henslowe recorded three performances at the Rose playhouse in January 1594 and two at the playhouse in Newington in June 1594 (the Newington entry adds the Admiral's Men to the companies with repertorial links to *Titus*). To these events may be added the following: a performance at the Manor House of John Harrington in Rutland on 1 January 1596; performances during a continental tour sometime before 1620; an illustration by Henry Peacham of what might be the play in performance; and seventeenth-century editions of a 1594 ballad (see Stern's chapter for more on the ballad). This apparently full record notwithstanding, *Titus* is missing significant evidence including a backstage plot, actors' parts, a playbill, a title or scene board (for more on these, see Steggle's chapter), an actual manuscript, and confirmation of co-authorship.

As co-editors of the *Lost Plays Database* we have often necessarily restricted the focus of our inquiries to the ontological status of play-texts. In this chapter we complement our work on plays by considering losses in records from both the playhouse and the larger world in which theatrical activity in England took place. We believe that the documents generated by plays in composition, performance, and print are beneficially contextualized by this wider view. Until recently, the study of lost documents has been a neglected field. In 1962 Bernard Beckerman asserted with the confidence of a scholar who knew the thinking of his peers that theatre historians 'need be grieved little by the disappearance of 75 per cent of the plays' on stage with Shakespeare's at the Globe because those lost plays were 'filler'; he praised the repertory system for 'winnowing out the chaff'.[2] We think about documentary losses differently. We argue that an awareness of gaps in the historical record enables us to assess extant evidence more shrewdly, as well as to be open to resources that have not yet exhausted their information on the early modern theatrical marketplace. Below, we consider the repertory system, playwrights and players, evidence from court and provincial performances, and the information in office books from various governmental agencies. In the process, we consider also absent documents and forgeries.[3]

Repertory documents

A play called 'Titus & ondronicus', which scholars have agreed is the *Titus Andronicus* so well documented earlier, first appears in Henslowe's diary along with other plays being performed by Sussex's Men at the Rose between 27 December 1593 and 6 February 1594. Because Henslowe listed the plays by title (there are twelve altogether), the diary provides the repertory to which *Titus* belonged during that run. Similarly, by naming the seven plays given at Newington in June 1594, Henslowe identified the repertory offered there over a ten-day period by the Admiral's Men and Chamberlain's Men (in some sense jointly, though Henslowe neglects to document the details of this arrangement).[4] But what of the other repertories in which *Titus* participated? Many theatre historians believe the play was new as early as 1589,⁵ but no evidence survives to locate it in any company's repertory at that time; likewise, no evidence identifies its repertorial mates after it migrated to the Chamberlain's/King Men.

Lamentable as the loss of repertory lists is for plays with extant texts and known company affiliations, it is even more regrettable for plays with neither. Consider the play *c*. 1588–89 for which Thomas Nashe implied an existence when he satirized poets who could spout 'whole Hamlets, I should say handfuls of Tragicall speeches' on command.⁶ Thomas Lodge also implied the existence of such a play in *Wit's Misery* (1596) when his narrator calls one of Beelzebub's devil-sons a 'fiend... [who] looks as pale as the Visard of ye ghost which cried so miserally at ye Theator like an oister wife, *Hamlet, reuenge*'.⁷ If Nashe and Lodge were referring to some play named 'Hamlet', the loss of its repertorial context in 1589 and/or 1596 deprives theatre historians of possible clues to its kinship with the *Hamlet* ascribed to Shakespeare that we know from editions in 1603, 1604–5, 1611, and 1623. But, sadly, that later *Hamlet*'s repertorial context is also lost. We do not have playlists from the Chamberlain's Men in 1599–1604 from which we might learn the titles of 'revenge tragedies' that may have shared the stage with Shakespeare's *Hamlet*; and we cannot say whether there were other contemporary offerings that complemented through comedic motifs or historical narratives conventional features in that *Hamlet*, such as a garrulous old courtier or a hastily remarried widow. Further, without repertory lists, we miss evidence that would show whether the King's Men returned *Hamlet* to the stage *c*. 1609–10, the success of which revival perhaps prompting its reprinting in 1611. Only one document locates a play featuring the character of Hamlet in repertory, and that is Henslowe's all-too-brief list of the Newington performances in June 1594. At present, we lack sufficient documentary evidence to determine the textual and commercial relationships of these 'Hamlet'/*Hamlet* plays.⁸

When Henslowe cast up his accounts 'frome the begininge of the world vntell this daye beinge the 14 daye of marche 1604',⁹ he sounded the death knell for a decade-long period of repertorial information in which he had recorded theatrical activities at the Rose and Fortune playhouses. The loss that theatre historians suffer by Henslowe's abrupt stop is illustrated most acutely with regard to the Admiral's Men (by 1604, Prince Henry's Men). Although occasionally Henslowe recorded the business of other companies (i.e., Pembroke's Men in October 1600; Worcester's Men in 1602–03), the primary focus of his accounting was the Admiral's Men, whose repertory he documented from 1594 to 1597 and whose expenditures for playbooks, apparel, and other company matters he listed from 1597 to 1603. Presumably, the company continued to play at the Fortune as vigorously as they had previously. However, it is not until 1624, when Sir Henry Herbert, Master of the Revels, entered in his Office-Book a list of fifteen plays newly licensed for the Admiral's/Prince Henry's Men (known as Prince Charles's Men by 1613) that a repertory list for the company resembling the fullness of one constructible from Henslovian data can be found. In that twenty-year gap, theatre historians have little more than printed editions to identify extant plays owned by this company and only one record, a note signed by the clerk of the Office of the Chamber on 15 June 1613, that provides the titles of lost plays. It names a pair of plays—parts one and two of 'The Knaves'– which were performed at court by 'the Princes servauntes' the previous March.[10] If Prince Charles's company repertory lists for performances at the Fortune playhouse in 1612–13 were not also lost, we would know more about the commercial environment of the two-part 'Knaves' than its plain-Jane title suggests. That wished-for repertory list, a decade into the Jacobean period, would also provide evidence on a topic hotly debated by theatre historians: the divide across companies between so-called 'citizen' drama at outdoor playhouses and classier 'elite' drama for indoor venues. Assuming 'The Knaves' was a 'citizen' drama, was its offering at court (an indoor venue for the elitist of the elite) therefore an aberration? If we had complementary information for the company repertory, we could provide an answer to this question that has some basis in historical data.

Such lacunae in the documentary record are a siren call to forgers, who recognize (1) the pragmatic opportunity to insert new repertorial information into a convenient gap and, more interestingly, (2) a scholarly yearning for supplementary data. Accordingly, at the lower margin of fol.11v of Henslowe's diary, the Victorian scholar John Payne Collier took the liberty of adding an entry for a play he called 'galfrido & Bernardo', which he subsequently transcribed into the edition of Henslowe that he published.[11] Collier's response to loss is fraudulent, even unethical, but it nevertheless points to the important question about how to respond to such documentary loss or absence. Scholars active today may not introduce forgeries to supplement an archival lack, but they do either ignore the lack altogether (yielding a distorted conclusion) or confidently supply conjecture as if it were fact. Such methodology puts at risk the wider community of scholars, who reproduce these dubious versions of the historical record because they trust the venerable reputation of their fellows.

Documents of playwrights

If Henslowe had acquired *Titus* as a new play in 1598, he probably would have written down the names of the playwright/s who wrote it. Switching in 1597 from the practice of recording daily performances at the Rose, he began instead to enter payments to specific authors for scripts (as well as other commercial activity); consequently, his diary from 1597 to 1603 is a rich source for names of playwrights in early modern England. Of special interest here are the men (including players) who are not identified elsewhere as writers of dramatic material, such as William Haughton, William Rankins, William Bird (Bourne), 'Mr Pett' (Haughton's collaborator on 'Strange News Out of Poland', 1600) and 'Mr Robinson' (Henry Chettle's collaborator on 'Felmelanco', 1602). These men, demonstrably known to the theatrical world of early modern London, are conspicuously absent from the current documentary record.

However, Henslowe's accounts are by no means complete; he did not always enter the details of his transactions with playwrights, despite having the opportunity to do so.[12] Consequently theatre historians rely on other documents to supplement the information the diary provides. One such is *Palladis Tamia* (1598), the moral, critical and literary reflections of Francis Meres. Meres claims that Thomas Heywood and Richard Hathway were accomplished writers of comedy, though no comedic titles can be associated confidently with Hathway until July 1598 ('Valentine and Orson') or with Heywood until December 1598 ('War without Blows and Love without Suit').[13] Meres also describes Thomas Dekker as being 'amongst our best for Tragedie',[14] though no tragic works by him dated 1598 or earlier survive under his name. Perhaps this is why Collier took pains to enlarge the credentials of Dekker as a tragedian by inserting a payment to him into Henslowe's accounts on 20 December 1597 for additions to *Faustus* and a prologue to *Tamburlaine*.[15]

In general, playwrights not recorded in Henslowe's diary fare badly in terms of archival preservation. An example is Thomas Watson (1555–1592), who is known to have contributed plays to the Queen's Men after their formation in 1583. Watson influenced fellow dramatists including Christopher Marlowe and Thomas Kyd, and was recalled fondly by Meres, Dekker, and others for his great learning. However, there is no surviving play, title, or even document that identifies a play as his in the archives.[16] Theatre historians even struggle to identify the dramatists who – with Shakespeare – wrote for the Chamberlain's Men. Andrew Gurr estimates that the company had '140 or so' plays now perhaps lost, plus 23 extant ones to 'match' the 161 staged by the Admiral's Men, 1594–1600.[17] The authors of some of these plays are identifiable through title-page ascriptions (e.g. *Every Man in His Humour* names Ben Jonson, *Satiromastix* names Thomas Dekker), but other plays were printed without authorial attribution (*A Warning for Fair Women*) or recorded by title in contemporaneous letters or diaries but subsequently lost ('Gowrie'). A pair of plays, 'Cloth Breeches and Velvet Hose' and *A Larum for London*, appear on a flyleaf in the Stationers'

Register in May 1600 where they are identified as Chamberlain's plays; both now are anonymous but in their own time the company would have known who the authors were (as might playgoers). The dearth of information about these plays is compounded by potential absences in the Stationers' Register entry itself: the heading, 'my lord chamberlens mens Plaies Entred', implies an intention of the clerk to add more titles, but the list stops. A similar phenomenon can be observed in a record of performances at court by the King's Men in the winter of 1604–05: they prepared twelve plays but performed eleven; the identity of the twelfth remains a mystery. The clerk of the Office of Revels simply recorded 'A playe provided And Discharged' on Sunday, 3 February 1605, but did not enter a title or author.[18] As with the apparently unfinished list in the Stationers' Register, the Revels record is one of documentary absence rather than loss: the document survives and the opportunity existed for the Revels clerk to record the twelfth play's details alongside its scheduled date of performance, but he did not do so.

Bleak as the prospect is of adding authorial attributions to lists of performances for the Chamberlain's/King's Men, it is bleaker still for companies without a Shakespeare, Jonson, or Heywood consistently in their employ. In the Jacobean period, companies under the patronage of the Duke of Lennox and the Duke of York included players from earlier decades; they must likewise have had experienced as well as (perhaps) new playwrights, but there is no record as to who they were. Even the records of the children's companies, which are comparatively well-documented in print in 1599–1608, do not identify more than a few plays in any given year by author. For theatre historians, this paucity of knowledge limits our ability to assess playwriting as a profession in the Jacobean–Caroline years; in particular, we are short of the information necessary to evaluate the versatility of individual authors in response to always-popular motifs as well as to the sudden emergence of new fashions in the theatrical marketplace.

A kind of bardolatry (or 'Shakespeare-effect') is observable in the realm of forgeries, where the desperate search for new information about Shakespeare takes precedence over exciting non-Shakespearean discoveries, as Estill's chapter in this volume explores. Such is the case with the 'Play of Oswald'.[19] A casual inspection of the British Library's detailed catalogue entry provides the impression that the manuscript warrants little attention: 'f. 37 William Shakespeare: Forged allusion to him: 19th cent.'[20] The reference here is to a suspected Collier insertion consisting of a cryptic reference to Shakespeare ('will shake') at the end of the document: 'yett the curre is of a good breede, *and to one hee knowes / will shake his tayl*' (the authenticity of the words italicized here has been disputed).[21] Whether a forged or simply implausible allusion, this manuscript is a red herring in terms of Shakespeariana; it is more interesting as a dramatic fragment in its own right. Its date and authorship are uncertain but it appears to originate from the late-sixteenth or early-seventeenth century public theatres. It contains material from the end of the play, in which Oswald's true identity is revealed through distinctive birthmarks; this bears an uncanny resemblance to the denouement of *Cymbeline*, though it is impossible at present to establish the direction of influence, if any.[22] The fragment preserves a not-insubstantial passage of dialogue, of obvious interest to students of Shakespeare's theatre, but the playscript as a whole is lost and the purported allusion to Shakespeare dominates what little critical discussion there is of the manuscript.

Provincial and court documents

Since 1979 when the first in a continuing series commissioned by the Toronto-based 'Records of Early English Drama' (REED) was published, theatre historians have had access to more data about theatrical activity in the provinces of England from the Middle Ages to 1642 than any previous generation of scholars. And yet, not a single REED item supplies the title of a London-based commercial play that was also performed in the country (though a letter by Edward Alleyn does; see later). However, one lawsuit known to scholars since 1942 hints at a touring repertory; it gives the titles of four plays belonging to a company arrested for sedition in Yorkshire in 1609.[23] REED records also do not add names to the list of dramatists who wrote for companies in the London and provincial marketplaces. What information, then, might we have if provincial records were better preserved and more detailed? We might, for example, know the titles of plays (and their playwrights) taken into the country by the Queen's Men, whose repertory carried the monarch's agenda in politics and religion to her subjects from Cornwall to Northumberland starting in 1583.[24] We might also track the entry of new plays into performance through the 1580s. At present, we know that *The Famous Victories of Henry V* was on stage in 1587, but we do not know if it was then new. It was printed with an advertisement of the Queen's Men in 1598, but that date was probably a decade after its maiden run.

Second, we might learn what shows Lord Strange's Men took on tour with 'Harry of Cornwall' in the summer of 1593. We know about that play because Edward Alleyn wrote to Henslowe in August 1593 and said that his company was 'redy to begin the playe of hary of cornwall'.[25] Henslowe had recorded this play as one of 24 performed at the Rose from February to June, 1592 (it was not then new). But provincial records are blank not only on the performance of 'Harry of Cornwall' but also on the names of other plays in Strange's summer touring repertory. Third, provincial records are largely silent on the titles of plays (and authors) given at the manors and castles of wealthy and titled families. According to Barbara D. Palmer, 'the Clifford and Cavendish accounts make up perhaps the largest continuous body of information available on visits of professional players to provincial great houses'; sadly, though, that massive archive does not name a single play seen by that privileged audience.[26]

Sometimes records from the court supplement other caches of documents. In 1583–84, the clerk at the Chamber Office entered payments for three plays given by the newly formed

Queen's Men at Christmastide, and two each by the Children of the Chapel and the Earl of Oxford's Boys; the clerk at the Revels Office complemented that record by specifying that six histories had been performed and one comedy.[27] But neither clerk named a title. In 1584–85, the Chamber clerk paid the Queen's Men for five performances, 26 December–23 February; and *this* year, the Revels clerk named the four plays ('Phyllida and Corin', 'Felix and Philomena', 'Three Plays in One', and 'Five Plays in One' [plus an 'Antick' and a comedy]). It is indicative of the fate of plays and the eccentricity of record-keeping that in such an instance – where so much information is provided – the plays themselves are lost. In an ideal world, clerks of the Chamber and Revels Offices would have done routinely what their counterparts did in 1604–05 and 1611–12, which was to enter the customary details (date, company, play title, payments to companies, royal audience). And, in that ideal world, the playscripts themselves would have survived.

Governmental documents

Theatre historians depend on records kept by governmental agencies and agents including those of the aforementioned Office of the Chamber and Office of the Revels; the Privy Council; the Admiralty; the Courts of Chancery, Requests, and the Exchequer; city and crown officials such as the Mayor of London and Bishop of London; and wardens of the guilds. A sample from just a few of these resources will illustrate how valuable surviving documents are and how frustrating their archival loss. An example is the infamous 'Isle of Dogs' affair. On 28 July 1597, the Privy Council issued a letter to the Justices of Middlesex ordering that 'no plaies shalbe used within London' and that the playhouses were to be 'plucked downe'.[28] On the same day, the Lord Mayor petitioned the Privy Council to do precisely that: shut down playing. Two weeks later (15 August) the Privy Council sent a letter to Richard Topcliffe to arrest Thomas Nashe and question him about a lewd play recently staged on the Bankside. And in between, on 10 August, Philip Henslowe made a note in the diary that William Bird had joined the Admiral's Men because there was a restraint against playing prompted 'by the meanes of playing the Ieylle of dooges'.[29] There are more official records and personal commentary on this disruption in playhouse business (e.g., players were imprisoned and released; Nashe, having fled to Yarmouth, complained about the charges against him), but absolutely nothing among surviving documents confirms the implication that the Privy Council ordered all playhouses to be 'plucked downe' *because* of 'The Isle of Dogs'.[30] In this case as in others, forgery supplements the conspicuous lack of evidence, thereby inadvertently identifying critical desires: a Collier intervention on fol.33v of Henslowe's diary purportedly documents a payment to 'the M^r of the Revelles man ... for newes of the restraynte beinge recalled by the lords of the Queenes counsel'; it follows earlier wish-fulfilment forgeries on fols. 29v and 33r which present a memorandum of payment to Nashe 'for the Iylle of dogges wch he is wrytinge for the company' and another to Nashe 'at this tyme in the flete for Wrytinge of the eylle of dogges'.[31]

Scholarly knowledge of licensing documentation has been enhanced by a series of serendipitous events. Extracts of the dramatic records of Sir Henry Herbert, Master of the Revels between 1623 and 1673, were published by Edmond Malone in the late eighteenth century, but by 1818 the papers had all but disappeared, as had the transcript Malone claimed to have made of Herbert's office-book.[32] Nevertheless, from Malone's notes we have some Herbert traces, meaning we know about such lost plays as 'Doctor Lambe and the Witches' and 'Buc is a Thief'. Craven Ord (1756–1832) also copied licensing transcriptions from Herbert's original manuscripts before they were lost; he did not publish his work but allowed other scholars to consult it.[33] A subsequent owner of Ord's transcription, Jacob Henry Burn (1793–1869), copied Ord's notes of play-licences into his own notebook (the anonymous

'The Lovesick Courtier' and Richard Brome's 'Florentine Friend' are known only through the Burn transcript).[34] When James Orchard Halliwell-Phillipps acquired the Ord transcript after Burn's death, he cut it into individual licence records, some of which are now lost; some are affixed in his various scrapbooks (including Folger MSS W.b.137–256). A further palimpsest layer is present in that these transcriptions (and copies of transcriptions) of Herbert's records sometimes also contain Herbert's records of *earlier* Master of the Revels' accounts; for instance, the record apparently made in 1661–62 of a note dated 20 November 1622 registers 'Seuerall Plays allowed by Mr Tilney In 1598. which is .62. years since' (including the lost 'Sir William Longsword', 'Fair Maid of London', and 'Richard Coeur de Lion').[35] The survival of multiple independent transcriptions of sections of Herbert's licensing records, and multiple copies of those transcriptions, is fortuitous in the extreme, but even so, caution must be exercised: these are transcriptions not primary documents.[36]

Another collection of official documents impoverished by archival loss provides information about the people associated with the playhouse world. Perhaps the most precious of these is the parish register. In 1536 Thomas Cromwell, on behalf of King Henry VIII, ordered that parishes keep registers of births, burials, and marriages.[37] For theatre historians the registers from parishes with playhouses are special because theatre professionals tended to live near their place of work: St Leonard Shoreditch (the Theatre), St Giles Cripplegate (Fortune), and St Saviour Southwark (Rose, Swan, and Globe). However, not all parish clerks noted more than name and date. At St Leonard, for example, the burial entry for Richard Tarlton on 3 September 1588 gives his address as Halliwell Street but does not add that he was a player, or playwright, or the most famous clown of his generation. James Burbage, a man of considerable commercial status in the parish (also a joiner and a player), was listed as buried on 2 February 1596/7 with no further detail; his son Richard, who was the star power of the Chamberlain's-King's Men for more than two decades (as Syme discusses in his chapter) was acknowledged merely as 'player' when buried on 16 March 1618/9. In contrast, the clerk at St Giles Cripplegate provides a thumbnail narrative in the entry of christening for 'Comedia base borne Daughter of Alice Bowker and as she saithe the fathers name is William Johnson one of the Queens plaiers' (February 1586/7). In the register of St Saviour, there is an entry of burial dated 31 December 1607 for Shakespeare's brother, 'Edmond Shakespeare, a player'; ancillary parish books, in this case the monthly accounts, record that he was 'buried in the church, with a forenoone knell of the great bell, 20s'.[38] The giant among parish supplementary books is the set of daybooks kept by Thomas Harridance at St Botolph, Aldgate, *c.* 1583–98; he recorded, over time, a family history for James Tunstall, a player with the Alleyns and their companies for most of his professional career.

Wills are another source. Tunstall's will survives, as do those of William Shakespeare, Edward Alleyn, and Christopher Beeston. Alleyn and Beeston are known to have owned plays, yet their wills do not mention a single book title. Even so, wills provide information not available elsewhere. The will of Simon Jewell (d. 21 August 1592) itemizes his debts and credits with his company; it also specifies bequests of his playing gear ('my playenge things in a box and my veluet shewes'). The will of Augustine Phillips (d. 4 May 1605) itemizes not only his gifts to fellow players but also to his former apprentices, Samuel Gilburne ('the some of ffortye shilling*es* and *my* mouse Colloured veluit hose and a white Taffety dublet A blacke Taffety sute my purple Cloke sword and dagger') and James Sands ('my base viall ... the some of ffortye shilling*es* and a Citterne a Bandore and a Lute'). Both apprentices remained in the profession as adults.[39]

*

Expertise, confidence, and certainty are desirable traits of academic research, but the latter is easily confused with the former two. Scholars often construct compelling narratives of early modern theatrical activity without being sufficiently shrewd in accounting for the loss, absence, and forgery of evidence. Previous chapters in this volume have demonstrated that a significant body of documentation survives, but simultaneously affirm that it remains a mere fraction of the theatrical activity of the period. That fraction is statistically atypical; it in no way guarantees that we know more about the masterpieces of dramatic literature. Indeed, the example of *Titus* illustrates that the greatest plays are not necessarily the best papered. In this chapter, we have stepped outside the playhouse to consider the loss of documentation beyond that on authorial composition, players' performances, and print culture to show how much more is additionally lost (and also how much remains to be discovered). Alongside a reinterpretation of surviving evidence, we recommend an openness to new sources of information (who knew that sewer records could yield data on playhouse architecture and players' daily lives?). As participants in the scholarly process of rethinking the contribution of documents from the court, manor house, Guild Hall, parish, and civic agencies, we are confident that further archival work will produce additional evidence to clarify and extend the narratives we currently tell about the literary and commercial world of theatre in the early modern period. Here, we highlight a few of the categories of documents historically perceived as ancillary to the study of theatre history in early modern England that could legitimately be said to be at its heart. Much of their data may indeed be lost, but perhaps the records are just waiting to be found.

Notes

1 Tiffany Stern, *Documents of Performance in Early Modern England* (Cambridge: Cambridge University Press, 2009, rpt. 2012), 1. In *Digital Humanities and the Lost Drama of Early Modern England: Ten Case Studies* (Farnham: Ashgate, 2015)

Matthew Steggle – co-editor with Roslyn L. Knutson and David McInnis of the *Lost Plays Database* (*LPD*) (2009): https://lostplays.folger.edu – suggests that the very title of a play can itself be considered 'a "miniature" document of performance' (19).

2 Bernard Beckerman, *Shakespeare at the Globe 1599–1609* (New York: The Macmillan Company, 1962), 16.

3 We define absent documents as lacunae in records where nothing has technically been lost because it was never entered; we consider forgeries to be barometers for evidence that is missing yet desirable enough to falsify.

4 In another instance of absent documentary evidence, Thomas Heywood similarly neglected to elaborate on his address to the reader prefacing *The Iron Age, part 1* (1632), wherein he notes that 'these were the Playes often (and not with the least applause) Publickely Acted by two Companies, vppon one Stage at once' (Heywood, *The Iron Age* [London: Nicholas Okes, 1632, STC 13340], A4v).

5 Gary Taylor and Rory Loughnane, 'The Canon and Chronology of Shakespeare's Works', in Gary Taylor and Gabriel Egan, eds, *The New Oxford Shakespeare: Authorship Companion* (Oxford: Oxford University Press, 2017), 417–602, esp. 490.

6 Ronald B. McKerrow, ed., *The Works of Thomas Nashe*, 5 vols (London: A. H. Bullen, 1904), 3.315.

7 Edmund Gosse, ed., *The Complete Works of Thomas Lodge*, 4 vols (Glasgow: The Hunterian Club, 1883), 4.56/62. Although Lodge omitted the title of the play, he provides details of costuming, dramaturgy, and script that point unmistakably to the Hamlet story.

8 We follow a practice now common in the field of theatre history to mark lost plays by quotation marks and extant plays by italics. For clarity and consistency, we standardize the spelling of titles to conform to usage in the *Lost Plays Database*. All lost plays addressed here have entries on that website.

9 R. A. Foakes, ed., *Henslowe's Diary*, 2nd edn (Cambridge: Cambridge University Press, 2002), 209.

10 David Cook and F. P. Wilson, eds, *Malone Society Collections VI* (Oxford: Oxford University Press, 1961), 54.

11 Foakes, ed., 28n. For a digitization of the forged entry for 'Galfrido and Bernardo', see the *LPD* entry.

12 Neil Carson claims that that the diary 'formed only part of Henslowe's accounting records, which included also formal bonds and very likely one or more ledgers', which he bases on Henslowe's lack of repayment records, inexplicable calculations of total outstanding debt, and sudden absolution of debts (*A Companion to Henslowe's Diary* [Cambridge: Cambridge University Press, 2005], 30).

13 Francis Meres, *Palladis Tamia* (London: Cuthbert Burby, 1598, STC 17834), Oo3v. To make sense of Meres's claim, Martin Wiggins (in association with Catherine Richardson) records untitled comedies by Heywood (#1044) and Hathway (#1068) in *British Drama 1533–1642: A Catalogue*, 10 vols (Oxford: Oxford University Press, 2012—). For the Hathway and Heywood payments, see Foakes, ed., 89 and 102.

14 Meres, Oo3.

15 Foakes, ed., 44n.

16 Michael J. Hirrel, 'Thomas Watson, Playwright: Origins of Modern English Drama', in David McInnis and Matthew Steggle eds, *Lost Plays in Shakespeare's England* (Basingstoke: Palgrave Macmillan, 2014), 187–207.

17 Andrew Gurr, *Shakespeare's Opposites: The Admiral's Company 1594–1625* (Cambridge: Cambridge University Press, 2009), 1.

18 W. R. Streitberger and John Pitcher, eds, *Malone Society Collections XIII* (Oxford: Oxford University Press, 1986), 9.

19 British Library MS Egerton 2623, ff. 37–38; see also the *LPD* entry and Wiggins #1260.

20 See http://searcharchives.bl.uk/IAMS_VU2:IAMS032-001983597.

21 E. K. Chambers, *William Shakespeare: A Study of Facts and Problems* (Oxford: Clarendon Press, 1930), 2.386; cf. Arthur Freeman and Janet Ing Freeman, *John Payne Collier: Scholarship & Forgery in the Nineteenth Century* (New Haven: Yale University Press, 2004), 2.1038.

22 See McInnis, 'Lost Plays and Source Study', in Dennis Austin Britton and Melissa Walter, eds, *Rethinking Shakespearean*

Source Study (London: Routledge, 2018), 304–307, for a discussion of the parallels.

23 Charles J. Sisson, 'Shakespeare Quartos as Prompt-Copies', *The Review of English Studies,* 18 (1942), 12–43. The plays named were 'The Three Shirleys' (i.e., *The Travels of Three English Brothers*), *Pericles*, a 'King Lere', and a St Christopher play.

24 Scott McMillin and Sally-Beth MacLean, *The Queen's Men and their Plays* (Cambridge: Cambridge University Press, 1998), 18–36.

25 Foakes, ed., 276.

26 Barbara D. Palmer, 'Early Modern Mobility: Players, Payments, and Patrons', *Shakespeare Quarterly,* 56.3 (2005), 259–305, esp. 271.

27 E. K. Chambers, *The Elizabethan Stage,* 4 vols (Oxford: The Clarendon Press, 1923), 4.159–160.

28 Chambers, 4.322.

29 Foakes, ed., 240.

30 William Ingram, *A London Life in the Brazen Age; Francis Langley 1548–1602* (Cambridge, MA: Harvard University Press, 1978), 167–196; see also, the *LPD* entry.

31 Foakes, ed., 68n, 63n, and 67n.

32 N. W. Bawcutt, ed., *The Control and Censorship of Caroline Drama: The Records of Sir Henry Herbert, Master of the Revels 1623–73* (Oxford: The Clarendon Press, 1996, rpt. 2003), 13–16; and Edmond Malone, 'An Historical Account of the Rise and Progress of the English Stage', in *The Plays and Poems of William Shakspeare,* 10 vols (London: H. Baldwin, 1790), vol.1, part 2, 1–287 (Malone quotes Herbert's office-book throughout this account of the stage, rather than reproducing lengthy excerpts of it in one location).

33 Bawcutt, ed., 17–19.

34 MS Osborn d1 (Beinecke Rare Book & Manuscript Library, Yale University; the *Lost Plays Database* has sponsored the digitization of the Burn transcript, excerpts of which are available on the relevant entries.

35 Bawcutt, ed., 249, item R29.

36 A cautionary example is the plot of '1 Tamar Cham', the original of which was lost after being transcribed by George Steevens in *The plays of William Shakspeare*, 21 vols (London: 1803), vol.3, foldout after 414. See that transcription in the *LPD* entry and W. W. Greg's scepticism of its accuracy in *Dramatic Documents from the Elizabethan Playhouses: Stage Plots, Actors' Parts, Prompt Books: Commentary* (Oxford: Oxford University Press, rpt. 1969), 160.

37 E. A. J. Honigmann and Susan Brock list 162 parishes inside and outside the City Walls in *Playhouse Wills 1558–1642* (Manchester and New York: Manchester University Press, 1993), xvii–xxii.

38 Edmund was christened on 3 May 1580 (see 'Parish register entry recording Edmund Shakespeare's baptism' in *Shakespeare Documented*, https://shakespearedocumented.folger.edu/).

39 Honigmann and Brock, 59, 73. Phillips is one of many theatrical people named also in the token books of St Saviour Southwark, which (along with more kinds of information) provide street addresses and household size (William Ingram and Alan H. Nelson, eds, *The Token Books of St Saviour Southwark*: http://tokenbooks.folger.edu/).

Afterword

'What's Past Is Prologue'

Peter Holland

'No people live longer than the documents of their culture'. 'Kein Volk lebt länger als die Dokumente seiner Kultur.' It is an unnerving quotation to begin with but Hitler's statement, in his speech on 11 September 1935 to the Conference on the Cultural Politics of the Nazi Party in Nuremberg, is intriguing. His solution, with its own finality, was to exterminate both people and their documents, be they Jews, Roma or gays. But his comment became a slogan that was worked into Third Reich art objects, like the tapestry that was placed in the SS-Ahnenerbe Haus in Berlin,[1] or on the catalogue for the Allach porcelain factory that opened in 1939,[2] or as the inscription on the Haus der deutschen Kunst in Munich that Samuel Beckett (of whom more later) saw in March 1937, noting in his diary that it offered '[p]leasant possibilities of application', a comment that Mark Nixon describes as made 'wryly'.[3]

As this collection has investigated documents of a past culture it has tried to bring something back to life, by rethinking the documents that constitute the material evidence of a particular moment in theatrical culture, the historical moment that we call, though no-one then did, 'Shakespeare's England'.[4] And what we call a document might not have been given the same label then either. As Tiffany Stern mentioned in the Introduction, referring to Claire Bourne's chapter, the word *document* meant '"teaching" or "instruction" rather than, as now, the inscribed paper that contains them' so that 'performance was itself a "document", and that theatrical events, for which there may never have been paper witnesses . . . are "documents" too' (p. 5). *OED* orders its definitions so that 'Teaching, instruction, warning' (document, *n*.1) precedes 'An instruction, . . . a lesson' (2) and 'That which serves to show, point out, or prove something; evidence, proof' (3), all marked as obsolete. Its earliest date for 'Something written, inscribed, etc., which furnishes evidence or information upon any subject' is 1728. *OED* is, as often, far from reliable about earliest usages – for instance, this 1695 statement about a work of historiography seems to be using 'document' in the sense familiar to us:

> It will be a Task, requiring great time, skill and pains, and the help of more knowing persons, by particular Treatises, going in order from the greater Antiquity downward, out of the most antient and approved Histories, most exact Collections and authentick Records and Documents, to describe the considerable and eminent Families . . .[5]

Nonetheless, the dominance of our current sense of the word can lead even *OED* into occasional error. When it offers a passage from Nashe's *Lenten Stuffe* (1599) as its earliest example for *documentize* (one of only 10 uses of the verb that even Anupam Basu's text-mining website, *Early Modern Print*, can currently offer) in the sense of 'To furnish with evidence' (2), it seems to me to mistake that for the usual early modern meaning,'to teach, instruct, give a lesson to' (1): 'Those that be scrutinus . . . let them reuolue the *Digests* of our English discoueries . . . and be documentized most locupleatly [richly]'.

Shakespeare is sure what a document is, at least in the single use he makes of the word, itself a somewhat surprising infrequency. Laertes describes his mad sister's linking of rosemary and remembrance, pansies and thoughts as 'A document in madness: thoughts and remembrance fitted' (4.5.176–7). Her actions are acts of teaching, fitting flower to meaning and fitting the combination of flower and meaning to recipient. Even the mad can instruct, can create moments that teach, so that her madness has method in it. By verbalizing the connections Ophelia creates a lesson, that act of teaching that *document*'s source in *docere* (Latin, 'to teach') still made its primary semantic space in early modern English.

Worrying at the word, even in Shakespeare, is not the point. Worrying at what the early modern senses might offer us as we rethink the (written) documents is more valuable. Much of this collection is concerned with what they might teach us and how they might instruct us. Later I shall be concerned with what the limits might or should be in what constitutes a document but I want first to emphasize how much this collection exemplifies a new and exciting interaction between book history and theatre history, for it has been far too rarely the case that scholars in each have connected in their consideration of their materials and the results are a major sign of the extent to which this collection marks an exhilarating step forward in our work.

In one of the most impressive of his long, long list of publications, W. W. Greg analysed (in one thick but normal-sized volume) and reproduced (in a second, gloriously huge volume) 'actual playhouse documents used in the original productions of Elizabethan plays'.[6] The purpose of the sustained analysis of these materials that Greg went on to offer was that they 'tell us something about the conditions of performance, and something about the nature of the texts in use' and the reason that might be worth doing is that their origins 'supply ... as it were a material scheme within the limits of which both the bibliographical critic and the textual editor must work'. The bibliographical critic and textual editor might be the same person, for they aptly describe the roles

Greg himself performed across his career and for which, twenty years after these two volumes were published, he would be knighted. Book history and editing early modern drama intertwine. Writing of those documents that he labelled 'prompt books', Greg argues that

> [t]hese thirty or so manuscripts afford a wealth of evidence that is of first-rate value, is indeed indispensable, to the textual critic and bibliographer, and there can be no question that its thorough investigation is among the most pressing tasks that await students of Elizabethan drama.[7]

Greg's own areas of study thus influence his own work here. The two volumes are an addition to the resources that he laboured to make available and to think about. But he defines the potential of this particular outcome only in terms of those same fields of work. There is no space here for the influence such study might have on literary criticism, something he rarely practised.[8] Nor can he imagine – for why would he have done? – that there would in the 1950s be a new academic discipline in the UK directly concerned with the study of theatre, with the University of Bristol's founding of the first UK Department of Drama in which Glynne Wickham would, in 1960, be the country's first Professor of Drama.

While many of the contributors to this volume might self-describe as theatre historians, interested in the cultural history of theatre and using textual bibliography and the editions of the dramatists prepared by Greg, his predecessors and successors as a way of understanding the material conditions for early modern theatrical activity, almost all of them work in departments of English. To the best of my knowledge, the McMeel Family Chair in Shakespeare Studies at the University of Notre Dame is the only permanent endowed chair in Shakespeare studies in the world not located in a department of English or Literature, being in the Department of Film, Television and Theatre.

There is a consequence for the nature of our work in the fact that we were all (or nearly all) trained through the discipline of English studies and that our approach to theatre history is driven by an interest in early modern performance, not measured against the longer tracks of theatre history or the broader geographies of global theatre cultures. The sharp and provocative new perceptions, large and small, that fill the pages of this volume are, nonetheless, to some extent constrained by our disciplinary training and practice. As we look forward to the work that may follow ours, we might consider the consequences of our disciplinary biases. When we examine the traces of early modern performance, are we alert enough to the documents that constitute the knowledge of, say, classical Greek tragedy and comedy, documents that include vase-paintings as well as papyri and inscriptions? Might a fuller knowledge of, say, the 'Texts, Documents and Art from Athenian Comic Competitions', as the subtitle of a magnificent collection of such materials describes itself, help us rethink how we interpret the texts and documents, not to mention the art and archaeology, of Shakespeare's theatres?[9] Even more significantly, the ways in which classical scholars have interpreted and rethought their corpus of documents might make us wonder whether we have been as sophisticated as we should be in the methodologies and theoretical frameworks we have been using. Not that I wish here to be especially privileging classical theatre. The more general problem is that the intense and fine explorations of how theatre historiography could and perhaps even should function have largely passed us by. To take just one leading figure in the development of the proper quizzing of historiographic evidence for theatrical practices with whose work we might engage – and whose writing we have shown comparatively little sign currently of engaging with – we could consider one introductory text and two collections by Thomas Postlewait and decide whether we have yet been sufficiently alert to the healthy scepticism that characterizes his thinking.[10] I am not, of course, proposing that this would necessarily and unequivocally transform our work – but it might.

To take the next step, we might also look at the work of those Shakespeare scholars whose focus of attention has been on later performances to see whether their ways of working with the material traces and documentary evidence available for their research might indicate approaches that could prove both relevant and fruitful for the early modern materials with which we grapple. I think here, for instance, of the brilliant last book by the late Barbara Hodgdon, *Shakespeare, Performance and the Archive*,[11] whose extraordinary grasp of theory and redefinitions of what constitutes our archive (photography, costumes, props, actors' scripts, stage managers' reports, fire safety concerns over candles and cigarettes onstage and the like) have been profoundly definitional of how performance might be researched and how it might be written about.

It seems to me that, perhaps because the discipline is so differently structured, book – and manuscript – historians are more aware of the potentials elsewhere in their field than theatre historians (and I count myself firmly among the latter, not the former). Paul Werstine's rethinking of the nature of theatre manuscripts is crucial here, in his *Early Modern Playhouse Manuscripts and the Editing of Shakespeare*,[12] itself building on Greg's achievements and always seeing those moments where Greg had not followed his own method.[13]

But Greg was always trying to be alert to what the documentary historical evidence can and, even more importantly, cannot tell us. As he said near the start of *Dramatic Documents*,

> Every item of historical evidence performs a two-fold function: positively it enlarges the basis we have to build on, and enables us to extend the structure of valid inference; negatively it is often of even greater service in limiting the field of admissible conjecture. That is why to a certain type of mind all fresh evidence is so extremely distasteful.[14]

I wish I knew whether that devastating last sentence was aimed at a particular fellow-scholar. *Rethinking Theatrical*

Documents is full of new items of historical evidence brought newly into view, from the smallest details of type-setting in early modern playbooks to the extraordinary amount that can be recovered about plays long lost and objects never preserved. It may be that we also need to rethink whether the archaeology of the theatres themselves constitute documents or at least documentary evidence, especially in the light of the fascinating report of excavations at the Globe and the Rose presented by Julian Bowsher and Pat Miller.[15]

But, of all the material newly available, the most exciting for our understanding of theatre practice seems to me to be Martin Wiggins's multi-volume project with Catherine Richardson, currently print only but urgently needing to be available as a website that can be easily searched, *British Drama 1533–1642: A Catalogue*.[16] There are many moments in our collection where authors use or negotiate with Wiggins's presentation of materials, especially over titles and details of lost plays – and reading his entries alongside the rich resources of the *Lost Plays Database* (https://lostplays.folger.edu) is always a fascinating and enriching experience. But I am especially intrigued by the way in which Wiggins's choice of what to record offers new ways of thinking about playtexts that are very well known indeed.

Take, for instance, the entry for *King Lear*.[17] Inevitably, as Wiggins records information according to the template he devised for each and every entry, there is much that is entirely familiar. It did not need the *Catalogue* entry to tell us that the Stationers' Register entry calls the play a 'history', Q1 a 'true chronicle history' and F1 a 'tragedy' but it is worth noting that Sir John Harington listed his copy of it under 'Names of Comedyes'.[18] Much more intriguingly for thinking about the play in performance is the list of props,[19] ranging from lights and a torch, the swords carried by Edmund, Oswald, Cornwall, Edgar and two servants, plus the 'bloody knife' of the last scene, money and letters, to furniture like a bench, a joint-stool and a chair. And the costume list also offers potential for our rethinking.[20]

Wiggins's entry records places that are represented but also ones that are spoken of. So we find in *King Lear* a list that covers Britain (Kent, Gloucester, Albany, Cornwall, Lipsbury, Salisbury Plain, Camelot, Dover and its cliff), Greece (Thebes and Athens), France, Burgundy, Germany and, in Asia, Scythia, Turkey and Persia.[21] If we are to understand the fictional geographies of early modern drama – and it is an area of study that seems to be much needed – then such speaking of place as well as speaking in places, places apparent only because they are spoken of, has promise for our work.

We are used to thinking about the characters who make up our editions' lists of characters. Wiggins finds 32–36 speaking parts in Q and 25–31 in F. We are also used to the resource that Thomas L. Berger and others compiled from another of Greg's astonishing research creations, his *Bibliography of the English Printed Drama to the Restoration*, as their *Index to Characters in Early Modern English Drama: Printed Plays 1500–1660* (1998). Their work enables us to find all the plays with doctors, French doctors, English doctors and any other varieties of medical professionals. But Wiggins also lists other characters in *King Lear*, ones only spoken of and never seen, such as Edmund's mother and Regan's mother, Gloucester's father, Goneril's and Regan's servants, the French spies in the households of Albany and Cornwall (present only in F) and Monsieur le Far, the French Marshal. Our future studies of early modern performance could, in the light of Wiggins's *Catalogue*, encourage different ways of pursuing early modern theatre costume – what *does* a French doctor look like and in what ways is that unlike an English one? – or peopling the play with the unseen characters each drama speaks of or researching the geographies of its imaginary.

In spite of the labours of so many scholars, I am still left with the enduring mystery of how exactly Shakespeare and his fellow dramatists constructed their plays, started planning, managed writing. Some early modern documentary evidence could usefully be reconsidered here, such as the materials Sisson presented long ago in *Lost Plays of Shakespeare's Age* (1936).[22] But it is a mystery for me only magnified by a fragment of a twentieth-century playwright drafting the beginnings of a play, a scrap that has intrigued me for years and that might help us rethink the abstract forms of some early modern drama, such as the chiastic shapes of *The Tempest*, a drama whose scenic design was brilliantly laid out by Mark Rose: 'Surrounding the centrepiece, accounting for almost the entire play, is thus an extraordinary triple frame comprised of distinct character groups'.[23]

At some point between February 1967 and April 1968 Samuel Beckett began outlining a play. He abandoned his first attempt. The second try changed the cast-list from two women to one man and one woman. Beckett sketched out a series of movements on and off the stage, creating four numbered sections:

1 Arrivée femme . . . Arrivé homme Reduction espace.
2 Femme seule.
3 Elle le ramène. Il l'expédie. Homme seule.
4 Il la ramène, ils s'expédient.

Then he wrote timing for each section: 10 minutes, 20, 5 and 10. Then he put a series of questions: '1. quel dialogue? 3. Que fait l'homme seul? 4. Quel dialogue? Et pourquoi decision l'en finir?' Finally, across the rest of the sheet there are some sketches of answers.[24] First, movement, then rhythm, then action. Or is the movement itself the action, as the parallel rhythms of the two acts of *Waiting for Godot* are or the form of *Play* with its astonishing stage direction near the end 'Repeat play'?[25] This sketch, something Dryden might have called a 'scenary', and we call a 'scenario', suggests a mode of forming a drama far from our usual models.

Beckett's fragment makes me rethink not only how he wrote but also how others, even Shakespeare, might have written – and the answer lies a long way from our most popular images of it, even when it appears most embedded in the material conditions of theatre as in the imaginings of the romcom screenplay for *Shakespeare in Love*. As we accustom ourselves to the brave new world that the innovative rethinkings of the contributors here have so thoughtfully and provocatively sketched, we can build on those insights in ways that they themselves have encouraged me to develop briefly here. The rethinking of theatrical documents is far from over.

Notes

1 See the image in the Library of Congress, available at https://www.loc.gov/item/2013650088/ [accessed 14 January 2019].

2 See the image at https://www.worthpoint.com/worthopedia/german-porcelain-factory-catalogue-1843324774 [accessed 14 January 2019]; see also Edmund de Waal, *The White Road* (New York: Farrar, Strauss and Giroux, 2015), 354.

3 Mark Nixon, *Samuel Beckett's German Diaries, 1936–1937* (London: Continuum, 2011), 87.

4 If the use of 'Shakespeare' in the title of this volume is in part a marketing ploy, it is also more accurately appropriate than in, say, the title of the two-volume collection of articles as *An Account of the Life and Manners of his Age* that finally appeared as a tercentenary marker in 1916, edited by C. T. Onions and others (Oxford: Clarendon Press, 1916).

5 William Camden, *A Second Edition of Camden's Description of Scotland* (London, 1695), sig. ¶2v, located through a rapid search of examples for 'document*' in 'EEBO-TCP Key Words in Context' at *Early Modern Print*, https://earlyprint.wustl.edu/toolwebgrok.html?corpus=plaintext_reg&searchPattern=document*&startYear=1692&endYear=1700&authors=&titles=&page=1 [accessed 14 January 2019].

6 Sir W. W. Greg, *Dramatic Documents from the Elizabethan Playhouses*, 2 vols (Oxford: Clarendon Press, 1931), 1: ix.

7 Greg, *Dramatic Documents*, 1: 190.

8 Though see W.W. Greg, 'The Function of Bibliography on Literary Criticism Illustrated in a Study of the Text of *King Lear*', *Neophilologus* 18 (1933), 241–262.

9 See Jeffrey Rusten et al., eds, *The Birth of Comedy: Texts, Documents, and Art from Athenian Comic Competitions, 486–280* (Baltimore: Johns Hopkins University Press, 2011).

10 I am thinking here, simply as examples, of his *Cambridge Introduction to Theatre Historiography* (Cambridge: Cambridge University Press, 2009); the very influential collection he co-edited with Bruce A. McConachie, *Interpreting the Theatrical Past: essays in the Historiography of Performance* (Iowa City: University of Iowa Press, 1989); and the more recent volume co-edited with Charlotte Canning, *Representing the Past* (Iowa City: University of Iowa Press, 2010).

11 Barbara Hodgdon, *Shakespeare, Performance and the Archive* (Abingdon: Routledge, 2016).

12 Paul Werstine, *Early Modern Playhouse Manuscripts and the Editing of Shakespeare* (Cambridge: Cambridge University Press, 2012).

13 See, especially, his article, 'The Continuing Importance of New Bibliographical Method' in *Shakespeare Survey 62* (Cambridge: Cambridge University Press, 2009), 30–45.

14 Greg, *Dramatic Documents*, 1: x.

15 Julian Bowsher and Pat Miller, *The Rose and the Globe: Playhouses of Shakespeare's Bankside, Southwark* (London: MOLA, 2009).

16 Martin Wiggins and Catherine Richardson, *British Drama 1533–1642: A Catalogue* (Oxford: Oxford University Press, 2012–), 9 of the projected 10 volumes published to date.

17 Item 1486, in Wiggins and Richardson, vol. 5 (1603–1608), 252–259.

18 Greg included Harington's lists in his *Bibliography of the English Printed Drama to the Restoration*, 4 vols (London: The Bibliographical Society, 1939–1957), 3:1306–1313. 'K. Leir of Shakspear' appears in the first list, the playwright's name included to distinguish it from 'King Leire.: old:' in the second list, one of only three playwrights' names in the first list (3:1310–1311). Harington heads the list 'Names of Comedyes' and marks some as tragedies within it, e.g., 'Mustaffa tragedy' and 'Byroun tragedy'. But he also leaves some self-evident tragedies without such a marking, e.g. 'Bussy D'Amboys' and 'Ferrex & Porrex'. It seems best to assume that 'Comedyes' here means no more than 'plays' and is not a genre marker.

19 Wiggins and Richardson, vol. 5, 257

20 Wiggins and Richardson, vol. 5, 257.

21 Wiggins and Richardson, vol. 5, 256.

22 Charles Jasper Sisson, *Lost Plays of Shakespeare's Age* (Cambridge: Cambridge University Press, 1936).

23 Mark Rose, *Shakespearean Design* (Cambridge: Belknap Press of Harvard University Press, 1972), 173. I explored this further in 'The Shapeliness of The Tempest', *Essays in Criticism*, 45 (1995), 208–229.

24 The sheet is described and reproduced in James Knowlson, ed., *Samuel Beckett: An Exhibition held at Reading University Library, May to July 1971* (London: Turret Books, 1971), #376, p. 118, and plate 6 following p. 30. '1. Woman arrives. Man arrives. Space narrows. 2. Woman alone. 3. She calls him in. He sends her off. Man alone. 4. He calls her in. They leave. . . . 1. What dialogue? 3. What does the man do on his own? 4. What dialogue? And why the decision to end it?' (my translation).

25 Samuel Beckett, *Play* (London: Faber and Faber, 1964), 22.

INDEX

Academy of Complements 168
actors' parts 2, 3, 6, 7–8, 18, 29, 52–67, 69, 72, 79, 194, 195, 242
Admiral's Men 35, 36, 38, 39, 40, 41, 47, 131, 132, 137, 242, 243, 245, 247, 252, *see also* Prince Henry's Men; Prince Charles' Men
Alabaster, William
  Roxana 119
A Larum for London 247
Alberge, Dalya 149
Alberus, Erasmus 136
Alcoran of the Barefote Friers 136, 150
Alleyn, Edward 28, 34, 35–6, 38–42, 47, 49, 50, 70, 79, 249, 250, 254
Alleyn, Richard 40, 42
Allott, Robert
  Englands Parnassus 171
Andrea, Bernadette 135
Andrews, Lancelot 31
Arber, Edward 235
Archer, Jayne Elisabeth 151
Aristophanes 166
Aristotle 132
Armin, Robert 70, 71, 227
Armstrong, Archie
  A Banquet of Jests 86

Astington, John 35–6, 48, 127, 169, 174
Atkin, Tamara 189

Baker, Gerald 123, 125, 127
ballads 2, 5, 6, 11, 70, 85, 133, 216–37
Barber, G. 212
Barry, Lording 177
Bastard, Thomas 159
Basu, Anupam 261
Bawcutt, N. W. 258
Beal, Peter 182, 184, 189, 191
Beaumont, Francis 196, 212
  Knight of the Burning Pestle 100, 108, 112, 125
Beaumont, Francis, and John Fletcher 49, 98–9, 109, 178, 179
  The Elder Brother 182
  King and No King 4, 13
  The Maid's Tragedy 108
  The Noble Gentleman 102
  Philaster 51
  Thierry and Theodoret 102, 109
  The Woman Hater 94, 102
Beckerman, Bernard 243, 256
Beckett, Samuel 260, 268–9
  Waiting for Godot 268
  Play 268, 271
Bednarz, J. P. 108
Bedwell, William 136

Beeston, Christopher 253
'Bellendon' 40
Bel-vedére 159, 171
Bence, John 178–9
Benfield, Robert 44
Bentley, G. E. 18, 31, 32 49, 173
Berger, Thomas L. 267
Bergeron, David M. 107, 212
Bernard, Richard
   Terence in English 165
Berry, Herbert 119, 236
Bertram, Paul 67
Bevington, David 49, 124
Bianco, Jamie 'Skye' 191
Bible 132, 133, 134–4, 151
   Bishops' 142, 145, 147
   Coverdale 145
   Geneva 140–2, 145, 147, 151
   Great 140–2, 145
   Matthew 145
   Vulgate 132
Bird, William 40, 246, 252
Birth of Hercules 94
Blackfriars Playhouse, London 22, 24, 95, 119, 193
Blackfriars Playhouse, Staunton, Virginia 116
Blayney, Peter 110
Bly, Mary 171
Boccaccio, Giovanni
   Decameron 19
Bodenham, John
   England's Helicon 235
book holder *see* prompter
book-props 4, 9, 128–51, 219
Bourne, Claire M. L. 5, 6, 10, 92, 100, 212, 213, 215, 261
Bowers, Fredson 102, 109, 170, 191

Bowles, Amy 214
Bowsher, Julian 266, 270
Boyd, Michael 149
Bradbrook, M. C. 125
Brandes, Georg 213
British Library Manuscripts Online (BLMO) 179–80
Britland, Karen 126
Britton, Dennis Austin 257
Brock, Susan 259
Brome, Henry 101
Brome, Richard
   Antipodes 76
   City Wit, The 112, 125
   Five New Plays 101
   'Florentine Friend' 253
   Jovial Crew, A 101
   The Lovesick Court 101–2
   The Weeding of Covent Garden 101–2
Bruster, Douglas 107, 131, 148
'Buc is a Thief' 252
Burbage, James 253
Burbage, Richard 34–40, 43, 45, 48, 54, 70, 83, 158, 253–4
Burn, Jacob Henry 252–3
Burnim, Kalman A. 51
Butler, Martin 49, 108, 124

Camden, William 269
Cane, Andrew 70, 71
Canning, Charlotte 270
Carlell, Lodowick
   The Deserving Favourite 44
Carlson, Marvin 149
Carson, Neil 132, 148, 257
Cartwright, William
   The Ordinary 231, 236

Castiglione, Baldassare 163
casting 34–51
Catalogue of English Literary Manuscripts (CELM) 178, 183–4, 187, 189, 190, 191, 192
Caveat for Cutpurses 226
Cavendish, William
   The Variety 101
Cerasano, S. P. 32, 36, 38, 49
Chamberlain's Men 37, 77, 230, 242, 243–4, 247, 248, 253, *see also* King's Men
Chambers, E. K. 94, 108, 257, 258
Chapman, George
   Blind Beggar of Alexandria 36, 40
   A Humorous Day's Mirth 42
Chartier, Roger 170
Chaucer, Geoffrey 19
Cheesman, Tom 236
Chen, Min 192
Chettle, Henry 246
Children of the Chapel 251
Children of the Queen's Revels 22, 27
Cholmley, John 231
Clarke, Hugh 51
Clayton, Thomas 66
Clegg, Roger 236
Cleveland, John 3, 12
'Cloth Breeches and Velvet Hose' 247
Cockpit/Phoenix Playhouse 95, 109, 119, 127
Cockpit-at-Court 127
Collier, John Payne 246, 247, 249, 252

commonplace books and commonplaces 2, 5, 6, 9–10, 85, 155–9, 163, 170
Commonplace Cultures 187
Condell, Elizabeth 19, 31
Condell, Henry 19, 37, 106
'Constantine' 40
Cook, David 256
Cooke, John
   Greenes Tu Quoque 70
Cordier, Mathurin 164
Corkine, William
   Second Book of Aires 235
Cotgrave, John
   The English Treasury 166–8, 174
   Wits Interpreter 168, 174
Coverdale, Myles *see* Bible
Cox, J. D. 110
Craig, Heidi, 6, 8, 172
Crane, Ralph 214
Crawford, Charles 171
Cromwell, Thomas 253
Crooke, Andrew 102
Crum, Margaret 181, 190
cue-scripts *see* actors' parts
cues 52–5, 57–64, 69, 73, 75, 77
'Cutlack' 36, 38
cutting plays 61, *see also* revision
Cutts, John P. 236

Dabourne, Robert 6, 17–32, 132, 183
   The Arraignment of London 17, 20, 25, 31
   The Bellman of London 17, 19, 20, 26, 31
   A Christian Turned Turk 26, 32

The Honest Man's Fortune
  17, 18, 20, 31
Machiavel and the Devil 17,
  20, 21, 22–3, 25, 28, 29
The Owl 17, 19, 22, 29
The She Saint 17, 29
Dabourne, Susanna 24
Daniell, David 140, 151
Danter, John 228–9, 242
Databse of Dramatic Extracts
  (*DEx*) 187–8, 192
*Database of Early English
  Playbooks* (*DEEP*) 189,
  191
Davenant, William 120, 178,
  212
  *Cruelty of the Spaniards in
    Peru* 119
  Siege of Rhodes 119
Davies, John 38
Day, John *see also* Dekker,
    Thomas
  Law-trickes 168
  *The Travels of the Three
    English Brothers* 83, 258
'The Dead Man's Fortune' 36
Dekker, Thomas 19, 22, 32,
  178, 179, 247
  Magnificent Entertainment
    126
  Satiromastix 247
  Wonder of a Kingdom 100
Dekker, Thomas, William
  Haughton and John Day
  The Spanish Moor's Tragedy
    41
Deloney, Thomas 227
Deodati, Isabel 31
Deodati, John 31
Depledge, Emma 213

Derby's Men 242
Dessen, Alan 130, 147
Deutermann, Allison K. 173
de Waal, Edmund 269
De Witt, Johannes 118
'Dick' (boy actor) 40
Dillon, Janette 107, 110
Dimmock, Matthew 115, 125,
  126, 136, 150
'Doctor Lambe and the Witches'
  252
'document' defined 5, 262
Donaldson, Ian 49, 124
Dorval, Patricia 172
Downey, Nicholas 3
Downton, Thomas 34, 39
Drayton, Michael 19, *see also*
    Munday, Anthony
Drury Lane 46
Dryden, John 268
DuBartas, Guillaume de Salluste
  31
Duffin, Ross 233, 235, 237
Dutton, Richard 67, 149

*Early Modern Manuscripts
  Online* 187, 192
Eccles, Mark 31, 32
Edmund Ironside 182
Edwards, Richard
  Damon and Pithias 104, 109
Egan, Gabriel 65, 256
Elderton, William 227
Elizabeth I 137, 138–47
Elsky, Martin 173
England's Parnassus 158
*English Broadside Ballad
  Archive* (EBBA) 220
English Short-Title Catalogue
  (ESTC) 183, 191

Enloe, Sarah 65
Enterline, Lynn 172, 173
Erasmus, Desiderius 164
Erne, Lukas 53, 65, 170, 171
Estill, Laura 6, 10, 155, 159, 171, 173, 189, 191, 192, 249
Evalyn, Lawrence 49
Evans, G. Blakemore 211
extemporisation *see* improvisation

Fabian, B. 212
Fairbrass, Valerie 237
Fair Maid of the Exchange 203, 214
'Fair Maid of London' 253
The Famous Victories of Henry the Fifth 74, 87, 250
Farmer, Alan 191
'Felix and Philomena' 251
'Felmelanco' 246
Fenn, Robert Denzel 126
Field, Nathan 17, 20, 28, 37, 38
'Five Plays in One' 251
Flecknoe, Richard
  Miscellania 172
Fletcher, John 17
  Faithful Shepherdesse 4, 13, 212
  Wild Goose Chase 44
Fletcher, John, and Philip Massinger
  Sir John Van Olden Barnavelt 66
fleuron 204–5
Florimène 119
Fludd, Robert
  De anime memorativae Scientia 118–19, 126

Foakes, R. A. 50, 127, 148, 256, 257, 258
Ford, John
  'Tis Pity She's a Whore 123, 127
Fortune Playhouse 36, 109, 245, 253
Foxe, John
  Actes and Monuments 137, 138, 143
'Frederick and Basilea' 38, 39, 40, 41–2
Freeman, Arthur and Janet Ing Freemen 257
Frolicksome Duke 229–30
Fumerton, Patricia 235

Gair, Reavley 126, 172
Galen 132
'Galfrido & Bernardo' 246, 257
Garrick, David 46–7, 51
Gayton, Edmund 71
  Pleasant Notes 86
Genest, John 51
Gernutus, a Jew 230
Gitelman, Lisa 211
Glapthorne, Henry
  The Lady Mother 183
Globe Playhouse 118, 119, 193, 243, 253, 266
Goffe, Thomas
  The Careless Shepherdess 71
Gold, Matthew K. 191
Goldring, Elizabeth 151
Gosse, Edmund 256
'Gowrie' 247
Greene, Robert 230–1
  Friar Bacon 80

INDEX

Orlando Furioso 38, 39, 79–80, 81, 88
Third and last part of conny-catching 236
Greene, Thomas 70
Greg, W. W. 18, 20, 31, 57, 62–3, 64, 66, 87, 92, 105, 109, 110, 193, 195, 259, 262–3, 264, 267, 269, 270
Grosart, Alexander B. 49
Guazzo, Francesco Maria 163
Guilburne, Samuel 254
Guilpin, Everard 38–9, 49
Gurr, Andrew 35, 48, 108, 125, 247, 257

Hakluyt, Richard
  Principall Navigations 150
Halliwell-Phillipps, James Orchard 253
Hardesty, John 106
Hardwick Hall 136–7
Harington, Sir John 266, 270
Harridance, Thomas 254
Harris, John 24, 32
Harris, Jonathan Gil 131, 148
'Harry of Cornwall' 250
Haryson, Goody 132
Hathway, Richard 247, 256, *see also* Munday, Anthony
Hatt, John 31
Haughton, William 246, *see also* Dekker, Thomas
  Englishman for my Money 41
Hayman, Francis 46
Heminges, John 34, 46, 106, 110
'Henry I, The Life and Death of' 41

Henry VIII 253
Henslowe, Philip 6, 7, 17, 17–32, 33, 41, 51, 122, 123, 131, 132, 231, 242, 243, 244–7, 249, 252, 257
Herbert, Henry 94, 245, 252, 258
Heywood, Thomas 182, 247, 248, 257, *see also* Shakespeare, William
  If you Know not Me 134, 138–46, 150
  Iron Age part I 256
  A Woman Killed with Kindness 168
Hibbard, G. R. 213
Hill, Aaron
Hillebrand, H. N. 32
Hinman, Charlton 66
  Zara 46
Hirrel, Michael J. 86, 257
Hitler, Adolph 260
Hodgdon, Barbara 265, 270
Holinshed, Raphael
  Chronicle 132
Holland, Peter 12, 110, 271
Honigmann, E. A. J. 235, 259
Hooks, Adam G. 170, 211
Hope, Jonathan 173
Howard-Hill, T. H. 213
Hunter, G. K. 171

improvisation 2, 8, 68–88, 162, 169
Ingram, William 236, 258, 259
instruction 95
Ioppolo, Grace 18
Irace, Kathleen O. 66, 67
'Isle of Dogs' 251–2

J. S.
　Wits Labyrinth 167–8, 174
Jaggard, William 235
James, Thurston 128–9, 130, 134, 147, 151
Jeffe, Humphrey 39
Jenstad, Janelle 190
Jephthah Judge of Israel 223
Jewell, Simon 253
jig 71, 85, 226–7
John of Bordeaux 80, 88
Johnson, Richard
　Golden Garland 229
Johnson, Robert 219, 235
Johnson, William 254
Jones, Inigo 3, 119, 120, 122
Jonson, Ben 3, 104, 122, 178, 179, 197, 214, 226, 231, 236, 248
　Alchemist 36, 37, 46, 51, 133
　Bartholomew Fair 37, 226
　Catiline 49
　Cynthia's Revels 112, 124–5, 127, 161–2
　Every Man In His Humour 49, 125, 247
　Every Man Out of His Humour 45, 49, 110, 157–8, 161–2, 171
　Poetaster 120–1, 127
　Sejanus 49, 110, 168
　Volpone 36, 37, 51
Jowett, John 66, 67, 110, 198, 213
Juby, Edward 40, *see also* Rowley, Samuel
Justinian 132

Kaethler, Mark 190
Kahrl, George Morrow 51
Kastan, D. S. 110
Kay, W. David 49
Kemp, William 70, 74, 77, 83, 227
Kermode, Lloyd 173
Keysar, Robert 22, 31–2
Killigrew, Henry
　The Conspiracy/Pallantus and Eudora 105–6, 110
Kincaid, P. C. 116, 126
King, T. J. 50, 51
King Leir 270
King's Men 27–8, 30, 37, 38, 42, 43, 45, 46, 47, 133, 214, 217, 219, 230, 242, 244, 248, 253, *see also* Chamberlain's Men
Kinney, Arthur F. 126
Kirsch, Arthur C. 170
Kirwan, Peter 213
Kiséry, András 5, 9, 172, 173, 176, 189
Kliman, Bernice W. 67
Knack to Know a Knave, A 39, 74, 81, 87
'Knaves' 145
Knight, Jeffrey Todd 211
Knight, Sarah 151
Knott, Betty I. 173
Knowles, Ronald 66
Knowlson, James 271
Knutson, Ros 6, 11, 31, 34, 41, 42, 48, 86, 101, 131, 176, 183, 189, 191, 211, 256
Korda, Natasha 131, 132, 148
Kyd, Thomas 247
　Soliman and Perseda 149
　Spanish Tragedy, The 36, 37, 57, 62

INDEX

Lady Elizabeth's Men 7, 17, 27
La ioyeuse et magnifique entrée de Monseigneur Francoys 126
Lamb, Jonathan 214
Langhans, Edward A. 211
Lawrence, W. J. 125
Lees-Jeffries, Hester 150
Leicester's Commonwealth 182
Leishman, J. B. 86
Le Neve, Oliver 180
Le Neve, Peter 178–80
Lennard, John 214
Lerer, Seth 213
Lesser, Zachary 149, 170, 171, 191, 211, 212
Levenson, Jill 179, 189
Lindley, David 234
Lodge, Thomas 256
  Wit's Misery 244
  Wounds of Civil War 203, 214
Lopez, Jeremy 173
lost plays 2, 11–12, 36, 38, 39, 176, 241–59
Lost Plays Database 183, 242–3, 266
Loughnane, Rory 256
Love, Harold 181, 186–7, 190, 192
Lovers complaint being forsaken 222
'Lovesick Courtier' 252
Lowin, John 37, 43–4, 51
Lust's Dominion see Dekker, Haughton and Day, *The Spanish Moor's Tragedy*
Lyly, John
  Sappho and Phao 100

McConachie, Bruce A. 270
McEvilla, Joshua J. 173
McGregor, Brian 173
McInnis, David 6, 11, 31, 41, 101, 131, 176, 183, 189, 191, 256, 257
McJannet, Linda 135, 212
McKenzie, D. F. 186, 192, 196, 212
McKerrow, Ronald B. 256
Mackman, Jonathan 32
MacLean, Sally-Beth 48, 258
McMillin, Scott 40–1, 48, 50, 54, 65, 258
McPherson, Kathryn R. 65, 215
Macray, William 189
Maguire, Laurie E. 66, 87, 125, 212
Malone, Edmond 131, 252, 258
Mann, Jenny C. 214
Manningham, John 158
Marlowe, Christopher 134, 221, 235, 247
  Doctor Faustus 38, 39, 76–7, 80, 87, 88, 130, 131, 132, 138, 247
  Jew of Malta 36, 38, 39, 123
  Tamburlaine 38, 39, 106, 110, 132, 134–8, 149, 247
Marcus, Leah S. 65, 151, 175, 189
Marino, James J. 6, 7, 29, 48, 65, 69, 86
Marotti, Arthur 191
Martin, Thomas 180, 184
Mary I 138–47
Mason, John
  The Turk 105
Masten, Jeffrey 212

Marston, John
  Antonio's Revenge 72, 87, 161
  The Dutch Courtezan 159
  Histriomastix 84
  The Malcontent 36, 37, 49, 158–9
  What you Will 130
Massai, Sonia 6, 8, 172
Massinger, Philip 17, 20, 178, see also Fletcher, John
  Believe as You List 44, 125
  City Madam 42
  The Emperor of the East 94, 95
  The Picture 44
  The Roman Actor 44, 45
Matar, Nabil 135, 150
Mateer, Dabbid 32
Mayer, Jean-Christophe 172
May, Steven W. 181, 190
Mazzio, Carla 213, 215
Melchiori, Giorgio 67
Menzer, Paul 65
Mercurius Britannicus 103
Meres, Francis
  Palladis Tamia 247, 257
Merry, Mark 183
Middleton, Thomas 81
  Mayor of Queenborough, The 133
  Viper and her Brood, The 22
Middleton, Thomas and Thomas Dekker
  Honest Whore, The 133
  Roaring Girle, The 211
Middleton, Thomas and William Rowley
  World Tost at Tennis 4

Miller, Pat 266, 270
Moncrief, Kathryn 215
Monfort, Walter
  Launching of the Mary 183
Montagu, Walter
  The Shepherd's Paradise 119
Montaigne, Michel de 159
Montedoro, Beatrice 189, 192
Montgomery, William 66, 67, 110
Morrisey, Robert 192
Moseley, Francis 102
Mossop, Henry 57
Most excellent Ditty of the Lovers promises 221
Mucedorus 73
Mueller, Janel 151
Mueller, Martin 49, 50
Mulcaster, Richard 202
  First Part of the Elementarie 214
  Queen's Majesty's Passage 150
Munday, Anthony, Michael Drayton, Richard Hathway and Robert Wilson
  Sir John Oldcastle 130
Munro, John 174
Munro, Lucy 6, 132, 172
Murad III 137
Murphy, Andrew 170

Nashe, Thomas 244, 251
  Lenten Stuffe 261
  Strange Newes 236
  Summer's Last Will 3, 12
Naylor, Ben 50

Nelson, Alan H. 32, 259
Nero 182
Newington Butts Theatre 242, 243, 244
Nixon, Mark 260, 269
Nobody and Somebody 224–6
Nobody his Counsaile to Chuse a Wife 226
Norman, Marc, and Tom Stoppard
    Shakespeare in Love 269
North, Marcy 191
Nungezer, Edwin 49, 50

'1 Tamar Cham' 28, 39, 259
Onions, C. T. 269
Ord, Craven 252–3
Orgel, Stephen 107, 110, 212
Orrell, John 126, 127
Ortelius
    Theatrum Orbis Terrarum 132
Ostler, William 38
Otway, Thomas 184–6, 188
    Alcibiades 184
    Friendship in Fashion 184
    The Orphan 46
Ovid
    Metamorphosis 132, 133, 230
Oxford's Boys 251

Painter, William
    Palace of Pleasure 132
Palfrey, Simon 46, 48, 51, 52, 65, 86, 87
Pallant, Robert 27
Palmer, Barbara D. 250, 258
Pangallo, Matteo 183, 191

parentheses 201–4, 214
Parkes, Malcolm B. 214
parts *see* actors' parts
Pass, Gregory A. 181, 190
Passionate Pilgrim 221
Patrick, Simon 178
patronage 25, 97, 186
Peacham, Henry 242
Peele, George 242
    Battle of Alcazar 38, 39
Pembroke's Men 242, 245
Pendleton, Thomas A. 67
Percy, William 9, 111, 115–18, 120, 122, 126
    Country Tragedy in Vacunium 117
    Cuckqueans and Cuckolds Errants, The 116
    Faery Pastorall 115–17
    Mahomet and his Heaven 117, 126
Peron, Jacques Davy du
    Luthers Alcoran 136, 150
Petersen, Lene 66
Pett, Mr 246
Phelps, Wayne H. 32
Phillips, Augustine 254, 259
Phoenix *see* Cockpit
'Phyllida and Corin' 251
pilcrows 204–6
Pilgrimage to Parnassus 72, 86
Pitcher, John 235, 257
Plautus 166
'Play of Oswald' 249
play ballads 2, 11, 216, 227–30
playbills 18, 34, 114, 122, 232, 242
plot, backstage 36, 49, 131, 194, 195, 242

INDEX

plot-scenarios 18, 20
Plutarch
  Lives 132
Pollard, A. W. 193
Pollard, Tanya 173
Porter, Gerald 223, 235
Postlewait, Thomas 264, 270
Potter, Lois 156, 170, 173
Potter, Ursula 173
Pratt, Aaron T. 211
Preiss, Richard 5, 8, 50, 58, 67, 86, 88, 211, 227
Prince Charles' Men 71, 245
  see also Admiral's Men; Prince Henry's Men
Prince Henry's Men 245
  see also Admiral's Men; Prince Charles' Men
prologues and epilogues 2, 6, 8, 81, 83, 91–110
prompter and prompter's book 3, 5, 61, 83, 86
props 9, 49, 128–51
Prudentius 178–9
Pudsey, Edward 158, 161–2
Purcell, Stephen 77, 87
Puttenham, George 202
  Arte of English Poesie 214
Pyramus and Thisbe 230

Qur'an 134–8, 149–50
Queen Anne's Men 70
Queen's Men 34, 138, 145, 247, 250, 251

R. D.
  Gratiae Theatrales 88
Raleigh, Walter 178
Randolph, Thomas 179
  Conceited Pedlar 178–9

Rankins, William 246
Rasmussen, Eric 75, 87, 124
Read, Tim 70, 71
Records of Early English Drama (REED) 249–50
Red Bull Playhouse 138
rehearsal 8, 68, 69, 79, 80, 81, 83, 84, 85
Renwick, William 88
repertory accounts 2
repertory lists (lost) 6, 7, 33–51
revision 7–8, 29, 30, 53–4, 57–63, 67, 69, 75, 104, 125
Reynolds, G. F. 125, 127
Rhodes, Ernest L. 126
'Richard Coer de Lion' 253
Richards, Nathaniel
  Messalina 119–20
Richardson, Catherine 50, 130, 148, 183, 257, 266, 270
Rieuwerts, Sigrid 235
Ringler, William 181, 189
Roberts, James 232
Roberts, Sasha 172
Roberts-Smith, Jennifer 190
Robinson, Mr 246
Robinson, Terry 51
Roe, Kathleen D. 190
Rose, Mark 268, 271
Rose, Mary Beth 151
Rose Playhouse 33, 42, 242, 243, 245, 246, 249, 253, 266
Rosenblum, Joseph 66
Ross, Alexander 136
Rowley, Samuel 40
  'Joshua' 36, 40
  'Samson' (with Edward Juby) 36, 40

Rowley, William
  All's Lost by Lust 100
Rusten, Jeffrey 270
Rutter, Tom 48

S. H.
  Sicily and Naples 3, 12
S. S.
  The Honest Lawyer 168
Salisbury Court Playhouse 109
Sanders, Julie 191
Sands, James 254
scene-boards 6, 9, 111–27, 242,
  see also title-boards
Schurink, Fred 172
Scott, Charlotte 148, 213
Scott, Robert 158
Scott-Warren, Jason 173
Scouten, Arthur H. 51
Seaman, Thomas 31
Seaton, Ethel 132, 149
'The Second Part of the Seven
  Deadly Sins' 36
Seneca 166
Seng, Peter 181, 190
sententiae 160–7
Sewell, Helen 235
Shakespeare, Edmund 254,
  259
Shakespeare, William 156,
  176–8, 180, 183, 186,
  188, 194, 218–37, 247,
  248–9, 254, 262
  Antony and Cleopatra 35,
    232
  Comedy of Errors 117, 148
  Coriolanus 35, 123
  Cymbeline 249
  First Part of the Contention
    55–6

folio 52–67, 105, 106, 108,
  213, 221
Hamlet (Q1 and F) 36, 37,
  46, 52, 54, 58–9, 72, 80,
  85, 87, 88, 131, 162, 166,
  223–4, 244, 256, 262
1 Henry IV 45
2 Henry IV 45, 233
2 Henry VI 55–6, 59, 61, 66
Henry V 35, 45
King John 46
King Lear 36, 37, 52, 63, 67,
  72, 87, 266–7, 270
Love's Labour's Lost 10, 11,
  84, 148, 159, 171,
  197–210, 213
Macbeth 35, 47
Measure for Measure 123,
  125
Merchant of Venice 230
Merry Wives 55, 57–60,
  62–4, 67, 133, 220–1
Midsummer Night's Dream
  47–8, 84, 117, 230,
  232–3
Much Ado About Nothing
  77–9, 82, 88, 162
Othello 36–7, 123–4, 166,
  221–3, 235
Pericles 178, 258
Rape of Lucrece, The 172, 179
Richard III 36, 37, 42, 47
Romeo and Juliet 63, 65, 66,
  67, 77, 88, 105, 227–8
Sir Thomas More 75–6, 86
Taming of the Shrew 229–30
Tempest, The 133, 148, 216,
  224–6, 234
Titus Andronicus 133,
  228–9, 241–4, 246, 255

Troilus and Cressida 108, 123
Twelfth Night 158, 227
Two Gentleman of Verona 72, 73, 87
Winter's Tale 218–19, 221, 233
Shank, John 70
Shapiro, I. A. 119
Sharpe, Richard 44
Sherrington, John 24
Shirley, James
　Bird in a Cage 3, 12
　Changes, The 102–3, 109
　Rosania 124
shorthand 53, 163
Sidney, Philip 179
　Arcadia 178, 182
　Defence of Poetry 112, 125
Silva, Andie 189
Simpson, Percy 214
Singer, John 42, 70
'Sir William Longsword' 253
Sisson, Charles J. 258, 268, 270
Skeaping, Lucie 236
Slater, Martin 40, 232
Slotkin, Joel 150
Sly, William 37
Smith, Bruce R. 230, 235, 236
Sofer, Andrew 133, 149
songs 5, 71, 80, 101, 113, 159–60, 175, 181, 184–5, 188, 195, 199, 216–17, *see also* ballads
Sorlien, Robert Parker 171
Spencer, John 13
Spenser, Edmund,
　Faerie Queene 19
Squier, Charles L. 191
Stallybrass, Peter 170, 171

Stationers' Registers 219, 220, 221, 224, 227, 228, 229, 236, 242, 247–8, 266
Steevens, George 259
Steggle, Matthew 6, 9, 99, 101, 109, 124, 125, 255, 257
Stern, Tiffany 5, 11, 13, 18, 20, 31, 34, 46, 48, 51, 52, 53, 65, 80, 86, 87, 88, 98, 100, 102, 108, 109, 110, 112–13, 125, 127, 129, 132, 133, 147, 149, 159, 171, 173, 175–6, 184, 189, 195, 199, 210, 213, 234, 236, 237, 241, 242, 255, 261
Stewart, Alan 172
Stone, George Winchester 51
Stow, John
　Survey of London 139
'Strange News Out of Poland' 246
Strange's Men 242, 250
Straznicky, Marta 172, 195, 211
Streitberger, W. R. 257
Stubbs, Philip 227
Sussex's Men 242, 243
Swan Playhouse 118, 253
Syme, Holger 6, 7, 59, 67, 80, 88, 149, 212, 214, 254

T. W.
　Thorny-Abbey 83, 88
Tarlton, Richard 70, 71, 73, 74, 253
Tarlton's Jests 87
'Tasso's Melancholy' 40
Taylor, David 51
Taylor, Gary 66, 67, 109, 110, 256

Taylor, Joseph 43–4, 51
Taylor, William 24
Teague, Frances 148
Terence and Terentian conventions 116–17, 164–6
The Theatre 253
'themes' 71, 85
Thomas of Woodstock 182–3
Thompson, Ayanna 235
Thompson, Craig R. 173
Thomson, Leslie 13, 130, 147, 210
Thomson, Peter 132, 148
'Three Plays in One' 251
Tilney, Edmund, 253
title-boards 2, 6, 9, 111–27, 242, *see also* scene-boards
Tomkis, Thomas
 Albumazar 163, 167
Topcliffe, Richard 251
touring plays 54
Tourneur, Cyril 17, 25
 The Atheist's Tragedy 41
Towne, Thomas 40
Traub, Valerie 87, 212
Travis, Edmond 24
Travis, James 24
Trevor, Douglas 213
Tribble, Evelyn B. 86
Troublesome Reign of King John 106
Trundle, John 224–6, 236
The Tryall of Chevalrie 73–4
Tunstall, James 39, 254
Turner, William
 Turners Dish of Lentten Stuffe 86
2 *Return from Parnassus* 83
Tyndale, William
 New Testament 145
 Pentateuch 145

type 10, 196–215
typography 10–11, 196–215

Udall, Nicholas 164–6
 Floures for Latine Spekynge 164, 165, 173
 Ralph Roister Doister 165
Urkowitz, Steven 67

Vadnais, Matthew 91
'Valentine and Orson' 247
Van Elk, Martine 173
Van Es, Bart 18, 31, 48
Vaughan, Alden T. 234
Vaughan, Virginia Mason 234
Vitkus, Daniel 135, 150
Vives, Juan Luis 164
Vulgaria quedam abs Ternecio 164

Wager, Lewis
 The Repentance of Mary Magdalene 97, 108
Wagner, Bernard M. 189
Walker, G. 108
Wallace, C. W. 32
Wallace, Hulda Berggren 32
Wall-Randell, Sarah 4, 9, 19, 219
Walter, Melissa 257
'War without Blows' 247
Warning for Fair Women 247
Watson, Robert N. 172
Watson, Thomas 247
Webster, John 32, 159
 Duchess of Malfi 36, 37, 38, 44, 51, 133
Weimann, Robert 107
Weis, René 66
Wells, Stanley 66, 67, 110

Werstine, Paul 64, 65, 66, 67, 265
Wheelock, Abraham 134
White, Paul Whitfield 97, 108
White, William 198
Whitefriars 231–2
Whitney, Charles 170
Wickham, Glynne 236, 263
Wiggins, Martin 31, 41, 50, 130, 148, 183, 191, 257, 266–7, 270
Wilkins, George 177
Williamson, Elizabeth 149
Wilson, Arthur
   The Swisser 44
Wilson, F. P. 256
Wilson, John Dover 193

W[ilson?], R[obert?]
   The Three Ladies of London 74, 87, 134,
   see also Munday, Anthony
Wily Beguiled 99–100, 105, 109, 112, 125
Winslow, Sean M. 173
Witmore, Michael 173
Wolfe, Heather 192
Woolley, James 190
Worcester's Men 245
Wotton, Henry 3, 13
Woudhuysen, Henry 213, 214
Wright, Abraham 170

Yates, Frances 119

www.ingramcontent.com/pod-product-compliance
Lightning Source LLC
Chambersburg PA
CBHW060944230426
43665CB00015B/2058